'A devastating account of English cricket and its short-comings ... The book describes the shocking lack of ambition, dedication, coaching and leadership in English cricket.'   Mike Brearley, *Observer*

'You will never read a better book about the bizarre circus known as county cricket ... a very funny, often outrageous book.'   Ian Wooldridge, *Daily Mail*

'The most honest and enjoyable account of a sporting life since Eamon Dunphy's football classic *Only A Game? ... A Lot of Hard Yakka* is one of the most illuminating sports books published in years.'
                                    Andrew Shields, *Time Out*

'Hughes may never have scaled the heights as a crick-eter, but he has become a wonderful writer on the sport ... gaspingly candid ... One thing is clear from this book – he had a really good time. So will anyone sensible enough to read it.'
                            Marcus Berkmann, *Daily Telegraph*

'A brilliant read.'   Hugh McIlvanney, *Sunday Times*

'The best written and most genuinely funny sports book in many years. Not that you need to be a sports nut – just curl up with it, and enjoy the anecdotes.'
                            Richard Martin, *Liverpool Daily Post*

'Startlingly candid ... a deserving winner of the William Hill Sports Book of the Year award.'
                                                              n

'In this remarkably entertaining memoir . . . Hughes colours in the reality behind the apparent drabness of the world's most gentlemanly competition.'

John Naughton, *FHM*

'Vivid and revealing . . . Hughes is tough on himself, detailing failures both professional and domestic, painfully recording a receding hairline and dwindling talent. Such honesty is rare in a sportsman's memoir.'

Andrew Baker, *Independent on Sunday*

'Original, refreshing, and has the unmistakable ring of truth.' Matthew Engel

'May be the first cricketer's autobiography ever to tell it like it is, from dressing-room to bedroom . . . Hughes is rivetingly unguarded.'

Tim de Lisle, *Wisden Cricket Monthly*

'Easily the best thing yet written about the life of county cricketers.' Geoffrey Moorhouse, *Daily Telegraph*

'Hughes' tale is vivid, funny and good-humoured but captures the insecurities, frustrations and mood-swings of the professional performer.'

Huw Richards, *Financial Times*

'Excellent . . . Hughes does not paper over the cracks, and his character assassinations and fly-on-the-wall observations make a fascinating read . . . his honesty is to be applauded.' Greg Struthers, *Sunday Times*

A LOT OF HARD YAKKA

Triumph and Torment: A County Cricketer's Life

Simon Hughes

HEADLINE

To M & D

ACKNOWLEDGEMENTS

Many thanks to Ian, Caroline, Gwen, my patient family, and all the
players who were such good sports.

First published in 1997
by HEADLINE BOOK PUBLISHING

First published in paperback in 1998
by HEADLINE BOOK PUBLISHING

10 9 8 7 6 5 4 3 2 1

ISBN 0 7472 5516 4

Printed and bound in Great Britain by
Mackays of Chatham PLC, Chatham, Kent

HEADLINE BOOK PUBLISHING
A division of Hodder Headline PLC
338 Euston Road
London NW1 3BH

Simon Hughes was born in Ealing in 1959 and won four Championship medals with Middlesex between 1980 and 1991, before joining Durham in their inaugural first-class season. He retired in 1994 to write for the *Daily Telegraph* and commentate for the BBC. He is the author of one other book, *From Minor to Major*.

The son of an actor, he is married to Tanya, a PR director, and lives in Hammersmith. They don't own any cats.

CONTENTS

BEFORE TIME

six million fans • an entertaining upbringing
• early visions of Cowdrey • Kent supporter
• the wrong costume for Hugh Grant • Dudley
Moore's Lamborghini • teenage fixation •
door ajar

HANGING AROUND

I haven't set the world alight, but I've hung around with people who have.

This story is about those people, and my struggle to remain alongside them. Once I'd elbowed my way into the mysterious world of county cricket, I became captivated by the close encounters of the game's greatest living players, and their rough and tumble on the professional stage. Lots of other times I sat in the wings transfixed by the stars off guard and the waffle of the stragglers in their shadow. The closer you look, the more you find.

You see, the thing is, cricket's an infatuating pursuit, but the ball is only actually *moving* for a small proportion of the day's play. And that's just when the players are out there on the field. Which leaves an awful lot of time for other stuff. Interesting other stuff. All those opinions and outbursts and antics that the public never hears or sees. How Ian Botham behaves after being out for nought, what he and Viv Richards talk about between overs; the sight of Mike Gatting piling into the teatime sandwiches or Dickie Bird getting into a Jacuzzi; the sound of team-mates winding up Curtly Ambrose.

Six million people are reputed to take an interest in county cricket. I say reputed, because only 0.0001 per cent of them ever turn up to watch. The other 99.9999 per cent follow the game in newspapers and magazines or on radio, TV, telephones and computer screens. They read *Wisdens* and *Who's Whos* and I-scored-my-first-century-at-seven-and-a-half-type autobiographies. All these sources faithfully record the facts but don't deal with the feelings, the psychology, the private melodramas, which to me are the most fascinating aspects of life spent cooped up with ten other noisy, itchy cricketers –

3

how the daily pressure of performance tampers with egos and relationships and condenses personalities into nuggety little comments and reactions.

My career puts these words and deeds in some sort of order, giving them a beginning, a middle and an end. It fluctuated between inspirational bowling spells in Lord's cup finals, and a virtual inability to hit the cut strip at Cleethorpes. It was like an Indian road – full of bumps and holes, often hazardous, but with the odd memorable highlight. I found the game compelling, whether I was in championship-winning sides or teams that came bottom of the pile. I've experienced and observed the whole gamut of sporting emotions. I wasn't particularly good and I wasn't particularly bad, but for fifteen years I was *there*.

Some people think professional cricketers live in a gentrified, uncontaminated world of polite clapping and summer pudding. My French aunt used to say, 'When's Simon going to get a proper job?' But sport vaguely reflects society, and during my time in cricket there have been dramatic developments in both. In 1980 there were still remnants of a sort of gung-ho amateur attitude and the game, like Britain, pottered along in its own quiet, eccentric way. By 1997 it was fully branded and sponsored, TV cameras poked into every nook and cranny and all the competitions were gradually being revamped. Everyone had to adapt, the run-of-the-mill journeymen most of all. Some hauled themselves into line, others fell by the wayside as diet, lifestyle and expectations evolved. *A Lot of Hard Yakka* is a snapshot of the way fat, thin, bright, dumb, sane, crazy, brilliant and useless individuals try to gel together as a team to satisfy the changing demands. It's mad, bad and sad.

If you've ever dreamed of being a professional sportsman, or wondered what it would be like, or want to find out the real reasons why we're lagging behind other countries, read on. It'll help you understand why, when cricketers retire, the thing they miss most of all is the 'crack', and that, in this particular life, love and hate can be just one ball apart.

4

SIMON

There's nothing exceptional about me; never was. I'm not tall or good looking or short or ugly. Neither clever nor stupid nor sad nor wacky. Just normal. You could have been me. I never wore an earring or got a girl pregnant; I don't have bizarre tastes or strange habits. I like Oasis and U2 and Rachmaninov; I love chicken Madras but I'll happily eat roast; I prefer John Smith's to Boddingtons, but I don't mind much either way. I wasn't a collector of anything except a reputation for being a bit clumsy.

My background was normal with a small 'n'. My parents weren't wealthy or poor, my sister and I didn't go to public school or on fancy summer holidays. But we did have a seaside cottage in Kent and quite a roomy, decorative house in west London close to the BBC, where my father often performed in TV sitcoms and dramas. He was a versatile actor, playing a psychopath in *The Saint*, a bank manager in *Bergerac* and falling off his bike in *My Wife Next Door*. He was the Dame in the Richmond Pantomime. Like the careers of many character actors, my father's fluctuated wildly. He'd often come back from interviews and auditions in an optimistic frame of mind, and never hear another word. But he persistently refused to be put off by the whims of directors and, after months of survival on fringe shows and business information films, he would suddenly land a plum job. Now in his seventies, he is still working. The satisfaction and energy he gets from performing is infectious.

My mother had also been in the theatre, and often there were well-known personalities in our midst: Dave Allen, my god-mother's husband; Derek Nimmo, a family friend; an old flat-mate of my father's, Leslie Crowther. We shared beach holidays with the Crowthers. I was brought up in a showbusiness environment but I had no acting ability whatsoever.

What I did have was a vision. From the moment I saw Colin Cowdrey on a black and white TV scoring a hundred against the 1968 Australians, I wanted to be a professional cricketer. Being a bit of a show-off, I liked the one-against-one nature of the game and the way a player raised his bat to the crowd when he'd reached a landmark. I practised the gesture a lot in the garden – which, appropriately, was 22yds long – and worked out a suitable autograph. I was so obsessed I read *Wisden* on the toilet.

OK, I also had some natural talent. I found from an early age that I could bowl fast. I don't know why. What I do know is that hurling a ball about outside with showbiz types meant I was never inhibited by celebrities, a great help later to any teenage whippersnapper suddenly thrust into a star-studded county team. At times my brazenness bordered on impudence. When I was ten, Dudley Moore arrived for tea in a sensational red Lamborghini. Imagining his fleet of spectacular Jensen Interceptors and Ferraris, I asked, 'Is that the *only* car you've got?' He looked rather hurt and replied, 'Well, yes, I'm afraid it is, actually.'

Sensibly, my parents steered me away from treading the boards – particularly after I slipped and destroyed half the set in the school pantomime. (Hugh Grant looked rather silly in this as a bunny girl with his hair tied up in little plaits, and he wasn't much more credible in the under-thirteen cricket team I captained.) Instead they fuelled my passion for cricket, taking me to Lord's and Canterbury and delaying summer holidays so that I could play Colts matches on Kew Green and Greenford Recreation Ground, running up as Snow or Greig, pretending I was Luckhurst or Cowdrey at the crease. I liked to believe I was playing a vital innings in the Gillette Cup final between Kent and Sussex, only betraying my real self by bursting into tears when I was out.

The life of a county cricketer appears rather glamorous to some young eyes, and to some old ones, for that matter. The grounds seem beautifully manicured, bedecked with bunting and marquees; there's a sense of occasion as the teams emerge clad in their smart outfits, laughing and joking. The players are always on TV or in the papers or appearing in pantomimes. They are better spoken and more suavely dressed than footballers, and eschew those affected haircuts. They drive swanky cars with their names on the side. People line up in orderly queues for their autographs, and blushing girls brandish newly signed pictures of them. They advertise Weetabix on ITV.

Ted Dexter lived nearby, and I marvelled at his grand house and his Aston Martin and his stunning wife. His daughter wasn't the worst, either. I assumed the Kent players I idolised in the 1970s had similar lifestyles – luxury homes, smart cars, constant recognition in the street. I imagined that when they walked into shops they were given complimentary goods and free access to the blonde assistants. (I later discovered that only the second bit was true.) I believed they were naturally fit and didn't practise much and spent their winters playing for England or on D.H. Robins' XI tours to South Africa. It sounded a perfect life, and I wanted to join in.

My father was an enormous help. He lived vicariously through my progress up the junior ladder, became a qualified coach and took over the running of an indoor cricket school. I spent winter holidays alternately practising in his nets and repainting the white tarpaulins between them. He was keen for me to do well and encouraged dedication and self-expression.

Having been brought up in the 1920s and 30s, he also had some old-fashioned principles. He stressed discipline and correctness, abhorred cross-batted slogging, no-balling and improperly dressed players with flapping shirts and floppy hats. 'I hope you're going to wear a proper cap today,' he'd say emphatically while giving my hair a little trim. He was slightly appalled by my preference for ripped jeans and my reluctance to strengthen my flimsy arms, and constantly badgered me to lop down large overhanging branches in the garden and cut them up with an old saw. At sixteen I was virtually a qualified lumberjack – and dressed like one, too.

By this time I had had a fair amount of success on the field and was already envisaging myself as a star player. I conceitedly wrote up my school performances in the third person in little report books. Against MCC: 'Hughes bowled at a tremendous pace so that it was even dangerous fielding in the slips. No one played him with any confidence as he blasted through, swinging and cutting the ball and making it lift.' I went to great lengths to achieve my ultimate goal: I lied about my age to get into reputable clubs; I messed about in the nets instead of revising the night before O-levels; I practised in car parks when the grass was too wet; I even behaved bolshily to umpires when a decision went against me. At eighteen I got a temporary job stacking shelves in M&S, not so that I could parade around in new DMs and a red Ben Sherman, but purely to raise the funds for a trip to Sri Lanka to play club cricket out there for a while. I was never interested in girls or clothes or Blondie or sculling pints of Harp lager down the Queen Vic. Only cricket.

I was selected for Middlesex Young Cricketers, invited to play for the county second XI and took a useful haul of wickets, though I was rather taken aback by the power of stroke at this level and let myself down slightly in the field. But I couldn't imagine anything more exciting than life as a cricketer and could think of nothing else in my first term at Durham University, where I'd been accepted more on the strength of my sporting reputation than for any educational ability. So when I noticed a letter marked 'Middlesex CCC' in my college pigeon hole, I could hardly contain myself. Dated 10 December 1979, in odd blue type, it read:

Dear Simon,
The Middlesex cricket committee are pleased to offer you a summer contract for the 1980 season. Your basic salary will be £45 a week, match fees and bonuses are still to be finalised. Please sign the enclosed copy of this letter if you accept the offer. Pre-season training is at the Barclays Bank Sports Ground, Ealing, beginning after Easter. Further details will be sent in due course. May I take this opportunity to wish you good luck for the season.
Yours sincerely,
A.W. Flower, Secretary

OPEN SESAME

Brearley and Gatting's handshakes •
Emburey's language • the birth of 'Group 4'
• first day at Lord's • hard yakka • the
Diamond and the blind physio • 'Spikes'

THE FIRST WEEK

Tuesday 8 April 1980

D-Day. I've had it ringed in my diary since January. My first twenty-four hours as a real, proper, professional cricketer; the day when my dream becomes reality. In ten long years of devotion to the sport, there have always been these vital questions swirling about in my mind: Where do you bowl to Viv Richards? If Michael Holding sends one down flat out, can you see it? Will I ever be on *A Question of Sport*? Now I am about to find out.

It's all very well clean bowling spindly teenagers and demolishing ropy club sides, but the County Championship is the real foundation of the game, each team rich in local talent and welded together by some of the greatest cricketers on earth. Somerset have Richards and Botham, Leicester David Gower, Lancashire Clive Lloyd, Gloucester Zaheer Abbas and Mike Procter, Hampshire Gordon Greenidge. Imran is at Sussex, though I've heard he is lately spending more time in Sloane Square. The prospect of squaring up to all these fabulous players is simultaneously exciting and terrifying.

That just about sums up what I felt today – exhilaration and apprehension bound together like hot beaches and cold sea. Experienced at once they give a pleasant sensation. Both states would have been heightened if the first day had been spent in practice nets on the Lord's Nursery in front of a gallery of eagle-eyed committeemen. However, we're at Barclays Bank Indoor Leisure Centre, Ealing – not the most auspicious place to begin a famous sporting career. It's an anonymous sprawl of 1960s buildings, five minutes up the road from my parents' house, resembling a secondary modern school in Telford.

I turned up early for once, despite Dad insisting I shaved

before leaving 'See if you can look at least vaguely presentable,' he said, wearing his tatty old gardening sweater. There was little sign of life when I arrived with an M&S bag full of training gear, only a decrepit old cleaner polishing the floor. After twenty minutes I was starting to get agitated. Had I got the date wrong, or the time or the place?

I detected voices above me and a faint echo of four-letter words. Upstairs, sitting at formica tables in the canteen, were a collection of casually dressed men dunking custard creams into cups of tea. Several were smoking, and one was addressing the others in strident tones. From the pudding-basin haircut and pointy nose I recognised him at once: the England spin bowler John Emburey. '. . . I tell you, it was fackin' pongo,' he was saying. He was describing the previous winter's Test match against India in Bombay, which Ian Botham had won almost singlehandedly, scoring a century and taking 13 wickets.

'The Indians kept calling him "Iron Bottom" but he wasn't – not after all that fackin' curry,' Emburey continued, not noticing me.

'Burnt Ring, more like,' someone else ventured. Not seeing anyone I knew, I leaned my plastic kit bag against a pillar. It toppled over, spewing out its contents, just as Mike Gatting came over. 'Always chaos when you quick bowlers are around,' he said, smirking. 'Howdoyoudo, old chap. I'm Gatt.'

'God,' I blurted out, gasping from the vice-like grip of his handshake, 'you look much bigger on TV.'

'Oh, cheeky as well. You'll do for us, then,' he said. 'Come and meet the Ripper.'

They seem to use a different language from the one club cricketers speak, but I guessed this was rhyming slang for skipper. Sure enough, Gatt took me over to meet the *éminence grise*, Mike Brearley. His handshake was much limper, his beard slightly unkempt and his beige corduroys a couple of inches too short. But he was very polite – apparently nothing like the Ayatollah he was depicted as by the Australians last winter – and introduced me to the other players before suggesting everyone got changed. The atmosphere was pregnant with reluctance.

We meandered downstairs to three rather cramped changing rooms. The group subdivided itself according to seniority. Most important players and coach in the first room, rank and file in the second, new boys in the third. I was quite relieved to be temporarily surrounded by people I knew. The other first-timers in our room were all team-mates from the Middlesex Young Cricketers: Richard Ellis, a dashing young batsman from Haileybury, wiry left-handed all-rounder Kevan James, and Kenyan-born spinner Rajesh Maru.

Already we had nicknames, the newcomer's rite of entry into any exclusive group of sportsmen. You aren't allowed in without one. Some are imaginative ('Creepy' Crawley, 'Legga' Lamb), some traditional ('Dusty' Miller, 'Smudger' Smith); others come from a middle name ('Ernie' Emburey, 'Henri' Edmonds) or highlight a personal characteristic – 'Bluey' Bairstow (red hair) or 'Paddles' Hadlee (flat feet). Those with no distinguishing feature simply get 'y' or 'o' tagged on to their surname. I was Hughesy, and James was Jamesy. Ellis, a cavalier sort with three initials, who already smoked and drank profusely, we all called Nepo because his dad was cricket and rackets pro at the school. Maru was known as the Rat for his small size and already well-developed aptitude for scavenging vital information – a sort of well-meaning team sneak.

Like me, they'd all tenaciously fought their way through the ranks of schools and Colts cricket. Jamesy, the gawky son of a Wood Green policeman, had hung on at Edmonton High School for an extra year just to play cricket all summer. His ultra-enthusiasm made him prone to blunders. One morning he was obliged to run himself out in an anonymous school match to get to a serious club game in the afternoon, but his contrived dismissal was a bit too obvious. The headmaster was furious and didn't forgive him for months. The Rat and his brother Pradip were forever in the nets at Wembley CC. Nepo was a demon sportsman with a world championship rackets title as well as various cricket honours. All of us were on one-year contracts and desperately anxious to impress. Today we were lumped together as Group 4 for training routines and sprint relays.

Warm-ups came first. Quite schoolboyish. We jogged continuously round the rather scruffy gym doing stretching exercises, hopping, jumping up to head an imaginary ball, running while doing a sort of bell-pulling motion or touching the floor in mid-stride. There was no sign of the masochistic routines I'd seen rugby players performing: one-handed press-ups, 800-metre piggy-back races. Most of the squad looked tanned and healthy, and some wore England touring sweaters and bright shorts. Several black players hung together near the back, all wearing four layers of clothing.

Left-handed batsman Graham Barlow, a qualified PE teacher, was in charge, wearing a smart blue tracksuit. Plenty of banter. 'Come on, Ern, don't lag,' he cautioned Emburey.

'Oi, Gladys, we're cricketers, not fackin' greyhounds,' Emburey grumbled.

'Greyhound? You move like a pregnant camel!' Barlow retorted. 'Right, stop, find a space. Ten burpees and ten squat thrusts, please.' Complaints all round.

Some put in more effort than others. The coach, forty-six and trim and sturdy, as befitted an ex-footballer, was as vigorous as anyone, but two of the senior players hardly moved a muscle unless he was looking their way. Another barely got his head off the floor doing sit-ups. There was much more enthusiasm when Barlow called out, 'Stump hole!' Everyone adopted the press-up position and lowered their pelvises to the floor, grunting like Neanderthals.

Grunts reverted to groans when Barlow shouted, 'Shuttles! Get in your groups.' These were relay races that became progressively harder. We Training Group 4 striplings were hampered by the presence of thirty-nine-year-old opening batsman Mike Smith, who wasn't very quick. Afterwards we played five-a-side football. In my keenness I managed to trip up the coach, who banged his knee hard against the wall bars. Jamesy helped him up.

I expected to find a special high-fibre lunch, the kind of thing Alan Knott apparently eats, but the only choice was stodgy steak and kidney. My mother, vegetarian and passionate about nutrition, would have been shocked – especially when I wolfed down a large helping and tucked into various people's leftovers, following that with two bowls of trifle. I was aware of being stared at by the older players, but reassured by the sight of Gatting ordering extra chips and smothering them in brown sauce. Later I found a large plastic bucket placed by my hook in the changing room. I noticed Nepo grinning smugly.

The rest of our two-hour meal break was aimless, though useful for stodge digestion. We flopped around the lounge area, grumbling about the shuttles, discussing last night's football and the assets of a plainish secretary in Reception. When we eventually returned to the gym, our numbers were depleted. Emburey had an 'appointment' and Phil Edmonds a 'business engagement'. We followed the same routine as in the morning, only shorter and slightly sharper. Began to feel slightly bilious after the thirtieth squat thrust, but managed to suppress the churning feeling in my stomach.

At 3 p.m. training was over. Standing wearily in the shower afterwards, I felt relieved, and yet slightly cheated. Your first day as a professional cricketer ought to be a momentous occasion, full of introductions, speeches, photographs and handouts of pristine kit wrapped in clear plastic. All I have finished up with is a bag of sweaty T-shirts, an aching body and a head full of slang. Still, at least I've been paid for it. Breaking down my summer's salary, I've already earned £9.

Wednesday 9 April

I woke up feeling as if I'd been run over by a JCB. Muscles ached, joints were stiff. After breakfast my mother went up the road to feed the stray cats that live under the cricket club pavilion; my father had already wobbled off on a rusty old bike to rehearsals for *Last of the Summer Wine*. Maybe he's hoping to take over from Compo. I was just about to leave for training when a blackbird flew in through the back door and careered repeatedly against the kitchen windows. No amount of yelling, creeping up on it, or threatening it with a tennis racket had any effect. Finally, after twenty minutes of this caper, I trapped it with a large bucket and tossed it outside, where it sat, totally stunned, until it was set upon by the neighbours' cat. The upshot was that I arrived late, and my excuse – 'There was this bird in the house' – was met with one or two sniggers and the remark: 'Did she have nice tits?'

Things were getting more sophisticated in the gym. Barlow laid pieces of paper round the floor to create various exercise stations, and then we did a circuit in pairs, taking it in turns to do a minute at each station. We performed such well-known, high-tech exercises as stepping up and down on a bench holding a fire extinguisher and doing sit-ups with a medicine ball.

Emburey seemed to be in constant occupation of the squeezing-the-tennis-ball station and Edmonds kept saying: 'Is this one really necessary for me? I am an exceptional bowler, you know.' He did some of the exercises rather half-heartedly. When it was time for the sprint relays, two players tried to sneak outside, and the Rat attempted to engineer Mike Smith a free transfer from Training Group 4 so that we could get someone quicker. Unfortunately Barlow overheard and made all four of us do twenty press-ups. Stayed in goal for the football.

More stodge for lunch: beefburgers and chips followed by apple pie (two helpings of each). 'Blimey, they don't need a garbage dump with you around,' Barlow commented. His tone was slightly admonitory, but there wasn't much else to do except eat. Ian Gould, the chirpy wicketkeeper, and Bill Merry, a long-haired fast bowler, were hogging the snooker table, Gatting was doing the *Telegraph* crossword, and a few others were leafing idly through yesterday's *Sun*. Some of the black players were dozing on a bench. Probably the best option.

Went on a run round the streets in the afternoon. Barlow wanted us to do five miles, but moans and whinges cut it to two. The route took us straight past my back garden, and when I mentioned this Barlow said, 'Cor, maybe we can pop in for tea with your mum afterwards.' He had a mischievous twinkle in his eye. I suspected he might be a ladies' man. The run wasn't supposed to be a race, but it ended up as one. I came in third, thanks to the practice I've been getting at college. The stragglers (mainly the seniors) were quite a long way behind.

'Well done, everybody,' Brearley said in the car park when the last of them had staggered back. 'Good effort. Thanks, Gladys. The chairman of selectors, Mike Sturt, is coming to talk to us tomorrow at ten o'clock. Don't be late.' He glanced in my direction.

Thursday 10 April
I made it – just. The closer you live to a place, the finer you always cut it, I tend to find.

I've met Mike Sturt before, when I was playing a club match, but not in his official capacity. He certainly looks the part. He arrived in a blue Rolls, dressed in an immaculate dark suit with gold cufflinks, spotted tie buffed forwards with a tie pin, matching handkerchief protruding exactly an inch above his pocket and patent-leather shoes. He looks like a Savile Row mannequin and has an authoritative aura about him – this man has the power to make or break. He knows it, you know it, and he knows you know. Even so, I heard a player muttering, 'One day I'm going to cut that wanker's tie off.' Perhaps there isn't much respect in the ranks, then.

The main reason for Sturt's visit was for him to announce an addition to the staff. 'Chaps, after extensive negotiations, we've decided to sign Paul Downton. He's an exciting young player who feels a lack of opportunity with Alan Knott blocking his wicketkeeping progress at Kent. He'll be joining us at the end of the Exeter University term. I think he'll fit in well.' Ian Gould, Middlesex's jaunty regular keeper, looked crestfallen. 'That's my cards and money,' he said later. 'One knife in the back now, the other in July. Fuckin' great.'

A Lot of Hard Yakka

By today, the fourth day, training has begun to drag. We all had aching limbs, and have done enough burpees to attract the attention of the RSPCC (Royal Society for the Prevention of Cruelty to Cricketers). I can't wait to actually get out there and have a bowl at some of these blokes. At least this time we did most of the work outside (mainly football) instead of being cooped in a stuffy gym.

At lunch, several players ferried their unwanted chips and the remains of their Black Forest gâteau in my direction. Could only eat three portions of each, but at least my eating habits have made me a few more friends. Afterwards, we had a team meeting. Brearley congratulated everyone on a good effort and ran through the programme for the next couple of weeks. On hearing the news that we are free to attend the Cricketers' Association AGM in Birmingham on Monday instead of net practice, the players reacted like schoolkids being told double history was cancelled. 'And by the way, Vincent and the Diamond are in on Tuesday,' Brearley finished.

This was not a reference to a gig by some musical double act, but to the arrival of our two overseas fast bowlers, the giant South African seam bowler Vincent van der Bijl, and the lethal Barbadian Wayne Daniel. There won't be much scope for opening the bowling with those two around, not to mention the former England seamer Mike Selvey. However, there is a murmur that Brearley isn't happy with the Van der Bijl signing. 'I wanted a fast and nasty, not a medium-pacer,' he is alleged to have said to the committee.

Monday 14 April, Edgbaston

Graham Barlow picked me up at 9 a.m. in a blue Fiat Mirafiori 131. It had his name on the side and flashy alloy wheels. 'Right, you're navigating,' he said as he eased the car smoothly on to the North Circular. He is a very energetic driver, nipping between lines of traffic, changing gear constantly. Quite a contrast to Dad pinking along at 30mph stuck in fourth. The car was spotless, and Barlow became irritated by a cassette case which slid around on the back shelf when he took a corner. A meticulous type, I noticed – an impression reinforced by the fact that when he gets dressed after a shower he always puts his shoes and socks on first, and then combs his hair and bends over to pack his gear before putting his clothes on. Not a pleasant sight.

The players' AGM took place in the banqueting hall at Edgbaston. There was a huge number of chairs laid out, but only a quarter of them were occupied. I recognised a few faces: Gooch, Amiss, Bairstow, d'Oliveira, and Phil Edmonds in a pair of ostentatious dark glasses. Each county had sent a small group and many of the representatives were in their team blazers. There were only three of us from Middlesex, none in official garb. The rest were too apathetic to make the journey. Everyone milled about drinking coffee for a while until the president, John Arlott, arrived. 'Sorry, men – plane was late from Alderney,' he warbled huskily, looking rather red in the face. His cheeks were more inflated than Dizzie Gillespie's and it looked as if speaking would be difficult . . .

Luckily, Arlott didn't have to say much. Edmonds did most of the talking, querying almost every point, whether it concerned salaries or the size of coloured logos allowed on pads. He argued a lot with the Derby captain, Barry Wood, who has a shrill, grating voice like a blunt saw on metal, and was equally ineffectual. At times the atmosphere got rather tense but I wasn't sure whether this was caused by irritation or boredom. Then, just as the conversation moved on to the bouncer law – something interesting at last – we broke for lunch. Plenty of wine and beer was consumed, which made the post-lunch assembly more genial but considerably less productive.

Tuesday 15 April, Lord's
A week into my career and my first day at Lord's. I caught the tube from Ealing to Marble Arch, then a 159 bus, quite an awkward journey with my kit, stuffed this time in two Harrods bags (a faint sign of upward mobility, although one had begun

to split). The pavilion doorman looked at me dubiously, and stopped me from going in without a tie. The fact that I was now a Middlesex player cut no ice. No one had prepared me for this. But the mere mention of the name Brearley was like saying 'open sesame'.

'Mind you wear one in future,' the doorman called out as I climbed the stairs, passing the swing bowler Mike Selvey going in the other direction in jeans, a T-shirt with 'No Wuckin' Furries' emblazoned on it and white trainers with red laces. Just understanding the rules, who enforces them and who keeps them will be a major step forward, never mind taking 5 for 20.

This was my first experience of the inside of the pavilion, and I was impressed by the highly polished floor, the wide staircases, the endless corridors and huge doors. I pushed one ajar to find some old fossil in white shorts and a vest practising shots in front of a mirror with a funny curved racket. In another room, an elderly man in a tweed suit was poring over a newspaper through a magnifying glass. 'Shh,' he hissed at the creaking door without looking up.

Eventually I found the Middlesex dressing room, which is unmarked, except for a notice declaring: 'Visitors not permitted without express permission from the captain.' My nerves weren't calmed by the incessant beating sound coming from within. Some strange initiation ceremony? No, Gatting breaking in two new bats by whacking them together. The huge room was strewn with an assortment of wooden tables and comfy armchairs and teeming with boxes of equipment, players' kit bags and new sweaters wrapped in cellophane. Every available hook seemed taken, but then I noticed a spare one in the corner and hung up my denim jacket on it. 'Oi, you'll be lucky,' said a stern voice behind me belonging to a player I hadn't yet met. 'You'll need a lot of hard yakka to nick my spot, sonny. Now piss off down the corridor and take your student's gear with you.'

A terrible hush had descended, and I suddenly felt stupid and conspicuous, brandishing my two plastic bags amid a sea of smart blue cricket cases emblazoned with 'England Tour of

Australia 1970–80'. I edged between them, catching my carriers on the corner of one. Last week's unwashed training gear spilled out. Gatting looked on pityingly. Someone pointed me in the direction of a small anteroom down the hall – Dressing Room 4 – which faced away from the pitch and contained old battered lockers and hard church seats.

There I found the other members of Training Group 4, along with the Second XI squad. It was a bit of a squash. Cricketers' unique slang rent the air: 'Hey, stop standing on my mums and dads – they were new out the packet yesterday,' Jamesy protested . . .

'Well, move your coffin over a bit then,' Nepo retorted grumpily, shoving the case with his foot.

'Come on, children, it's a bit early to be losing your trolley,' an older second-team player cautioned. The Rat peered round the door. 'Watch out, Coach is coming,' he warned. He summoned us back into the main room.

'Right,' said Brearley, silencing the dressing-room commotion. 'As the weather's good, we'll get straight in the nets. There'll be four groups, two seamers and a spinner in each. The list's on the wall. Hopefully the Diamond'll turn up at some stage.' At that precise moment the door burst open and in came a hulking, beaming West Indian in blazer and white shirt with several buttons undone to reveal a glistening gold chain. He carried a maroon holdall and a bat under his arm.

'Sorry, am I late, Rip?' he asked, the beam fading to a grin.

'Yes, you are,' Brearley said gruffly. Then a wide smile spread across his face. 'Doesn't matter a bit. We're all very glad to see you, Diamond. Welcome back. We're just off over to the Nursery. Get over there when you're ready, no hurry. You can leave the bat behind, though.' Obviously batting practice for Wayne Daniel is a waste of time.

We walked through the Long Room, a daunting rectangular space with vast windows overlooking the ground. There are oil paintings of W.G. Grace hung about, and dark stained high chairs and tables. 'Those stools look antique,' I said to the veteran batsman Mike Smith.

'They're nothing compared to some of the old duffers who sit in them,' he replied.

We tried to walk across the outfield to the Nursery, but some official shouted at us from a top window and we had to go back round behind the stand. 'Stupid old fart,' said Gatting, hard on our heels. The MCC hierarchy is renowned for not wanting its beloved grass walked on. Ever, preferably.

The rest of us were already in a circle doing neck-stretching exercises when a car arrived bearing Emburey and Edmonds. Too lazy to walk, they had driven round from the pavilion, a distance of probably less than 200yds. 'Well,' Emburey said when Sergeant Barlow remarked on this, 'if you haven't got any muscles, you can't fackin' strain anything.' My image of the supremely fit professional cricketer is gradually becoming distorted.

The attitude of the batsmen in the nets was very responsible, though. There was none of the slogging and heaving you normally associate with practice, at least not until Gatting laid into Emburey a few times, lofting him on to the roof of the new indoor school, to much exclamation. I have never seen the ball hit as far in my life. Big hits were retrieved by Daniel, who spent the morning performing elaborate stretching exercises in a fetching red tracksuit and chatting up passing MCC secretaries.

Generally, the batsmen's faces were clenched in concentration, notably that of the opener Wilf Slack, who took time to settle before each ball and asked the bowlers to set imaginary fields, then claimed runs if he felt he'd worked the ball between the men. The pitches are much harder and drier than the club ones I'm used to, and one or two of my deliveries bounced shoulder high. One, unfortunately, ended up as a vicious bumper which shaved Edmonds' nose. He came marching down the wicket and swore at me, but Brearley said, 'Well bowled.' There are plenty of rumours that they don't get on.

We adjourned for lunch before I'd had the chance of a knock. So much for lugging two new bats and the pair of pads Slazenger have given me over from the pavilion. While capped players made their way up to the pavilion dining room, the rest of us trooped to the pub round the corner for sausages and beans.

Wednesday 16 April

My first stint as a professional cricketer is over. This was my last day before going back to university. 'Off up to Butlin's again, are you?' said Gatting, chewing on a cheese roll. I am leaving as the gargantuan South African fast bowler Vincent van der Bijl arrives. The moment I saw him today he reminded me of a huge, balding headmaster, which is exactly what he is back home, even if his name, pronounced 'Fander bale', makes him sound like a machine for collecting hay. He is thirty-two – quite old for an overseas player – 6ft 8ins tall and walks in wide, measured strides. He takes size 15 shoes.

Still, he seems a gentle giant. He has a rich laugh, and spent a lot of time today helping younger players in the nets. He bowled only a few overs himself, but his accuracy, bounce and prodigious movement are phenomenal. He has a smooth, curving run and a double whirl at the crease, which seems to happen almost in slow motion. By contrast, there is nothing slow about Wayne Daniel's bowling. He grimaced every time he released the ball, and beads of sweat flew off his forehead as he slung it down. I can't imagine how anyone manages to move the bat in time.

Watching with interest behind the net was a vital man, the Middlesex scorer Harry Sharp. He has a dual claim to fame. He was the teenage Ian Botham's coach and mentor on the Lord's groundstaff, and before that, in the 1950s, he had a reputation for slow play when opening the batting for Middlesex. One day a member came up to him before a match and said, 'Hello, Harry. Are you playing today?'

'Yes!' he replied proudly.

'Well, I'm off home then,' the bloke said.

Brearley introduced me to him. 'This, Simon, is the Admiral,' he said, refusing to be drawn into tacky nickname-speak. Sharp looked me up and down and nodded sagely.

'Mmm. Slip of a lad, inn'e?' he muttered, temporarily re-moving half an extinguished cigarette from his mouth. 'Whippy action.' He slipped the dead fag back between his lips.

Lunch was abbreviated because of an important meeting. All twenty-four playing staff gathered in the main dressing room for a briefing from members of the committee. There was dead silence when they walked in, Sturt again immaculate, with the treasurer, Mike Murray – a pleasant man handicapped by a voice like a dying drone. We are to get a £6.50 meal allowance on away trips, they said. Petrol 8p a mile. Claim it from the office after the match. Prize money was discussed, contracts and registration forms handed out. They must be back signed by Friday, or we'll be ineligible. Any questions? The younger players were all far too overawed to speak up, but Edmonds, of course, was in his element. 'If we claim our expenses after the match, that means we'll be out of pocket for three days,' he pointed out, brandishing a copy of the *FT*. 'Surely we should get the money up front?' His request was deftly quashed.

Finally at 2.37 p.m. on my eighth day, I got a bat. I soon regretted it. The net pitches were worn after two days' solid use and the ball kept darting back and slapping into my right, unprotected inner thigh as I played defensively. I hopped about in pain, which caused quite a bit of merriment, and resorted to slogging, narrowly missing the coach's head with one scything heave. 'Haven't you got any common sense?' he called out in a narked voice, and went back to tossing lobs for Gatting to drill into the side netting.

Gatting soon diverted the spotlight on to the Rat, launching his best flighted deliveries miles out of the net so often that Jamesy felt obliged to comment, 'Blimey, Rat, the umpires better keep a box of balls handy for when you come on.' Jamesy, an innocuous medium-pacer, steadfastly refused the coach's offer of a rest. He dropped his next delivery too short and Gatting pulled it over a wall into St John's Wood Road, narrowly missing a number 9 bus. 'Make that a *bucket* of balls in your case, Jamesy,' Nepo weighed in. I wanted to laugh but my thigh hurt too much, and so I went to see the physio, Johnny Miller.

I expected to find a rippling young enthusiast in a tracksuit behind the door marked 'Physiotherapist'. I was slightly shocked to come upon a frail, elderly man wearing a grey nylon shirt and tie and fiddling with medicine bottles by a sink. The room reeked of TCP. When I first went in he didn't notice me. I coughed loudly and he turned in my direction. 'Oh, hello, who is it?' he asked, even though I was only 6ft away. He moved about like Ray Charles, and I realised he was almost blind.

While Johnny rubbed some substance into my bruised leg, which looked as if it had been used for target practice, he told me his life story. He was a test driver for Vauxhall in the early 1960s, but one prototype car went out of control on a circuit and his injuries were so bad he nearly died. He emerged from hospital some months later with his eyesight seriously impaired, so decided to train himself to be a physio. He read physiology in braille, ending up with twenty huge volumes he didn't know what to do with. So he wallpapered his flat with them. 'I used to have parties for other partially sighted medical students, and we'd feel round the walls for different bits of the body and test each other on them.' These days people who do that sort of thing end up in court. Then he became physio with Tottenham Hotspur, moving to Lord's in 1977.

Hobbling back to the junior players' anteroom, I emerged into a full-scale verbal war, all because Nepo had borrowed Jamesy's bat without asking.

'That's got to last me all summer, you know.'

'The number of runs you make, that shouldn't be a problem,' Nepo replied.

'I go in higher than you.'

'That's only 'cos you're an arse-licker. You've been so far up the coach's rectum we ought to call you Spikes – it's the only bit of you we can still see.'

I departed feeling quite glad that I was on my way back to college.

SUMMER 1980

Middlesex reserve • a busy twelfth man •
Nancy • first-class debut • man of the match
• Imran winds up Daniel • Brearley's degree
in people • double champions • Zimbabwe
with 'John Cleese' • dead men floating

CRICKET AND SEX DON'T MIX

May

Anyone who says they didn't enjoy university is either barmy or lying. Why would anyone in his or her right mind complain about putting reality on hold for three more years? You don't have to plan anything, or push the trolley around Sainsbury's on Saturday mornings, or fill in your tax return, and you can wear jeans and a T-shirt whenever you like. (Ironically, when there's no dress code, people's clothes seem to be more uniform than ever.) University is a holiday of indulgence. It doesn't quite fit Mike Gatting's comparison with Butlin's: that's more like conscription.

Sid Vicious's anarchic version of 'My Way' was still everyone's favourite record in 1980 and at some louche party his accomplice, Johnny Rotten, said that sex was 'two and a half minutes of squelching'. Sadly, by the end of my first year at Durham, I was still unable to confirm or deny this. Most of my mates were constantly claiming conquests, but the girls I cornered were either ace teasers or 'just wanted to talk'. In the bar I couldn't even get to first base with Climax Kate or Holly Hotlips, and when I was clogging their route to some hunky rugby player I was made to feel like one of those irritating Welsh terriers that get under your feet. I didn't have a second hand Alfa Romeo, floppy hair or a rugged physique.

Why do the Carlings and Winterbottoms of this world get the best-looking women? Because they are available, that's why. Rugby takes up half an afternoon followed by a raucous free-for-all in the bar. Cricketers, on the other hand, are immersed in their own little world for days on end, then disappear into some exclusive zone to relive it all again. Most females think cricketers are sexually retarded, so it's not surprising they plump for other types of sportsmen. It's only later that they admit that losing their virginity to a beered-up second-row forward with a hairy back put them off sex for ten years.

Playing sport for a northern university was a much more practical education than sitting reading sociology books. You learned how maddening travel on the M62 is, why Yorkshire people rave about fish and 'clerks' with HDTs (hand-drawn Tetley's) and are so scathing about southerners (we are pompous and unfriendly, and our beer is like piss, they say gruffly). You visited places like Hull and Lancaster, on the surface unappetising towns that a spoiled Londoner like me would make a beeline for only if we were selling biographies of Tony Benn or researching urban degeneration. Behind the façade they were equally unappetising, but at least we could witness that at first hand.

Without sport I would have been a social cripple and a physical wreck. I thought parties of dopeheads, drunks and snogging couples were stupid, mainly because I wasn't participating. But I still went, drinking far too much and drawing attention to myself by fleecing people's pockets for an imaginary lost gerbil. It didn't endear me to many of them; neither did the pictures of Brearley and Boycott above my bed. It made a change from Debbie Harry, I argued.

Bitter was 25p a pint, which meant you could get incoherent for a quid. To sober up we played space-invaders for hours, having worked out how to take the perspex front off the machine and clicked up a hundred free credits. By the time you went to bed, the characters were marauding through your subconscious. I wrote to my parents that I was spending most of my time in the library. If they hadn't cottoned on before, they did when I got 14 per cent in my prelims.

Culture and sport do cross paths occasionally, of course. To raise money for a cricket tour, we organised a strip show in college, but on the night of the event we discovered the venue had been double-booked with a lecture by the Bishop of Durham. The strippers, arriving in the usual fake-fur coats and suspenders, had to be sneaked out of a back entrance. The tour never came off. However, good university cricket is a perfect way to prepare for the first-class season. There's plenty of time for practice, it's not too demanding, you're in good company, and the student support is stimulating and witty. And there's beer at lunchtimes.

THE COMFORT ZONE

June

When I came down from Durham at the end of term I hit the ground running. My summer contract with Middlesex had officially begun with a series of midweek Second XI matches, there was club cricket on Saturdays and Durham were in the knock-out rounds of the inter-university championships. That added up to fourteen days cricket in sixteen: no time to think, get nervous or be prompted up large chestnut trees by my father.

Arriving back in London on the overnight mail train was not the best preparation for the first match of an arduous fortnight, but I wasn't going to miss the last night of term. College irresponsibility had eroded any lingering remnant of discipline and I was buoyant after a fruitful university season. So instead of a restful eight hours' sleep at home, I snatched about two in between the grinding of the train's brakes and the droning of a fellow passenger wittering on about locomotives.

The West Indian Joel Garner always said he bowled better after a late night on the rum and Cokes, and initially, the same approach seemed to work for me. By day I took a stack of wickets in the Second XI and various opposing players and officials complimented my bowling. I shrugged it off, it was all coming pretty easily. By night we roamed the pubs and bars of middle England. Apart from perpetual lateness and a tendency to bowl no-balls, my only genuine blemish was running out the coach without facing against the Royal Navy. Apparently, he used to enjoy his little bat, so trying to give him the strike I called for a risky single and couldn't turn back because there was no grip on my trainers. All he said to me when I came in unbeaten a few minutes later was: 'You prat. Wear studs when you bat in future.'

Many of the Second XI players, known universally as the Dinky Doos, had a surprisingly complacent attitude. Their kit bags were full of porn mags and their preparation was sloppy – idle hits against pavilion fences, casual fielding practices, filling each other's gloves with shaving foam. Some tended to coast on the field unless an important person was watching. Spikes became neurotic about the whereabouts of officials. He always ran in extra hard if the coach was conspicuous beside the sightscreen, or added an extra flourish to a defensive stroke. Significantly, it was often at these times that his bowling got spanked to the boundary or he nicked one to slip.

There was also a lot of messing about on the field, which I hadn't expected. Slip fielders pretended to read newspapers when some of the more innocuous bowlers were running up, and young trialists in the opposition were given a fearful verbal assault when they came to the wicket. One was close to tears after being asked if he'd got his mother's permission to be out and what the brown stain was on the seat of his pants.

In a way you could understand them trying to liven up proceedings. They had been on the second-team treadmill half a summer already, some of them for several years, and couldn't see any way of getting off it. They travelled around in each other's clapped-out cars, stayed in nasty hotels and frittered away their meagre expenses on card games and beer, surviving on greasy takeaways to save money – something the hierarchy disapproved of. One night Spikes rested his bag of chips on the coach's car outside the hotel. The coach happened to be on his way back from dinner. 'Take that off there, you pillock!' he snapped.

They played on some ropy wickets at usually deserted club grounds and complained that the first-teamers never took any notice of them. If it rained they had to help the groundsman with the covers (on one occasion a committee member polished off my lunch while I was away doing my duty). Some of their gripes were justified – what is life if you haven't got something to moan about? – but this was no excuse for the generally lacklustre attitude.

I found the lack of naked ambition baffling, but I wasn't affected by it. I concentrated on bowling fast, fielding enthusiastically and regularly winning the Dick of the Day award for some naïve remark. I was a sucker for silly wind-ups.

Me: 'Has anyone got a stud screw?'

Colleague, opening his bag: 'What, you mean one of those metal devices with a little handle?'

Me, eagerly: 'Yes, great.'

Colleague: 'No.'

I practised hard with Wilf Slack and Paul Downton (also recently arrived from university) and keenly watched the team bat while others spent more time lying about inside inventing new rhyming slang and sharing in-jokes. Cricket was rarely the topic of conversation. I was relatively blasé about my early success, not giving any thought to the fact that I was only 5ft 9ins, played in a pair of old boots that wouldn't even qualify for a parish jumble sale and had to resit my university exams in August.

LAW AND ORDER

English cricket has a sort of feudal hierarchy. Capped players are allowed to eat in the special Lord's dining room because they are established in the team and have earned their stripes. They've served their apprenticeship and as a rule they get all-inclusive salaries, sponsored cars and a locker with their name on it. On the field they wear special caps and sweaters which distinguish them from the hoi polloi. It's the only sport in which seniority is actually visible on the field. I mean, you don't see Cantona wearing a different Man United shirt from Beckham just because he's been in the First XI for longer.

But in cricket the uncapped players are the also-rans. They

receive a low basic salary (about £8,000 in 1996) and then get match bonuses (£50 a day). If you're injured or ill, you don't get paid. They wear odd Roman-numeral 'II's on their cricket sweaters. They share twelfth-man duties for the first team, leave tickets at the gate for senior players' families and are also expected to play for a reputable club side at weekends.

How they get around is their problem. Shanks's Pony or the Frankie Lane, Mike Selvey said. Mind you, anything was better than a ride in the thing our second-team wicketkeeper, Chris Goldie, drove. It was a scratched blue Morris vegetable van that reeked of rotting cabbage and fag ends. It'd been refused entry at the Grace Gates twice. 'You can't bring that tin can in here,' said the gateman, with customary Lord's civility.

'If I park it outside it'll get towed away,' Goldie reasoned.

'Who by, Steptoe and Son?' the man retorted, and shut the gates.

The MCC laid out most of cricket's structure and remains the game's guardian. It is arguably the largest private club in the world, with a reputed 20,000 members, though considering they last had a head count about twenty years ago, it's a fair guess half of them are dead by now. The MCC owns Lord's and rents it out to Middlesex for about £60,000 a year. They insist on 'proper white clothing' even when players are knocking up on the Nursery. Anyone caught outside the dressing room wearing blue tracksuit bottoms would be hung, drawn and quartered.

The contrast between Middlesex and the MCC was best illustrated by their office facilities. The secretary of the MCC and his cohorts had fabulous rooms to one side of the pavilion with solid, mahogany furniture and panoramic views of the ground. In 1980 the Middlesex secretary and his administration staff were confined to an ill-equipped prefab behind the pavilion in a serious state of disrepair. The crevices in the floor were a health hazard for staff and players popping in to collect mail from their pigeon holes, and part of the ceiling had fallen in. It was a shambles.

On the other hand, the MCC did provide the most palatial

washing facilities in London. The pavilion dressing-room annexe had wonderful turbo-powered showers, each with rose heads the size of breakfast bowls; baths deep enough to stage sub-aqua lessons and unlimited supplies of hot water and towels. There was even a bloke to run the bath and fetch drinks and shampoo and answer the big red payphone behind the door. The corridors reverberated to the cries of 'Roy, can we have some tea?'

'Roy, we're short of towels.'

'Roy!'

'Rrrooyyy!'

All the regular players gave him the runaround even though he looked at least seventy.

TWELFTH MAN

Saturday 5 July, Middlesex v Northamptonshire, Lord's
Whenever the first team were playing at Lord's on Saturday, the whole staff was expected to be in to help at nets, run errands and generally be on hand. When I arrived at 9.45 a.m., there was a buzz of expectancy in the air, and the pavilion was filling up with elderly men hobbling about and fathers and sons, the boys looking distinctly uncomfortable in their jackets and ties. We still had to change in Room 4. Today the coach came in and told me that I was twelfth man. I immediately thought this meant I was close to making the first team, until Spikes said, 'You're the only one of us who hasn't done it yet,' which was rather deflating.

I assumed I was in for a cushy day watching the cricket and taking the odd sweater out on to the field like I'd seen in Test matches. I was in for a shock. As soon as I walked into the dressing room I was hit by a barrage of requests.

'Twelthy, put tickets on the gate for Mr and Mrs Johnson.'

'Twelthy, get my second pair of batting gloves out of the drying room, can you?'

'Tell Roy to bring the tea in, Twelthy.'

'TWELTHY!'

'So you're Harry Twelthers today,' said Gatting. 'Could you go up to Nancy's and order me a chicken salad, please?'

'Just two cheese rolls for me, thanks,' said Edmonds. 'I'll have them down here.'

'Save my lunch until tea will you?' said the Barbadian-born batsman Roland Butcher.

And before long I had a list like a Chinese takeaway menu of different requirements, some of which had to be brought downstairs so the recipient could eat in the dressing room. In my wide-eyed enthusiasm I found the job intriguing.

At 10.30 an old wooden trolley was trundled in bearing baskets of chocolate bourbons, custard creams, digestives and a teapot the size of a garden watering can. 'Oh, it's crude oil again,' said Gatting, surveying the dark brown liquid choked with teabags. 'Cuppa rosy, Rad?'

'You bet. Two sugars, Gatt-boy.'

The whole team added 'boy' to everybody's name. Gatting tipped up the pot and poured tea into several cups in one continuous flow, saying 'Look, British Rail,' as he sploshed it about.

As soon as the team had trooped on to the field, I set off in search of Nancy. After a number of wrong turns I came across her sitting at a table behind a door marked 'Players' Dining Room'. She was writing figures in a book. She had a tight perm, wore large rectangular glasses and held between her fingers an inch and a half of ash which clung desperately to the butt of a cigarette. I'd heard that Nancy stood no nonsense, gave pompous committeemen a right ear-bashing and answered to the same description as Billy Bremner: 5ft 4ins of barbed wire. Considerably shorter, if anything, I noted. But I could see a twinkle in her eye.

'Now den,' she said in a heavy Irish brogue, 'yeh'll be de new twelfth man. Wha they call yeh, Soimon, is it? Yes, and Moike wants a chicken salad, Wayne'll have his downstairs, and rolls for that Edmonds. I suppose dey'll be wanting puddins down dere as well, and tea and cakes I should tink. Jaysis, don't de wives ever bleedin feed 'em? All roight, all roight, de tray'll be ready at whun o'cloch. And tell 'em, no shorts in my doining room.'

I turned and left, mildly impressed.

While Middlesex fed Allan Lamb's square cut out in the middle, the old red payphone behind the door rang persistently. It was usually some girl or other for Wayne Daniel, who spent most of the lunch interval wrapped in a large white towel, saying into the mouthpiece, 'Helloo, how arrre yoooou. Mmmm, what are you doing tonight?' and caressing his genitals.

As I was on official duty, I was allowed to eat in the dining room. I couldn't believe the amount of food served up. Two thick slabs of beef dangled over the end of each large plate, with carrots, cauliflower cheese, boiled cabbage and crisp roast potatoes loaded on top. Most players were also chewing on white baps smothered in butter. They then consumed ample slices of apple pie dolloped with ice cream and custard. Six different cheeses were passed round with the coffee. It was on a par with the Café Royal. The teams had a table each, and there was another for scorers and umpires. When they all got up to leave I checked the clock. The feeding frenzy had taken less than fifteen minutes.

I tucked into my own lunch with gusto and was a little late back into the dressing room. 'Twelthy, you're supposed to be here to tell us if the umpires have gone,' Barlow said tetchily. 'Get your arse into gear.' The day continued in the same vein. When I wasn't asking one of Daniel's harem to ring back, I was hanging up one of his vests in the drying room, ferrying extra sweaters or orange squash out to the bowlers or taking the short-leg helmet and shin pads on and off. At tea I went to speak to a spectator and returned to the dressing room to find everyone ranting that the tea hadn't been poured out. 'There were no drinks ready for the bowlers, either,' Barlow added. 'You're pissole.'

By the end of the day, after, in addition to all the fetching and carrying, I'd run baths for the bowlers, collected two of Edmonds' guests from the Grace Gates, made a list of after-match alcoholic requirements and helped Roy bring them in, I felt downright bushed. I hadn't expected being twelfth man to prove harder than playing, and wished I'd had some advance warning. But in professional sport, no one tells you anything of much value.

BLIND MAN'S BUFF

Monday 7 July, Lord's

Nothing could have prepared me for what happened today, however. I was having a breather on the balcony after the morning chores, watching Wilf Slack bat. Suddenly, he larruped one straight into the Northants short leg's head. The fielder sank to the ground in agony and all the Middlesex players looked at me as if it were my fault. 'Go on, hurry up, get the physio – he might be dying,' said the coach. Johnny Miller was in his room and when I burst in, he sensed something was wrong.

'What is it, mate?' he asked. 'An MCC member with convulsions?'

'No, something serious – Geoff Cook's been hit on the head.'

'Quick, lead me out,' he said, panicking, and grabbed his first-aid satchel, knocking bottles off the medicine cabinet in the process.

I helped him downstairs and through the Long Room, but when we were out on the field he let go of my hand and suddenly blundered ahead. He lurched towards a group of players crowded round the stricken Cook, then suddenly veered off course and made straight for the wicketkeeper, George Sharp, who was minding his own business by the stumps. 'Where's the problem, mate?' J.M. asked, and started feeling Sharp's face. 'Oh yes, a nasty bump there.'

'That's my gumshield,' said Sharp. 'The injured player's over here.'

Thankfully, Cook only suffered a cut ear and was led off for repairs – or rather, he finished up showing Johnny the way off. As I was about to leave the scene, the Northants captain, Jim Watts, said, 'Excuse me, we haven't got a twelfth man – can you field for us for a bit while Cooky has some treatment?'

This was a nerve-racking and puzzling prospect. Should I let runs through my legs, deliberately not try for catches and annoy Northants, or dive for everything and be ticked off by Middlesex? It was a no-win situation, but I thought it was infinitely preferable to being the dressing-room dogsbody. That is, I did until Watts spoke again. 'Oh, er, would you mind doing short leg?'

'No, not at all,' I replied, minding very much. I was to discover over the next couple of years that the youngest player is always put at short leg as he is both the most expendable and the least likely to kick up a fuss.

I donned Cook's blood-spattered helmet, but wasn't required to do anything much except block my ears every time Clive Radley called for a run. His cries of 'YEEESSS!' and 'WAAAAYYT!' could have been heard in Holloway. When a couple of his batting partners were out, I went and chatted to him at the non-striker's end rather than falsely join in the Northants celebrations.

Knowing which team to sit with at lunch posed a problem. Seeing as I was fielding for them and seeking to glean some useful strategic information, I chose the Northants table, but they only discussed a night out at Stringfellow's and I got some funny stares from the Middlesex players. Barlow said, 'We're obviously not good enough for him,' in front of everyone else. It was a good thing the match was washed out shortly afterwards – I was getting thoroughly confused.

UP THE LADDER

Thursday 17 July, Nottinghamshire v Middlesex, Trent Bridge
Rain and more twelfth-man duties meant I spent days
alternating between twiddling my thumbs and careering
around like a blue-arsed fly. In a lull while Middlesex were
fielding against Hampshire, I saw the gallumphing South
African Van der Bijl take a wicket, and the genial Barbadian
Daniel race up from long leg to embrace him. It was like a
bear hugging a giraffe, and it was symbolic of the warmth
most West Indians showed South African players. Whatever
Peter Hain was blethering on about on Radio 4, black cricketers
weren't remotely tempted to ostracise white ones brought up
on apartheid.

No one, not even Hain, could fail to be impressed by Van
der Bijl. Not only was he a fearsome bowler with incredible
accuracy, genuine penetration and an lbw appeal like an
enraged triffid, but off the field he was also gentle and
disarming, intelligent and funny. Bowling at an inspired Sunil
Gavaskar in a Benson & Hedges group match, he got a pasting.
In one over, after seeing several decent deliveries disappear
for sumptuous boundaries, he groaned as another forcing
stroke slid off Gavaskar's bottom edge past leg stump for
four. It was his first blemish in two hours. Following through
all the way down the wicket, the 6ft 8in bowler towered over
the diminutive Indian, 120 not out. 'Oh, you 'orrible little
man,' he uttered in mock ire. 'Why don't you *concentrate.*'

Van der Bijl's magnificent bowling inspired the team to a
series of victories, and he won Man of the Match in the first
round of the Gillette Cup. During second-team practice at
Lord's the day before the next round, against Notts, the coach
wandered over to me as if he were going to ask me to pad up.
He said, 'Philippe [Edmonds] is struggling a bit for tomorrow,
so they want you up at Trent Bridge.' I had a sudden surge of
butterflies as emotions clashed. I visualised bowling Middlesex
to a Gillette Cup victory on my first appearance, and yet
instead I could run up and, seized with nerves, fail to hit the

cut strip to be discarded forever on the mound of Players Who Didn't Have the Bottle. The realisation that I might just be carrying the drinks calmed me down.

I didn't sleep much that night. It may have been anxiety, or it may have been because we were staying in a breeze-block hotel about 30yds from Junction 25 of the M1. Probably both. I arrived at the ground to find only ten other fit players. Edmonds had a bad knee and was still in his civvies. 'Oh, you're up the ladder, are you Henri?' said Emburey, pulling on his whites. About forty minutes before the start, as we limbered up on the outfield, Brearley took me aside and said: 'You're taking the new ball with Diamond. Good luck.' I tried to mask my nerves by nodding nonchalantly, but my stomach was churning so violently it must have been audible.

The rest is a blur. So was the ball to the Notts opening batsmen, as they couldn't reach most of my stuff. After three wides in my first over I began imagining myself hanging from a crane over that pile of arms and legs on the bowlers' scrapheap, their sad voices wailing, 'Just one more over, pleeease, Skip.' But afterwards the umpire was more forgiving, even if the partisan spectators weren't. Every time the ball strayed outside the off stump there was a chorus of '*Wide!*' from the members' enclosure. For this reason – and because the Trent Bridge scoreboard displays individual bowling figures in all their dreadful entirety, overs bowled and runs conceded in large fluorescent numbers – I have never had a particularly soft spot for the home of Nottinghamshire cricket.

Van der Bijl's presence was vital at that point. The gladiatorial nature of cricket – that sequence of duels within a team game – can make it lonely out there on the field. Especially on your county debut in a knock-out competition on a large, unfamiliar Test ground with local supporters willing you to fail. He told me to forget about the crowd, the match, the batsmen, Emburey with his hands in his pockets at slip. To concentrate on my own game and imagine that I was bowling at two ginks in the park. It was a bit like the suggestion my mother once made that I should visualise a gruff head-master in his underpants. It made the ogre manageable by cutting it down to size. My bowling improved dramatically and I never forgot that piece of advice. Indeed, I discovered as time went by that most great players followed the same philosophy. 'I don't care if they've got Goliath in their team,' Ian Botham said in the dressing room before Durham's NatWest quarter-final against Leicestershire twelve years later. 'If we all do our job they can't do theirs.'

I have two other memories from my first game, which we won, thanks to a bullish innings from Gatting: meeting the Notts bowler Peter Hacker, whose glass eye made him appear to be talking to someone over your shoulder, and seeing Ian Gould's crestfallen face at being out for 0. He had been batting and keeping well, but he knew that his smoking and drinking, and his laddish image at the time weren't particularly appreciated by the men in suits, who were itching to replace him with the newly signed, dapper, public-school-educated Paul Downton. A week later Gould was dropped and hardly ever played for Middlesex again.

COME ON DOWN

Monday 28 July, Middlesex v Kent, Lord's
For a while I thought I wouldn't, either. I hadn't exactly set the world alight at Trent Bridge, though I enjoyed the big-match experience. I went back to the Second XI, where I was booted around like a son who'd gone off leaving the washing up unfinished. One day the coach arrived slightly later than usual, and finding us lounging about ogling page-three girls, ordered everyone outside for several laps of the outfield and then wielded the bat slightly sadistically during fielding practice. His aggression galvanised the team, though, and we annihilated Warwickshire Second XI.

Downton and I had both done well in that game and were

called in for the championship match at Lord's the following day. It was against Kent, his old county. On the first morning a deep depression descended over London, the ground was flooded and at 11 a.m. it was so dark it felt like the Apocalypse. All the street lights came on and several Canada geese settled on a small lake in front of the Mound Stand.

The dressing room was a hive of activity, each player reacting in his own idiosyncratic way to being cooped up. Gatting was trying out various bats by bouncing balls on them and banging them loudly on the floor as if he were waiting for the bowler to arrive. Butcher was rehearsing his stance in a mirror. There were porn mags overflowing from Wayne Daniel's bag, while Emburey's voice could be heard above the rest in the card school. 'Royal flush beats a full house, Dildo,' he was saying. He commanded huge respect as vastly well-endowed men usually do. Barlow was doing sit-ups. The umpires came in and said there would be an inspection at 2 p.m., and that they would probably call it off for the day. The mood became even more upbeat. Only Edmonds and Selvey, on opposite sides of the room, were indulging in anything vaguely sedate. One was immersed in the *FT*, the other flicking through *NME*.

By Monday the ground had dried out, and Middlesex won the toss and elected to bat. Brearley hadn't announced the batting order, so everyone was caught by surprise when he opened with himself and Downton, making his Middlesex debut and usually a tail-ender. 'Blimey, he's off his rocker this time,' Selvey said of the captain when the openers had disappeared down the stairs. Barlow added: 'I always thought the man was crackers.' Brearley and Downton put on 160 for the first wicket.

Because the match was now a two-day affair, Middlesex declared after tea with only four wickets down, hoping that Daniel could work up a head of steam and knock over the Kent top order. In my twelfth-man role, I had become his enthusiastic lackey and I bustled around fetching his boots and shirts from the drying room while the rest of the team got ready to field.

As they were going out of the door, Brearley stopped and stared at me, reclining on the balcony in tracksuit bottoms and trainers. He said: 'Why aren't you coming out with us? You are *playing*, you know.'

Have you ever heard of anyone being unaware he was making his real, proper championship debut until the match in question was a day and a half old? Probably not. Neither, I imagine, have you ever witnessed a distinguished leader anxious for a breakthrough putting every fielder on the boundary, then sending down an over of ridiculous lobs the like of which is never seen outside the annual match between the Tube Drivers and the Ticket Collectors. But Brearley was no ordinary captain, and 1980 was no ordinary summer.

MR MOTIVATOR

For the next two weeks my feet hardly touched the ground. Whenever I ran up and turned my arm over, batsmen did silly things, and I got first-class wickets through nervous energy and beginner's luck. Strutting bit hitters were deceived by my small, chaotic appearance. Brearley wrote later: '[Hughes] is no human mountain, no muscular giant nor a superb Athenian discobolus ... You would hardly quiver in your boots at the sight of this unprepossessing, slight man of below average height and self-deprecating expression. But put a new ball in his hand ...'

He helped enormously by giving me a bowl early in an innings so that the tension didn't have a chance to develop; by encouraging me to go all out for wickets and by setting such cryptic fields that the batsmen were totally confused. (He sometimes countered a sequence of legside boundaries by moving extra men to the *off side*, for instance.) He also translated some of the team's slang. Clive Radley kept asking for the 'Acker' (milk) and the 'housemaids' (cheese) at lunch, and Barlow moaned about pain in his 'Staffords' (hips). People talked about trolleying (losing your temper) and being up the ladder (faking injury). Understanding Emburey was easier. Removing the expletives cut his dialogue by half. He once said to an unsuspecting journalist who had popped in to ask about his dodgy back: 'Well, to be honest, the fackin' facker's fackin' facked.'

The team was an extraordinary mixture of characters. The Cambridge-educated duo of Selvey and Edmonds were diametric opposites. One had an unkempt, rocker sort of image and his favourite piece of clothing was a Bruce Springsteen 'Born to Run' T-shirt; the other was smart, conceited and always monopolising the phone to take business calls. Barlow was all bulging pectorals, Radley the crafty stalwart with the lived-in face; Gatting and Emburey were constantly trying to outdo each other in the nets or at backgammon, and Daniel told outrageous ribald stories about his female conquests to an infatuated audience of Butcher and Slack. Van der Bijl loomed large accompanied by a pinched Natal accent and a rich, booming laugh. I was the nonchalant, chaotic student with my supermarket carrier bags and skidding bouncer.

Brearley heaped all this flotsam into the melting pot and somehow siphoned off the best bits to the benefit of all. His techniques were varied. He coaxed extra overs out of Daniel by promising an introduction to the attractive brunette in the Tavern; he worshipped Radley; he reacted tersely to Edmonds, or replaced him with the Rat, who was showing promise. Sometimes he was intimidating. He'd give me a severe bollocking if I fell into the old British habit of not wanting to be seen to be trying too hard. He wouldn't tolerate negligence or people holding something in reserve through fear of failure. Once he strode on to the pavilion balcony above a gaggle of slumbering MCC members after Butcher had stupidly run out two batsmen and yelled right across the field: 'YOU CUNT, BUTCH!'

Occasionally he threw a wobbler in the dressing room if the team had been underperforming. When he did so he commanded the utmost attention. He once ranted that players weren't paying enough interest to the game when we were batting; they were always too busy watching telly or playing cards, he said crossly, and the gag from the next batsman in, to 'leave the cards be, I'll be back in a minute', had gone beyond a joke. 'I want more dressing-room attention on the match when we're batting,' he demanded, 'and less on silly games of pontoon.' There was dead silence when he'd finished and everyone looked ashamed of themselves. Then, with perfect timing, Emburey said, 'OK, whose deal is it?'

Brearley joined in the general levity, but a decade earlier, before he took over the captaincy from an impenetrable clique of Peter Parfitt, Fred Titmus and John Murray, this sort of banter would have been sternly received. The hierarchy in those days had a stricter pecking order and adhered religiously to the old cliché 'Youngsters should be seen and not heard.' Thank God those inflexible Victorian values had been cast out. Realising that lateness was just an attention-seeking exercise, Brearley didn't utter one harsh word when, after a mental aberration, I wandered in only ten minutes before the start of a Sunday League game. But that summer I could do anything and get away with it.

His best motivational ploy was to make everyone feel valued and involved. He was always canvassing opinion among the team, and no one was left out. The day he came over during an opposition run riot and asked me, aged twenty, who I thought should bowl next, I felt 10ft tall, particularly when he took up my suggestion. The idea didn't work, but I was prepared to run through treacle for him for the rest of the summer.

Compare that with the treatment Devon Malcolm received from the England management in South Africa at the end of 1995. They shamelessly sniped at his technique, almost as if they suspected all the township adulation was going to his head and he needed taking down a peg. He must have felt knee high to Paul Daniels. No wonder he had a lousy tour and shot his mouth off afterwards.

It's not as if Malcolm was the first, either. The refuse tip has been overflowing with talented but complex characters –

Lewis, Ramprakash, Tufnell, Hick – who, with sensitive, imaginative handling could all have produced so much more. But no, we go on blindly stating that 'If three lions on your chest doesn't motivate you, nothing will' and dismiss people with 'He's just a show pony,' without ever comprehending why they often fail to deliver. I'll tell you why. Because they're all wracked with self-doubt.

SHARED PLEASURE

Wednesday 30 July, Worcestershire v Middlesex, Worcester
How we'd all love to bottle the confidence and enjoyment of a purple patch for later use. Mine was just beginning. Revelling in the animated atmosphere, I won the Man of the Match award in my third game, a televised Gillette quarter-final, taking 3–23 on a juicy Worcester pitch, and bowling them out for a paltry 126. I had a huge advantage being a stranger on the scene, and Brearley flaunted it. The batsmen didn't know what to expect from me, nor I from them. Apprehension only properly materialises once you've had your fingers burned.

The morning after I was fêted by the press, made all the newspaper headlines and was interviewed by radio and TV. I'd been in the professional game a matter of weeks, but on the evidence of the previous twenty-four hours I would breeze through county cricket. And when I got home with my £100 prize to find Dad chuntering about a cheque for £1.30 for a *Some Mothers Do 'Ave 'Em* repeat in Hong Kong, I thought I'd really arrived.

Early success can go to your head, but the Middlesex dressing room kept me docked to reality. I was reminded that awards were shared out and that I was still a student at heart. 'Don't change anywhere near me,' Emburey would say, guarding his neatly folded kit. 'I don't want to end up with a bag full of your reeking socks.'

'He'll probably tip tea in it first,' added Radley, smirking.

A Lot of Hard Yakka

I was given several silly nicknames, including Heinz (they said I had 57 varieties of delivery) and Yozzer (an old Lancastrian term for Hughes, as with David Hughes in their team).

And children will always keep your feet on the ground. A small boy rushed up to Brearley and me as we walked off the field and asked excitedly for the England captain's autograph. When he'd obliged, the boy looked at me doubtfully and, handing me a pencil, said: 'Sign here, mate.' When I returned the book he read what I'd written, then methodically rubbed it out.

Fortunately, I wasn't erased from the team, but I was beginning to realise how cavernous the gap between the Second XI and the first-class game was. Build-ups were much more serious; so was the standard of the opposition. There were overseas superstars everywhere – Miandad, Rice, Procter, Glenn Turner, Gavaskar – quite apart from all the England and West Indies players. The leading cricketers had four or five bats, and Gatting had six pairs of gloves, all numbered. Edmonds had three lockers, each containing unused items of sponsored equipment, mostly footwear. I had paid £11.50 (trade price) for my one Slazenger bat, and had to borrow things like helmets and thigh pads. At least in the first team you didn't have to change round the back in a dingy anteroom. And on the field you didn't spend any time checking to see if the coach was watching. You were far too immersed in the game to worry about that.

Everything followed a firm routine, though. You got to the ground for 9.45 a.m., did the warm-ups, which Barlow always began with a bark of 'Gregories' (after Gregory Peck, the slang for neck-stretching), loosened up in the nets and sat down for a cup of tea and a biscuit at 10.30. Then, after a post-match snifter in the dressing room and a couple in the pub, you were back home by 9 p.m. Celebratory piss-ups were infrequent, and even after our exciting win at Worcester, most of the team only stayed around long enough to allow the spectators to get their cars out.

THE INCREDIBLE HULK

Tuesday 12 August, Gillette Cup Semi-Final, Hove
In fact, if we had had a session after every victory that summer, we'd have been certified alcoholics and I'd never have done a stroke of anthropology revision. Middlesex forged ahead in all competitions, leaving in their wake a wave of destruction mainly perpetrated by Wayne Daniel. The mere sight of his rippling physique and beadily perspiring forehead at the end of a 25yd run-up was enough for some batsmen. Despite being constantly late on the field owing to a habitual need to visit the toilet as the umpires emerged from the pavilion, he worked up a ferocious pace with new ball, old ball, wet ball, dry ball, at any time of day against anybody. He was a gem, invaluable in any era. No wonder they called him the Diamond.

Jon Agnew, then Leicester's number 11, was so frightened he came out protected like the Michelin Man and deliberately took guard a foot outside leg stump. 'I owe it to my side to be fit to bowl,' he said. From my regular position at short leg (expendable, unprotesting), I could see great trepidation in the eyes of Essex's last man David Acfield as he prepared to face the Caribbean music. 'Tell him just to bowl a straight one and he can have my wicket,' he said tremulously. The Rat, who overheard from mid-on, obliged.

At Hove in the tense Gillette semi-final against Sussex, Imran Khan foolishly let Daniel have a bouncer at the end of the Middlesex innings. I was the non-striker and it was the most terrifying delivery I had ever seen at first hand. Imran thundered to the wicket – muscles taut, features clenched – leaped into his delivery stride and propelled a murderous bumper which came within a wafer of decapitating Daniel. The sight of Imran tearing fearsomely down the hill and the baying of the excited crowd made me realise for the first time that adrenaline was sometimes brown.

Daniel wasn't in a fit state to bat after that and gave me the strike. Thanks very much. But it had the opposite effect on his bowling. He took 6–15, blitzing Sussex from the competition. Two batsmen were bowled before they'd twitched, another was forced so far back he trod on his wicket, and Imran himself took rapid evasion from several ferocious bouncers before succumbing tamely at the other end.

Daniel's vigorous effort in delivery dragged his sweater up over his head and left his rolled-up sleeves flopping, so there were endless delays while he rearranged his clothing. There is a wonderful photograph of him receiving the Man of the Match from a toothy Ken Barrington. Daniel is beaming and glistening with sweat, the collar of his shirt flat across his shoulders like wings, revealing a gold chain and an expanse of rippling torso. Presumably the snapper was a woman.

His influence was far-reaching. Two days later in the nets, a ball he sent down flew up and accidentally hit me on the chin, causing a large swelling, though not much actual pain. As luck would have it, the incident got me back into Durham University. I still had to sit my retakes, but with a swollen jaw, a doctor's note and some uncharacteristically good acting, the results were ignored. Anyone who was playing for the best county side in the country was good enough for them.

TOP OF THE FORM

By early September Middlesex were leading the championship and in the final of the Gillette Cup. The last hurdle was a three-day match at Cardiff, a straightforward journey down the M4 for most of the team. I'd been in Durham doing exams, so wasn't expecting to play. Van der Bijl was doubtful, however, having slipped, three-quarters drunk, in the hotel bathroom and badly bruised his hip on the toilet bowl. He played in the end, hampered by what the spectators had been told was a 'groin strain'. So did I, and between us we took over half the Glamorgan wickets on a crumbly old pitch in front of a handful of despondent Welshmen, to give Middlesex an unassailable lead in the championship. With one – now meaningless – match to play, Van der Bijl had taken 85 wickets, and everyone agreed that he had made all the difference.

At Cardiff there were celebrations, albeit rather short-lived ones, since we were due at Canterbury the following morning for our last game. Beer followed the champagne, and even Brearley, who usually drank only Darjeeling, clasped a full pint glass proudly to his chest. Barlow got quite carried away with jubilation and was semi-plastered by the time we set off into the night for our anti-climactic trip to Kent.

The vision of a blue souped-up Fiat Mirafiori throbbing down the M4 at 120mph was irresistible to the Reading Police, and after a seven-mile chase they pulled us over. Barlow tested positive and was taken down to the station to provide a blood sample, while another policeman drove me in his car. Barlow apprehensively entered the building and was met by the duty sergeant, whose stern face suddenly brightened. 'Cor blimey,' he exclaimed. 'You're Graham Barlow, aren't you? You Middlesex lads have just won the championship, haven't you? Congratulations! I've been a Middlesex fan for thirty years, you know . . .' There was a nervous pause. Then he said, 'Do have a safe trip, sir.'

Within four days the Gillette Cup was ours as well. The final was played in a marvellously cordial spirit. When the Surrey captain, Roger Knight, passed me on his way to the wicket, he wished me good luck and almost apologised when he clipped my second delivery through mid-wicket for four. Gatting retrieved the ball, and brought it all the way back by hand, presenting it to me as if on a salver. 'Keep going. Don't worry about a thing,' he said, smiling. 'Just enjoy yourself.'

Because of the capacity crowd and a large TV audience I was rather conscious of an unsightly spot on my chin and more nervous of dropping a high catch than about being hit for a lot of runs – a lone fielder on the boundary is so much more conspicuous. So when Intikhab Alam launched a skier towards me at long-on, I was relieved that Van der Bijl, fielding on the other side of the sightscreen, called for it. He ran 30yds and made a despairing lunge, but didn't lay a hand on the ball. Instead it plopped to the ground about 10ft from where I was standing. The crowd oohed but no one on the field said anything. There was more consternation that an 18st South African had just made a small crater in the hallowed turf.

Five hours later, we were on that famous pavilion balcony collecting the medals. I looked down at the assembled throng on the field below, waving coloured hats and banners, and saw my own image in among them: a twelve-year-old in red jumper and corduroys gazing admiringly upwards and clutching a scorecard and a rosette. At that age I had visualised the excitement of standing up there acknowledging the fans' cheers; now, seven years later, it had happened. This, I realised, was what people meant when they said you had the world at your feet.

How the metamorphosis had happened I wasn't entirely sure. All I had done was run up from some vague mark and let go of the ball, not always entirely sure whether it would swing in or out, end up short or full. I worked on the confident assumption that if I didn't have much idea what the ball would do, then what chance did the batsman have? Botham had made a success of the liquorice-allsort style, after all. Bowlers like this might be hellish to captain, I knew, but Brearley seemed to revel in the challenge. He rubber-stamped his approval when he chose me as his bridge partner on the coach trip back from our last Sunday game.

Basking in the glory of becoming the first county ever to win both major trophies in one season, the rest of the team accepted my unpunctuality, poor dress sense, clumsiness and no-balling as a novelty, sometimes even finding it amusing, like a wife enjoying a new husband's foibles for the first few weeks of marriage. The press reacted with customary hyperbole, writing me up as a future England player, and there were all sorts of lavish headlines: 'SIMON TOP OF THE FORM', 'SIMON – IT'S SO SIMPLE', 'HUSTLING HUGHES THE HERO', etc. I even believed some of them. I had also accumulated three cash prizes, two winners' medals and a new video recorder as a result of my first two months in county cricket – unreal, and a considerable advance on my original £45 a week. I had also failed to score a single first-class run in five championship matches, and despite twice remaining not out, had achieved the distinguished average of 0.00.

STRANGLING HEADLESS CHICKENS

I had a whole new vocabulary as a result of my opening season in first-class cricket. I made a list of the jargon I'd learned.

Aerosol bowler: Someone, usually a paceman, who 'sprays it everywhere'.

Bunsen (burner): Turning pitch. Raging bunsens are often found in India.

Cafeteria bowling: A load of dross, so the batsman can 'help himself'.

Cardboard cut-outs: Immobile slip fielders.

Crusted: Batsman hit on head by a bouncer.

Dinkies: Second team.

Dollies: Stumps.

Donks: Outfielders, usually lumbering fast bowlers.

Filth: Bowling that promotes a flier.

Flier: Rapid run-scoring at the start of an innings.

German general: Batting side encouraging the ball to boundary (after Goebbels).

Gnat: Seam bowler of negligible pace.

Grabbers: Slip fielders.

Headless chicken: Bowler who tears in wildly with a crazed expression.

Jaffa: Unplayable delivery.

Jugged, going for the jug: Bowler savaged by a rampant batsman.

Knacker: Ball, delivery.
Lenny: Batsman who favours legside shots.
Nick: Faint edge, or another word for 'form'.
On 'em: Batsman arriving for the second innings having got nought in the first.
Pongo: Rapid scoring.
Rabbit: Hopeless tail-ender.
Sawn off: Dodgy umpiring decision.
Spitting cobra: Delivery that rears abruptly from a length.
Strangle: Wicket with rotten delivery. The bowler is often labelled 'Boston'.
Trolleyed: Player (usually the captain) losing his temper.
Up the ladder: Injured player suspected of hypochondria.
Xs: Captain's allowance for a round of drinks after a day's play.

COMMONWEALTH TUTORIALS

Autumn 1980

It could be said that the performance of the swanky Phillips video machine I won as the Bowler of the Month for August became a microcosm of my entire career with Middlesex. It employed a complex new system different from that of other videos and was rather nifty for several years. Then it started to go on the blink, was impossible to reprogramme and ended up some time later on the tip.

But there was no time to look at reruns of the summer's successes as we were about to be whisked off on a trail-blazing tour of Zimbabwe, pausing only to play a charity match. This marked Ossie Ardiles' first attempt to master the perplexing art of overarm bowling, which in his case involved running round in circles and releasing the ball skywards from several yards behind the umpire. John Cleese also played, impersonating Mike Brearley in prematch photos with fake beard, wide-brimmed sunhat and turned-up collar. When we arrived in Zimbabwe mugshots of our leading players were displayed across the back page of the local paper. The photo captioned 'Mike Brearley' was actually a picture of John Cleese.

The official objective of the Zimbabwe tour was to forge a sporting relationship with a newly constituted state, and to encourage their cricket development. The main objective of some of the players was to soak up some rays and get laid. The influence seeps through to almost everyone eventually, I'm afraid, and, well . . . it was about time one or two of us got our feet wet. I'll spare you the details of my discovery of the Honey Trap, except to say she was a nineteen-year-old hairdresser whose name I've forgotten and I withdrew in the middle to turn over the Donna Summer tape.

There was no doubt that the Zimbabwean players had both sporting ability and a wicked sense of humour. They were expert practical jokers. They circulated a story that the brother of one player had broken the world record for consecutive press-ups. When you mentioned it to the player he said, 'My brother hasn't got any arms,' and looked utterly downcast, eliciting a spluttered, profuse apology. Then he would burst out laughing, indicating that it was all a load of cock and bull. They had an obese 21st left-arm spinner called Richie Kashula, whose shorts were so large that Gatting and Emburey each got into one leg and waddled round the boundary like Siamese twins. He took revenge by imprisoning Emburey in a cage of baby leopards on his family's game reserve and threatening to free the growling mother from her pen.

The warmth and generosity of the people we met (at that time, almost exclusively white) made their hospitality hard to refuse, and every morning Emburey wandered into the changing room bleary-eyed saying, 'Right. I'm not going out or drinking any more this trip.' He was always to be found at two o'clock the following morning pissed as a newt. The grounds were superbly appointed, surrounded by blue and white striped marquees and blooming jacaranda trees. There was an area of open seating called Castle Corner, from which tanked-up men hurled friendly abuse: 'Oi, Hughes, lend us your brain – I'm building an idiot.' We stayed in luxurious five-star hotels, were chauffeured about in large executive cars (though most players preferred sleeping to sightseeing), taken to countless receptions and dinners, where the steaks were a foot long, and generally treated like royalty.

Towards the end of the tour, as we were travelling back from the tranquil Vumba Mountains, Brearley mentioned casually that he'd been asked to assemble an international XI for a five-day match in Calcutta over New Year, and would I like to play? I nearly bit his hand off before he'd even mentioned the fee of £125. The team, containing top players like Wayne Larkins, John Lever and Frank Hayes, was to fly out, business class, on Air India on Boxing Day.

I had spent four months in Sri Lanka two years before so I was somewhat au fait with Asian lifestyles, but the squalor and deprivation of Calcutta hit me like a kick in the stomach. Whole families lived in cardboard lean-tos beneath flyovers choked with traffic and acrid black fumes. There were beggars everywhere with deformed limbs, and some with no limbs at all, lying slumped in dark recesses with empty begging bowls beside them. The roads were bedlam. In the filthy Hoogley River, we saw a bleached dead body floating close to where women and children were washing themselves.

Our hotel was the ultimate contrast. You got to it by walking straight off the main street, down a long, wide corridor and into an airy marbled reception area with chandeliers and palms in brass pots. The staff wore white tunics with gold braiding and elaborate headdresses. Each room was large and white-washed and was allocated an individual bearer, who was at your personal beck and call twenty-four hours a day. They dozed on stools outside your room but stood bolt upright and saluted whenever you walked past. The bedrooms all over-looked a glistening pool surrounded by tables and chairs with parasols. When you sat at one all you could hear was the swaying of the palm trees and the lapping of the water – no hint of the chaos and deprivation only 30yds the other side of a high concrete wall. It was like prison in reverse.

The Indians certainly seemed to regard English cricketers as VIPs – until they got on the field. There the Brearley International XI got a good thrashing. The match was to celebrate the golden jubilee of the Bengal Cricket Association, and the Indians put out a strong side captained by Venkat, the Test off-spinner. They were all in the middle of their season, whereas most of us hadn't played for three months. It showed.

The Indians batted for most of the first three days on a wicket as flat as a pancake and I finished up sending down 49 overs. I'd never fielded for even one whole day before. The vast Eden Gardens ground – rows and rows of concrete terracing towering above the pitch – was only a third full, but still the crowd numbered over 25,000. They were very noisy and kept pushing bits of paper, cardboard and even dried leaves through the security bars for us to sign. One afternoon the whole stadium erupted in the middle of my run-up and wouldn't stop clapping and cheering for several minutes. I pulled up and we all glanced at each other quizzically, looking for giveaway brown stains down the backs of trousers or other unfortunate evidence. It emerged later that everyone had been listening on miniature transistors to the Australia–India Test match in Sydney, and Kapil Dev had just taken his fifth wicket.

The best bit was the lunches. About half an hour beforehand, waiters would ferry into the dressing room a number of heavy iron cooking pots and gas rings and prepare an elaborate spread of meat and fish curries, chicken tikka, spicy potatoes and cauliflower and a pungent yellow mush which was apparently made of lentils. There were enough chapatis and rice to feed a small army. Some of our team picked listlessly at the bread and complained that there were no chips. Why are Brits so unimaginative when it comes to foreign food? I ate so much it was quite a struggle to bowl afterwards.

Tea, something I assumed would be especially good in India, was a disappointment, though. Spoonfuls of brown dust, powdered milk and sugar were ladled into a large kettle, which was then filled with water and brought to the boil. It tasted like toffee-flavoured Carnation milk. The sandwiches were almost bereft of filling, which caused more indignation.

On the final day the teams were presented to Indira Gandhi, who actually stayed and watched the play for half an hour. She had a graceful air and an even limper handshake than Brearley. It's just as well Mike Gatting wasn't there – he'd have accidentally broken her wrist.

After all this early fame and fortune, I was gaining quite a reputation back at university. I was written about in student magazines, sports-mad lecturers let me off geography practicals and I was given free use of the Athletic Union phone. On the social front, people I'd never met claimed acquaintance, various girls came and went and 'So many people come to my room,' I wrote home, 'that a packet of chocolate digestives only lasts four and a half days.' High living or what?

Some time during the second term, a letter arrived from Middlesex offering me a three-year contract. It was far more than I had expected and gave me the security of one full season after I'd finished college. The other members of Training Group 4 had done enough – in the Rat's case considerably more than enough – to be given another go the following year. But neither Nepo nor Spikes had yet made their first-class debuts. What a pleasure awaited them.

LAISSEZ FAIRE: 1981

THOMMO GOES BUST

For Middlesex 1981 began contentiously. Despite the presence of several promising home-grown fast bowlers, the county had signed the Australian legend Jeff Thomson for one season. How were we going to nurture young talent if the path was blocked by two overseas spearheads? some outraged members demanded. Others correctly realised that it was a temporary measure which gave Middlesex potentially the most fearsome opening attack in the country.

Thomson himself was pretty oblivious to the debate. He was perpetually cheerful, said 'Shit, yeah' a lot and fitted easily into the Middlesex regime of jeans and T-shirts. He wasn't used to the far reaches of England in April, though, and shrouded himself in multiple sweaters on the Darlington balcony during a friendly match against Durham. 'Jeez,' he said, 'it's not even as cold as this in my fridge back in Brisbane.' He soon cheered up at the sight of a blonde waitress carrying a tea tray to the dressing room. 'Cor blimey, I wouldn't mind catching it off that,' he muttered, rather too loudly, and the girl blushed.

Because I was still at university, I missed most of Thommo's early-season performances, but his duel with Viv Richards was often re-enacted by Wayne Daniel over the following months. 'First knacker, Thommo send down a bungcer – real quick,' Daniel would say in hushed tones, obviously awe-struck. 'Vivvy, he all shook up. Blinks, touches he cap. Second knacker fly from a length, hit he on de tumb. He no problem. Third short, *reeaall quick*. Vivvy he go forward, he rock back, he hit it back *harder*! Past Thommo head high! Jesus Chris' man, Viv can play, *he can play*!' At this point Daniel always looked as if he was about to burst into tears, but somehow regained his composure to add: 'And you should have seen

61

his piece of crumpet in the Tavern . . .' This was just in case you had forgotten that West Indians most admire great batsmen for their pulling power *off* the field.

I had a great term of cricket at Durham. Captained by Worcester's Tim Curtis, we comfortably won the British University Cup after a nerve-racking semi-final, and as a second-year student with no summer exams, I didn't even have to feel guilty about not doing a stroke of work.

Coming down to London at the end of June, I was resigned to a spell in the Middlesex Seconds, and constant entreaties from my father to build up my strength. 'You know it's the only way to improve,' he had written for the fiftieth time in a letter to me at college, 'and for God's sake get your run-up sorted out.' Why can't parents understand that labouring a point just makes the child more resistant?

Instead, the day after getting back I was summoned to the first team at Trent Bridge because Thomson had suffered a hernia. As it turned out, he wasn't to play again that summer. He was last seen on a Kon Tiki coach bound for Amsterdam. I had been drafted in for a three-day championship match over a weekend, which rather upset my plans. I had a smart party to go to in Hertfordshire on the Saturday night and now I'd be stuck in Nottingham without any transport. A decade and a half later, it seems a pretty strange attitude to have adopted, but when you've just spent ten weeks wallowing in the warm bath of student life, sudden, unforeseen responsibility is like a freezing cold shower.

RANDALL THE HAPPY HOOKER

27 June, Nottinghamshire v Middlesex, Trent Bridge
But after the initial shock cold water is invigorating, and the match was memorable. It had a frightful, numbing beginning, though. The covers were removed at 10 a.m. to reveal the closest thing to a mangrove swamp you're ever likely to see

in first-class cricket. Or a smallholding of spinach at the very least. It was damp, lush and rutted. A wicked smile crept across Richard Hadlee's face when he heard that Notts had won the toss. A couple of hours later we were 118–9. Hadlee had just sent Daniel's off stump cartwheeling through several revolutions as I shuffled out to the wicket, having hurriedly borrowed Phil Edmonds' helmet. It was too big (what else would you expect?) and kept slipping sideways. Hadlee was not amused.

Imagine being enclosed in a small, illuminated space and being fed a barrage of searching questions by an indefatigable examiner. Your responses are nervous gibberish. It soon became clear that facing Hadlee was a bit like that. His bowling was a kind of interrogation. 'How d'you cope with outswing?' his expression seemed to ask. 'Here, try this one.' Grope. 'Mmmm, not too good, have another.' Desperate block. 'Dear, dear, you're lunging at it now. Try a short one round the ribs.' There's no perceptible change of action, not a flicker in that steely stare. You get the feeling he won't relent until he's found a way to break your physical and mental resistance, probing and analysing like someone from MI5. After surviving for what seemed an eternity but was actually only ten balls and, I assumed, his complete repertoire, he sent down what looked like a rapid beamer. I ducked instinctively but was astonished to feel the ball crash into my toe right in front of middle stump: a brilliantly disguised slower ball. I was amazed at his powers of deception, and even more amazed when the umpire gave it not out.

As often happens in a last-wicket partnership, the more accomplished player was out first, leaving me unbeaten on four (an edge through the slips) – my first runs in county cricket. As I was walking through the members enclosure, a grizzled local supporter with a mouth full of bun muttered, 'Eee, me dook, yer was never really in, was yer?' and belched loudly.

Later I endeared myself even less to the Notts followers. I took the first Notts wicket, which brought in their hero Derek

Randall at number 3. He was cheered all the way to the wicket as he practised his forward defensive, mumbling, 'Coom on Rags, coom on.'

'He's a nervous starter and a compulsive hooker,' Brearley whispered. 'Give him a bouncer second ball.'

Randall hoiked it wildly into the hands of Edmonds at deep square leg and departed for a duck, head bowed. There was a dense hush around the ground. I was engulfed by elated colleagues, but I couldn't help feeling a bit of a spoilsport. W.G. Grace's voice echoed in my ears: 'They've come to see me bat, son, not you bowl.'

I bowled 23 overs that afternoon and took five wickets, though it must be emphasised that the pitch was a cabbage patch. It emerged later that one of my wickets the umpire thought was a snick to the keeper was actually the sound of Clive Rice's gold chain clanking against his perspex visor. Fashion triumphing over common sense in his case, I suppose. Still, I led the team off the field at close of play to comments like, 'Top drawer!' and 'You'll do for me.' It gave me the nerve to ask Edmonds if I could borrow his car to pop out for the evening. I didn't tell him I was going to a posh party a hundred miles away.

Having cavorted around half the night with a girl I'd got off with in the back seat of a DAF, I was rather bleary-eyed when I returned to pick Edmonds up at the hotel next morning for the Sunday League match. I was made twelfth man, and once the team had gone out on to the field, I subsided into a deep sleep. Throughout the Notts innings I was completely oblivious to the Middlesex fielders' frantic signals for sunhats and drinks and got some dark looks when they returned. 'That was a pisshole effort,' said Barlow, self-appointed youth-bollocking officer. 'We were waving all afternoon and Eddie Hemmings had to bring us our gear in the end. And now you haven't even poured the tea out or got the bowlers a drink.' No wonder he was on his third marriage.

The atmosphere had become a shade frosty and I realised that returning to a team after a long break was like going home to your parents for Christmas. Initially they make quite a fuss of you, cooking your favourite meals, giving you the best chair, but it isn't long before they start ticking you off for being a messy eater and getting mud on the carpet.

If negligence is bad, clumsiness is worse. When the championship match resumed the next morning, I dropped a dolly which deprived us of an extra bonus point – a precious teapot shattered on the kitchen floor. At lunchtime the players' irritation had turned to despair, and they sat in the dressing room glumly munching egg and cress baps and idly flicking through disintegrating copies of *Men Only*.

But on county cricket's restless rollercoaster, you can soon get back on track. When Randall came whistling into bat for the second time, I was in the middle of an over. 'Try a bouncer second ball again,' advised Brearley. 'He's a nutter – he's bound to have another go at it.' The trap ostentatiously set, I bounced, Randall hooked, and the ball looped down deep square leg's throat. He had fallen twice, second ball, for the most transparent ploy in the game, each time without troubling the scorers. It had to go down as the most foolhardy pair in history, made even more absurd by Brearley's later admission that he had actually outlined the ploy to Randall himself when they'd had dinner together the previous night. It is this self-inflicted vulnerability that makes players like Randall, forever walking the tightrope between triumph and calamity, so deeply treasured.

Such events can transform group morale – even the normally morose Emburey managed a smile after that wicket – and Middlesex surged to an unlikely victory on a tide of optimism. Back on the M1, my heart jumped at the mention of my name on the Radio 2 cricket scoreboard as a possible for the third Test against Australia. Stupid overreaction, totally premature, I thought, and for the remainder of the journey to Maidstone, I could think only of the girl in the back of the DAF.

THAT'S GOT TO GO DOWN AS A CHANCE

Wednesday 8 July, TCCB XI v Sri Lanka, Trent Bridge

Yet the BBC weren't so far off the mark. Two days later, as I picked splinters out of my socks in the dilapidated eyrie of the Maidstone pavilion, I was handed an official letter from the TCCB inviting me to play in an England trial XI against Sri Lanka the following week. I hadn't yet played in ten county matches, yet the England selectors were already trying to haul me up the ladder. I came over all bashful and tried to play it down, but Brearley was all for the idea. 'The Rip thinks there's a bit of Botham in you,' Clive Radley mumbled. 'Swingers, bouncers, experiments. You're the dog's bollocks. Don't stop now Yoz-*booyy*!' It was an ill-timed comparison. Botham had just been out for a pair at Lord's, bowled indifferently and had jumped from the England captaincy before he was pushed.

I should have been uncontrollably excited, but through a combination of youthful nonchalance, uncertainty and high testosterone, I wasn't. I was far readier for nights of hot passion than for days of Test cricket – well, what young lad isn't guided to some extent by his knob? – so this extra expectation I could do without. And it was another away game (Nottingham *again*) which meant more nights up north sharing poky hotel bedrooms with burping, farting cricketers.

Here there was one consolation, however. The hierarchy had allocated us single rooms in the Nottingham Albany, so at least I wouldn't be woken by a team-mate running a bath or cooing to his wife at some unearthly hour. As it turned out, this didn't mean I got any more sleep, though. There were reputedly five girls to every man in Nottingham, which accounts for the nudge-nudge, wink-wink attitude of cricketers destined for a few nights in the city. Two females had been enticed into the next-door room by a couple of players on the first night, and I was kept awake until 3 a.m. by laughing, screeching and the rat-a-tat-tat of a headboard banging against the wall. At times it sounded as if someone were digging the road rather than having sex.

The culprits regaled us with a dramatised description of events the next morning, which lasted a lot longer than John Barclay's team talk. 'Go out and enjoy yourselves,' was about the gist of it.

'Some of us obviously already have,' a voice piped up, and there was a lot of loud narfing. I thought it was all rather sordid, and decided I wasn't really cut out for après-cricket at this level. But in Nottingham you can't avoid it. After the first day's play we gathered in the Trent Bridge bar and were soon joined by a woman in her thirties with permed hair whom everyone seemed to know. Several people made a beeline for her and bought her drinks, and eventually she was introduced to me. 'Hello, I'm Grace,' she said. 'You're new up here, aren't you? Maybe I can show you around.' And she took my hand and placed it on her warm breast. Then she brushed her hand lightly across my crotch. I shrank away in embarrassment, but she was egged on by others. 'Ah, he's a bit shy,' she continued. 'We'll see what we can do about that later.'

'Amazing Grace has got a bloody good team,' one player said afterwards. 'You're no one unless you're in it. She likes new boys. We'll bring her up to your room later. You don't mind putting a show on for the lads?' Well, I did mind very much, actually, but it was a difficult situation. I didn't want to seem like a Mummy's boy to the others, but neither did I relish the thought of revealing my sexual inarticulacy in front of them. I didn't fancy her, either, to be honest. I stayed out late to avoid an awkward confrontation, and woke several times in the night after unpleasant dreams about dominant school matrons. I didn't perform well in the match, and at the time I was quite relieved.

Now I understand what forty-year-old fathers mean when they say to their twenty-year-old sons, 'If only you knew what I know now.' At that age, boys aren't interested in dedication or sense or going to bed early. They want time off the leash to experiment and find themselves. At least ten years elapse before they appreciate the golden opportunities created by their lack of inhibition. By then, the chance is lost. It's so infuriating that the true realisation of our own sporting potential materialises only when all we're equipped with is the aptitude for mowing lawns in neat stripes.

Looking back, it was the closest I came to playing for England, and if I'd been less self-conscious and not so afraid of responsibility and a bit more willing to listen, I might have taken part in the most memorable Test series of the decade. Brearley, after all, was about to be reinstated as England captain and we spoke the same language. But my attitude infuriated him. 'Why do you bowl four perfect balls in an over, then two easy leg-stump half-volleys?' he asked me one day, perplexed.

'I don't think I'm good enough to bowl *six* good balls an over,' I replied with a baffling trace of self-satisfaction.

He smiled, but inside he was seething. He hated complacency and lack of ruthlessness. He was quite un-English in that way, and fought against our embedded inclination to hold something back rather than go all out to win. He virtually ordered bowlers to intimidate tail-enders if they hung around and forever sought to stimulate players by giving them extra responsibility and self-belief. By galvanising Ian Botham like this he resurrected England that summer in perhaps the most sensational Ashes turnaround ever. Sadly, we Middlesex players didn't see much of it – we always seemed to be labouring in the field towards some meaningless draw. We were preoccupied with trying to winkle out Worcestershire during Botham's barnstorming century at Headingley, and retrieving boundaries glided and caressed by Zaheer Abbas while he was taking 5–1 at Edgbaston.

EDMONDS – BRILLIANT ECCENTRIC OR ANNOYING BASTARD?

29 July, Lancashire v Middlesex, Southport
At least back on the county treadmill I felt safe and reassured, like a local rep returning to his own patch after a management

training week. Even sharing a room seemed suddenly more acceptable, though not with Phil Edmonds. I had been lumped with him for the three-day match against Lancashire at Southport in the sort of 1920s hotel where coachloads of pensioners stop off for lunch. Lots of flowery wallpaper, padded seating and toilets in public areas, but seriously neglected upstairs. The beds were lumpy, musty and squeaky, but not nearly as disturbing as Edmonds himself.

As a confirmed insomniac and an information junkie, he kept the telly on until the national anthem had finished and the set was making a nasty high-pitched bleep. Then he'd set the alarm for 6.05 a.m., and when he woke switched on Radio 4 for *Farming Today*. Music would have been just about OK, but trying to doze as some Cornishman waffled on about milking methods was too much. After two nights of this, I secretly disconnected the radio while he was out of the room, thinking I would at least get a bit more kip. But when he discovered the radio wasn't working the next morning, he made a great commotion complaining to Reception, and in the end an odd-job man was sent round to fix it, which involved turning on the light and moving my bed as well as making even more noise. 'Fools rush in . . .'

I never totally endeared myself to Edmonds, a feisty but intriguing character, which was a shame, since he was captain when Brearley was on Test duty. On the first day of the Southport match, he gave the new ball to Mike Selvey, who usually aggravated him, and constantly yelled at me on the boundary to move 2ins this way or that. He even threw the ball at me once when he thought I wasn't listening. It ended up in the crowd, ten deep round the boundary. This was the day Charles and Diana got married and it had been declared a national holiday. Most of the spectators wore ties and patriotic hats and were in high spirits. Oh, the romance and blind optimism of those times.

Some punters were following the pageant on transistors but nobody dared take their eye off the middle because between the time Charles entered St Paul's as a bachelor and emerged as Diana's husband, Clive Lloyd progressed from 0 to 91. I was bowling at him for most of that innings, slightly apprehensively at first, until he'd blocked four successive maidens. Just as I was starting to feel I'd got him cornered, he swayed on to the back foot and pulled a perfectly respectable ball into some distant allotments as if he were swatting a pesky fly that had suddenly woken him from a mid-morning nap. After that he went berserk.

Being toyed with by someone who looks such a misfit is very humiliating. The loping gait, the round shoulders, the thick-rimmed glasses and the sunhat like a German helmet totally belied Lloyd's awesome power and feline reflexes. When he suspended the carnage temporarily to have a drink, I picked up his bat. The handle had six rubber grips, the edges were 2ins thick and it weighed a ton. It was like wielding a railway sleeper, and from the bowler's point of view, that's what it looked like.

He hit Wayne Daniel, who was no slouch, for a straight six which shaved the bowler's head, never climbed more than 12ft above the ground and was still rising when it clattered into the sightscreen 60yds away. Daniel went as white as a sheet, if that is possible for a man as black as night, and joked afterwards that he'd never chat up Lloyd's 'crumpet' again.

Apart from Lloyd, Lancashire weren't much of a side in those days, and many of their players were rather sluggish and overweight. 'Too much beer and black pudding,' my Mancunian aunt said. We had far more skill and spirit and won the match comfortably in spite of, rather than because of, Edmonds' leadership. Mostly his captaincy was a dead loss. He was often fractious, set strange fields and omitted players he disliked, e.g. Selvey, a skilled seamer, even on a pitch the colour of a billiard table. If his spinning partner suddenly found some turn on a particular wicket he would bring himself on from that end, relegating his colleague to the opposite one. He became irked by Daniel's prolonged absence having ankle treatment at The Oval and was then informed by the umpires that the Barbadian wasn't permitted to bowl for half an hour once he'd returned. 'Oh, just fuck off then, Diamond,' he said, and sent the bemused player back to the dressing room. They nearly came to blows at tea.

Sometimes Edmonds was deliberately provocative, and on occasion this backfired. At Hove, Imran Khan had batted competently for some time and I, the only fit fast bowler, had spared him the bouncer, chiefly because the wicket was fast and our batsman feared severe reprisals (and so did I). When Edmonds gave me a rest, Imran said, 'Can I take my helmet off now, then?' to which we both nodded.

Seeing the Pakistani prince now sunhatted, Edmonds said surreptitiously, 'Go on, have one more over and stick it up him.' Imran parried the surprise bouncer with his glove and was caught in the gully. As he jerked his head back his hat fell on the wicket, which kept us amused for a while. But we weren't laughing when he came haring down the hill later that afternoon. He took 6–52 and we lost by a mile.

And yet Edmonds' personality was addictive. He was articulate, sharp and brilliant in the role of devil's advocate. His outright audacity was enviable, and he had supreme confidence in his ability and judgements, epitomised by his arrogant stroll on to the field and affected upturned sunhat. It was presumably that inner strength which enabled him to overcome an embarrassing outbreak of the yips in 1980, when for a time he couldn't manage anything except a double bouncer or a high full toss and only regained control by completely doing without a run-up.

He was sometimes intensely irritating, bowling a whole over deliberately down the leg side if Brearley didn't give him the field placings he wanted, or lying down at mid-on because he was bored, but it usually made us laugh in the end. He was a skilled mickey-taker, admonishing the black players with mock prejudice for the obsessions they had with their looks and their female conquests. 'Why don't you guys just get your cocks out and measure them?' he would say. He scoffed at Wayne Daniel's lurid stories about his sexual exploits, yet the two were firm friends and always travelled together. If he wasn't reading the *FT* or a biography of Macmillan he was formulating new sponsorship deals – boxloads of Patrick footwear kept arriving in the dressing room, for instance. Frequently he sat on the balcony talking telephone numbers with some pinstriped acquaintance. There was rarely a dull moment.

MEN OF LETTERS

For me the season had gone better than expected. I had bowled erratically at times, but that was down to inexperience or overexuberance and generally the ball seemed to be coming out of my hand pretty fast. People asked how a 5ft 9in pipsqueak like me could bowl so quick, but I had no idea. I just ran up and let go with no real fear or apprehension, clanged the odd helmet and made a mess of the Gloucester batsman Phil Bainbridge's ear. I experimented with different deliveries and sometimes was applauded for surprising some distinguished player with a brilliant in-swinger when, to be honest, it had been a complete accident. MCC members and other spectators nodded their approval as I walked through the Long Room and most of Middlesex's committeemen were almost deferential.

I got plenty of encouragement from the Godfather himself, Gubby Allen, the respected former England captain and selector who hobbled backwards and forwards between his MCC-owned house and the Lord's committee room. He had a private entrance into the ground from his back garden, his own key into the pavilion and a special high chair with the best view in the house. The older players bowed and scraped whenever they encountered him in the corridors and always called him sir. His word was gospel. If Gatting was making too much noise hammering the dressing room lino with his bat, Gubby would thump his stick on the committee room floor below in protest.

Initially he took a great interest in me, because, he said, he had been a similar sort of bowler (he was the one who refused to bowl leg theory in the Bodyline series). He suggested I tried a shorter run, and passed on useful advice about swing. I was flattered by his attention. But he could be brusque and had a rather eccentric manner. Once he drove round to the Nursery Ground in his grey Bentley to watch a friendly match I was playing in. While we were batting I ambled past his car, unaware that he was inside it. Suddenly the electric window was lowered just long enough for him to say, 'Hughes – too many no-balls!' before it whirred back up again.

His lifestyle epitomised the tsars-and-serfs arrangement at Lord's. His splendid house was provided rent-free in return for his services to cricket, and he had a housekeeper to look after him. The groundstaff were expected to prune the roses and mow his lawn in their lunch hours and never got a penny for it. They were paid a pittance by the MCC and had only a broken down old AA caravan behind the sightscreen for tea breaks or to take refuge in when it rained. It wasn't fit for a dog.

The hardships of a groundsman's life made me aware of how privileged I was as I headed back to university in the first week of October, somewhat mystified by Brearley's suggestion that I should give it all up and play cricket full time. This advice seemed particularly odd coming from a man with a double first from Cambridge. But not half as odd as the letter which I found in my college pigeon hole on 7 December 1981. I was just off to play football for the college against Newton Aycliffe and read it while squashed in the team Land Rover on the way to the game. Written partly in note form, it said:

Dear Simon,
I'm tidying up a deskful of unanswered letters before going to India tomorrow. This note is to ask if I told you you'd got yr cap. Did I? I hope so. And hearty (really) congratulations.
Yrs, Mike (Brearley)

A Lot of Hard Yakka

* * *

Talk about a bolt from the blue. Most cricketers have to wait years to get their county cap, and eventually it is awarded to mark an excellent series of performances in the first team and a reputation for reliability and quality – a sort of stamp of approval, like becoming an officer in the army, I suppose. Usually it's officially presented by your captain on the pavilion balcony in full view of team-mates, public and photographers, and there's champagne and canapés with the committee afterwards. You don't have to wear a silly 'II' on your sweater any more and you get a nice, secure all-inclusive salary and permission to eat in the Lord's dining room whenever you want. And you never have to change in poky, neglected Dressing Room 4 ever again.

I may have been deprived of the familiar ceremony, but I had earned my stripes after only eighteen first-team matches, which was wonderfully satisfying. Especially when you compared it to the fate of the others from Training Group 4 who began their Middlesex careers on the same day as me. The three of them managed only one first-class appearance between them in the whole season (Spikes scored 5 not out and took 0–34 on his debut against Gloucester). I'd hardly seen any of them for three months.

After a promising first year, the Rat was having second-season blues, which were not helped by Edmonds having rediscovered his form after his 1980 yips. He wasn't sniffing out as much nifty info as before, either, although his unconventional approach to fielding at short leg – scurrying up the wicket alongside the batsman if he danced down the wicket – had won him a few admirers. Nepo was so frustrated by his inconsistency and lack of opportunity that in one Second XI match, having nudged a scratchy 30-odd before lunch, he removed his contact lenses and went out again and deliberately slogged. He made a brilliant 168, but all the batting places in the firsts were tied up, and he failed to maintain a challenge. Spikes had a singularly unproductive year and became so anonymous that one morning Brearley came up to me looking perturbed and said, 'Our twelfth man today is that chap on our staff who bowls and bats left-handed . . . I can't remember his name.'

They were pretty disconsolate. They spent their days playing in front of a handful of pensioners at Sittingbourne or Nuneaton, their nights in crummy hotel bars or monitoring team-mates' exploits with a girl known as the Bournemouth Flier, and only came to Lord's on Saturday mornings to bowl at the first team or for Naughty Boy nets after they'd played badly. The future was extremely uncertain for all of them. Whereas, to all intents and purposes, I had made it. I was a capped player, I already had two cup-winners' medals and had been recommended for the England tour party to the West Indies by John Woodcock of *The Times*.

My father certainly wasn't allowing me to get complacent, though. At 8.30 a.m. the day after I got home from university for the Christmas holidays, he was in my room with the saw. 'Come on,' he said. 'They're demolishing a house up the road and there's some lovely wood to cut up before breakfast. It'll build up your biceps for next season.' All I got for my efforts were bemused stares from the neighbours and a palm full of splinters.

THIRD DEGREE: *1982*

the Jackson Five • banned stars • rain games
• big bangs • Botham and Richards
vanquished • Titmus recalled • Brearley's
final triumph • Springbok supremacy

SLOW CHANGE

Friday 2 April

The season had an inauspicious beginning. I was already depressed by Mike Brearley's decision to retire the forthcoming September when I discovered that my brand new Renault 5, bought with the proceeds of two seasons' success, had been rammed overnight outside my parents' house. No one had owned up to it. The garage replaced the damaged wing with one a different shade and the car never looked the same again. A day later I attended the Middlesex committee's 'Meet the Players' dinner, a deadly pass-the-port-old-chap sort of affair at the rather worn-out Cricketers' Club in the West End. Denis Compton kept the place just solvent with his daily five-hour lunches.

I thought there might be a presentation of my county cap there, but it was never mentioned and I detected slightly negative vibes from some of the players, as if it were an offence to jump rank so quickly. Then one of the more out-of-touch committee members cornered me with, 'I say, I used to put clay in my wicketkeeping gloves. What d'you put in yours?' before launching into an interminable monologue about life behind the wickets in the 1930s. He thought I was Paul Downton. Mind you, mistaken identity was something Roland Butcher, Wayne Daniel and Wilf Slack, all of whom were black, had to put up with all the time.

They were joined on the staff by two other players born in the West Indies – Norman Cowans and Neil Williams – and the whole lot of them always sat together in the dressing room. We called them the Jackson Five. They spent an inordinate amount of time preening themselves after training, dousing their bodies in creams and lotions, and Cowans seemed to have inherited Daniel's habit of standing around swathed in white towels handling his goods, of which he was, understandably, very proud. As a ditherer myself, I was often last in the dressing room with them and we all got on well. I was constantly amazed at the length of time they could sustain a conversation about the assets of Noelene the lunch waitress. Occasionally they inadvertently lapsed into a patois which I could only half understand.

'Mnnn, she raggin' it, her body smooth, her tighs dem luksha-ree.'

'Wha's happenin', you bin chattin breeze, Raas-ole?'

'Listen up, I ain't no Raaaas-ole, Bamba Claart!'

And then they'd all purse their lips and make that distinctive sibilant sound with their mouths that women do to pet cats.

If the Jackson Five weren't conspicuous, the chances were they'd assembled in the physio's room. One of them would have some minor ailment, or need a massage, and the others followed to loll about on a treatment bed or cut out extra bits of padding for their boots, or use Johnny Miller's binoculars to spy on girls in the stand. Why he had binoculars at all was a mystery to me as he could barely see past the end of his nose. Once, when he was winding crepe bandage round Daniel's thigh, he got his tie caught up in the strapping and accidentally cut it off three inches below the knot.

With six graduates on the staff and lots of players with overseas experience, there was plenty of informed discussion about the South African situation. Fifteen county players had just come back from the first rebel outing, labelled Boycott's tour, and had subsequently been banned from Test cricket for three years. John Emburey was one, but there were no hard feelings towards him – not on the surface, anyway. Maybe the Jacksons felt a bit betrayed, but even they thought the three-year ban was harsh. Emburey certainly did – he was rucking about it for weeks, often while sitting on the toilet with the door open. But then he'd have moaned if he'd just won the pools. Anyone who supports Millwall gets like that.

Mike Gatting had to cope with an early-season ban as well. During the three-day match against Cambridge University he had been lured into a college bar by the dangerous Mr Stephen Henderson, a man well known for his revelry and liquid intake – a sort of public-school version of Ian Botham. Henderson had just thrashed an unbeaten 209 off the Middlesex attack and engineered a lock-in from which Gatting eventually extricated himself at 1 a.m. Seeing his car parked on a double yellow line, he attempted to move it to a meter 100yds down the road, but halfway along the kerb he was apprehended by a WPC. He was next seen emerging from the station at dawn, and was disqualified from driving for a year.

HAZARD WARNING

Meanwhile, in a Durham University library revising for my finals, I made a list of the overseas fast bowlers in county cricket that summer. It read:

Essex:	Norbert Philip
Glamorgan:	Winston Davis
Gloucestershire:	Franklyn Stephenson
Hampshire:	Malcolm Marshall
Kent:	Eldine Baptiste
Lancashire:	Colin Croft
Leicestershire:	Andy Roberts
Middlesex:	Wayne Daniel
Northamptonshire:	Kapil Dev and Sarfraz Nawaz
Nottinghamshire:	Richard Hadlee and Clive Rice
Somerset:	Joel Garner
Surrey:	Sylvester Clarke
Sussex:	Imran Khan and Garth le Roux
Worcestershire:	Hartley Alleyne

The first thing batsmen do at the beginning of the season is to look at the fixture list, note down when they'll need their arm guards and extra thigh pads and wonder if there's any hope that the odd imported headhunter will be worn out by the time they're encountered. There didn't appear to be too many escape routes in 1982.

Temporarily, mine was a final term at university. In previous years, coming into the Middlesex side midway through the season fresh from two and a half months of healthy gallivanting had been an advantage. This time it was a drawback. A combination of owning a car, compiling a dissertation, pandering to a possessive girlfriend and dealing with the fallout after finals took its toll on my fitness, and when I came down in July I was pallid, out of practice and couldn't stop bowling no-balls, which to my father, above all, was a heinous crime. I think he would have been more tolerant if I'd declared I was gay. Going on my previous rather than my current form, Middlesex shoved me straight in the first team and initially I wasn't up to it. Brearley lost his temper when I messed up his master plans with lousy concentration or clumsy fielding, and when he stared at you daggers and exclaimed, 'What the *fuck* are you doing?' he was actually quite frightening.

I couldn't even produce much at Nottingham, almost my second home, but there were other influential extraneous factors. One was the re-emergence of Amazing Grace at our hotel, this time with a friend called the Poison Dwarf. We were again holed up in the characterless Post House by the M1. There was a lot of coming and going in the room next to mine, and various (unmarried, of course) team members sneaking about with one of those minuscule face towels wrapped round their waists. I jammed an armchair up against my door and took my phone off the hook.

Another hazard was the fact that one of my bowling boots had completely worn out. I'd reinforced it with white tape, but every so often my foot burst out of the side as I was letting go of the ball. Clive Radley came to my rescue in the end by giving me one of his spares, so I played in one Patrick and one Mitre. I don't think Geoff Boycott would have been very complimentary if he'd been commentating.

At least returning to Lord's would settle my mind, I thought.

Now I was a capped player I'd get complete respect and a comfortable place in the Lord's dressing room. Naïve. My ten-week absence at college meant that all the hooks and lockers and armchairs had been claimed and everyone had their own favourite space, so I had to make do with the back of an old chair which was often used as a wicket for dressing-room knock-abouts.

These usually took place during lengthy rain stoppages and involved negotiating a spinning tennis ball with a stump or a bat, using the edge rather than the front. During other delays we played cards or an idle catching game bouncing balls off the tops of coffins or had impromptu boxing bouts in batting gloves, or selected Fat, Ugly XIs from the *Who's Who*. Relaxation was out of the question.

One person did enjoy a comfortable spot – and he wasn't even a player. Eddie Dawe had been a committed Middlesex supporter for fifty years and on Sundays he used to bring boxes of peaches or mangos or toiletries for the team, the remains of which often ended up in my kit. The best armchair was drawn up for Eddie to watch the game from, and he often stayed for several hours. Edmonds also introduced Sir Phil Harris of Harris Carpets fame, and he was accorded a prime viewing spot on the balcony. Later he supplied us with colourful little holdalls with 'Harris Queensway' on the side, but they fell to pieces quite quickly. So did the company.

The dressing room was a circus of intrigue before matches, and during them if we were batting. Brearley mulled over tactics with the chairman; Gatting would be in noisy mock stance, practising the little cough he always exhaled after hitting a boundary. Butcher was experimenting with a new backlift in front of the mirror. Edmonds was discussing some financial business on the phone beside Slack, who was easing an extra rubber grip on to his bat handle. In the other corner Radley made clicking sounds as he nudged imaginary balls through the leg side and Daniel did sit-ups or rubbed his sore Achilles' with acne cream while Emburey needled him. 'That's all just fackin' bullshit,' he said good-humouredly. Selvey entertained Barlow with satirical Australian commentary.

The general hubbub was suddenly quelled when a dismissed batsman returned to the room – a sort of respect for the dead. That hush hung like a pall over The Oval dressing room – like the one at Lord's, large, Victorian and festooned with pictures of old players – in a knock-out match against Surrey. The gallumphing Sylvester Clarke produced a terrifying spell with the new ball, bulldozing through Middlesex's top order. Brearley began the procession, getting out in the first over caught behind off a flier, and his simmering mood was inflamed by Ted, the old Cockney attendant, saying innocently, "Ere Mike, wot you doin' back so early? Ain't they started yet?' Brearley nearly wrapped the bat round him. It takes a handful of games in a team to learn which batsmen tend to return to the dressing room trailing blue touchpaper.

IN FOR A SHOCK

Explosions certainly seemed to be on the agenda that summer. After the Falklands War came an atrocity much closer to home which put life and death into stark focus. As we were sitting down to Nancy's chicken chasseur at lunchtime on the last day of a match against Notts, there was a massive bang and all the pavilion windows rattled alarmingly. At first we thought it was an earthquake; then someone suggested it might have been Gatting tripping on the stairs on his way up. But after no more than ten minutes the air was rent with sirens and news filtered through that there'd been an IRA bomb under the bandstand in Regent's Park, about half a mile away as the crow flies. We had been for a jog there only three days before and remembered the old folk reclining in the blue and white striped deckchairs listening to the band.

For a while after that I got a bit obsessed by perspectives. What did cricket matter compared to this? I said. How could we get shirty about a bad decision or a low score or a dropped catch when people were being maimed left, right and centre? Were we justified in getting all uptight on the field just because a loose ball had been spanked to the boundary? 'Yes, because when you're bowling it seems to happen about twice an over,' railed Nepo, who'd recently been drafted into the squad.

This wasn't quite true, but my free rein lasted only one more game, a bizarre affair at Southend. We stayed at a non-descript hotel by a wharf with shared bathrooms and a communal TV room. We spent most of the evenings at the local nightclub, where one evening Gatting was asked to judge a local talent contest. Afterwards he was jigging about innocently on the dancefloor when a man came up and, for a reason which never became clear, laid him out. Gatting's face was all puffy the next day and he had a black eye. Graham Gooch whispered good-humouredly to his mate Emburey, 'Cor, looks like the bloke's done him a favour.'

The umpires for this match, Don Oslear and the Pakistani Khizar Hayat, turned it into a complete farce. Batsmen kept getting out hooking and then being reprieved because the delivery had been deemed above shoulder height. (The worldwide prowess of the West Indian fast bowlers had forced the ICC to introduce the one-bouncer-per-over law, but the umpires were hopeless at implementing it.) Brearley lost his rag several times, though I was never sure whether it was because I was buggering up his championship aspirations with too many hittable short balls or because of the ropy decisions.

The game was heading for a dreary draw when heavy rain came to the rescue on the last day. After lunch everyone started to get changed into civvies – surreptitiously, so as not to appear too presumptuous. Some umpires are bloody-minded. Sure enough, Oslear kept us there until 4.55 p.m. and then, with no possible chance of a result unless most of the Middlesex batsmen were suddenly assassinated, declared the ground fit for play.

Both teams were incensed, and as a protest Keith Fletcher took the field in blue tracksuit bottoms until he was ordered to change. In keeping with the daft nature of Essex teams, Gooch then bowled an over of left-arm to Brearley (batting left-handed), and Brian Hardie, who was totally mad, sent down an over of lobs, removing a sweater after each ball and ultimately his shirt as well. Mercifully, the umpires called a halt after that.

So did Brearley to my immediate progress. He walked over to me at the nets before the next game and I knew it wasn't to ask if I'd prefer the Pavilion or the Nursery end. 'I'm really sorry, Yozzer,' he said, 'but we've decided to leave you out today. The Diamond's fit and Norman's been bowling well, and it looks like it might be Selve's wicket rather than yours. Don't be disheartened.'

It was my first experience of this situation. He tactfully didn't mention the word 'dropped', but I knew that was the reality all the same, and it hurt. To make matters worse, I would now be lumbered, as twelfth man, with the repulsive task of collecting everyone's dirty whites, socks, shirts and Daniel's jockstraps, skidmarks and all, and taking them down to Sketchley's in Marylebone High Street where our dry-cleaning was free.

In between the monotonous fetching and carrying and shouting 'Diamond – Eau de Cologne', having answered the batphone in the corner, I dwelled on a ragbag of emotions, including resentment that someone else had been preferred to me and frustration at my own inconsistency. I was a grumpy twelfth man because I was desperate to play, unlike some of the guys you meet, who are just along for the ride and are relieved at not having to actually perform. An added frustration was the fact that we were top of the championship, and playing pulsating cricket. When that happens the dressing room is a rich source of high-octane banter, never mind the odd win bonus. Secretly, I hoped the team would continue to flourish but at the same time look slightly deficient in the fast-bowling department and would suddenly realise what they were missing. These are unsavoury thoughts, but real sportsmen don't eat quiche.

In any case, no matter how chummy you are with other players, you're never really part of a performance as twelfth man. You witness all the success and failure, the excitement and despair, but if you haven't actually *felt* the pain, you can't appreciate the pleasure, and vice versa. A strange sort of distance develops between you and the participants, a subconscious cold shoulder that can only be retracted if you're welcomed back into the fold. It's the same sort of unspoken ostracism you get at a party dancing opposite a girl who doesn't fancy you.

MIDDLE ENGLAND SUBSIDES

7–10 August, Somerset v Middlesex, Weston-super-Mare
My demotion didn't last long, in fact. It was only one game – a great relief as the next match was against Somerset. For several years I'd aspired to play on the same park as the two greatest cricketers in the world, Ian Botham and Viv Richards, not to mention the tallest – Joel Garner. We were in a park, too – Clarence Park, Weston-super-Mare. Hardly an auspicious stage for Beefy, Smokin' Joe and Bird, as they were known to anyone who'd played for England (most of the Middlesex team).

Weston was the quintessential county cricket venue. It had a sloping wicket, a bumpy outfield (which for most of the year was a public dog toilet), marquees, deckchairs, temporary stands and the constant hum of generators powering beer pumps and ice-cream vans. And the world's smallest pavilion, actually an enlarged park-keeper's hut, but barely adequate to keep chickens in. The dressing rooms were full of shrapnel-sized splinters, but it didn't matter: once everyone had wedged their cricket cases in there was no floor space visible anyway. The lack of elbow room resulted in me jogging a tin of whitener off the seat, splattering the contents simultaneously into several bags. It wasn't an enthusiastic welcome back into the fold.

A Lot of Hard Yakka

The bowling attacks pitted Cowans, Hughes, Emburey and Edmonds against Garner, Botham, Vic Marks and Colin Dredge, a loping seamer who ran in like an arthritic chasing a pickpocket. It was easy to see who the weak links would be, and Richards, strolling in with a mouth full of gum around 11.30, cast a cursory glance round the field then quickly sent a couple of my less than probing deliveries rasping through the covers. He leaned on his bat, chewing contentedly, but over-confidence got the better of him for once and he was out for 35.

Botham exuded a similar aura of self-satisfaction when he strode in, helmetless, after lunch. He'd recently taken 208 off the Indians, for God's sake. 'Go-orrrrnnnn, Ian,' the crowd burred. 'We love you, Both' (pronounced to rhyme with moth). I always got lumbered with the overs immediately after lunch because all the other bowlers tended to lapse into post-prandial lethargy. I was more curious than frightened of Botham, despite his opening salvo, a back-foot thump which nearly took gully's head off. When he tried to repeat the shot, he got a thick edge to third slip which Gatting clung on to.

As with most Botham terminations, there was a fair amount of pain involved and Gatting's congratulatory handshake was a good deal limper than usual. It didn't dim my exhilaration as I was engulfed by my colleagues. I.T. Botham c Gatting b Hughes 7 was a proud moment, and I wasn't afraid to show it. At least I'd made some progress, then; two years before I'd have recoiled with mild embarrassment at claiming a wicket with a less than perfect ball, and Brearley would have berated me crossly with, 'I suppose you want to call him back then, do you?'

Neither Botham nor Garner were much cop with the ball on this occasion and, like most westerly teams playing Middlesex that summer, Somerset failed to put up much of a fight. In fact, they were totally spineless. Needing 200-plus in their second innings to make us bat again, they folded to Cowans and me for a pathetic 57 all out, and all 10 wickets went down in the space of 8 overs. Richards, flabbergasted at a flier from

Cowans which shaved his nostrils and which he later described as 'seeerious', poked at my out-swinger and went for a duck; Botham ran down the wicket to his first ball, heaved mightily and was bowled all over the place. 'Pah, he's blimmin' rubbish,' echoed the same group who'd given him a rapturous welcome twenty-four hours earlier. Their irritation was understandable. In glorious sunshine, play was over by midday.

But Botham and Richards were a special kind of hero. Invariably failures were quickly forgiven and long queues of maturing men, schoolkids and old ladies stood gawping in adulation as they waited for their idols' autographs. (I signed a few and kept hearing the recipients whispering 'Who is he?' behind my back.) That night there was an indoor skittles evening for Richards' benefit in a cavernous local pub. The place was heaving with ruddy-faced supporters and holidaymakers with burned necks and the function raised a few thousand quid. Botham wasn't even there. Neither, for that matter, was Richards.

The Middlesex machine rumbled on. At Cheltenham a mind-numbingly brilliant innings by Roland Butcher, whose August scores – 1, 0, 1, 173, 11, 11, 197 – made an articulate career statement, should have seen off Gloucester but the weather saved them. And our ten-day ramble through the shires' temporary sporting venues ended at a neglected ground in Coventry owned by the Courtauld textiles company and sometimes hired by Warwickshire. It mainly staged matches against teams like Viyella Nomads and Halifax Woollen Mills, and certainly wasn't equipped for professional cricket. The pavilion was ramshackle and full of what appeared to be the former contents of a church hall. The jumble of furniture left very little room for manoeuvre and when I pulled a muscle in my back the only area big enough for the physio to treat me lying down was underneath a grand piano. Honestly.

Middlesex won this match by an innings, helped along the way by an extraordinary disease that suddenly afflicted Gladstone Small. In his third over he sent down eleven no-balls in addition to five legal ones and was in such a state by the end of it he opted to deliver the last off a three-pace run-up. It was a wide. I don't think anyone has accidentally bowled a longer over in first-class cricket. 'Well, captain, you asked for three good overs to start with,' the bowler said wryly afterwards, 'so I gave you them all at once.'

Small was a consummate professional, but county cricket was riddled with people who were a good deal less team oriented. This may have blunted the game's competitive edge, but it added to the fun. When Yorkshire visited Lord's there was a symbolism about their batting order with Boycott at number 1 and Illingworth at 11 – as far away from each other as possible. That was how they liked it at work and play. Coming in first wicket down was Bill Athey, a fearless young player who, it was well documented, was pretty fed up with Yorkshire's shenanigans and fancied a spell with a decent county. Like Middlesex. They had their eye on him, too, and were on the point of offering terms.

Athey was that Jekyll and Hyde, the teetotaller who can't resist a complete bender every six weeks or so. 'Tonight's the night,' sang Rod Stewart on the radio as I parked outside the Tavern, and it was. Both teams had been invited to Mike Selvey's benefit cheese-and-wine, an altogether more sober affair than Richards' skittles night. Except in Athey's case. He didn't bother with the cheese; he made a beeline for the plonk de la maison and sculled several bottles on an empty stomach.

When he'd drunk the place dry I drove him to his hotel and during the journey noticed my Renault was making strange wrenching noises. Then I realised it was Athey, leaning out and chundering down the side. Now both wings of my precious new car were tarnished. It was nothing compared to how Athey suffered. He was in such a bad way he couldn't take the field at all the next day. He spent the entire time prostrate on a bench, looking like death, and was subsequently fined. Middlesex's interest immediately evaporated and Athey stayed where he was. A while later he joined Gloucester, and a promising career hiccupped into obscurity for some time.

THE CONJUROR'S FINAL ACT

Richie Benaud once said, 'Captaincy is ninety per cent luck and ten per cent skill. But don't try it without that ten per cent.' In Brearley's case, the ratio was more like 60–40. He was a brilliant leader with great vision, but even he couldn't have prospered without fate's helping hand. He won more tosses than he lost; he was lucky to captain England in the prime of Willis and Botham, and when Australia were rebuilding after Packer. At Middlesex he was fortunate to inherit the best two spinners in the world, not to mention a battery of enviable fast bowlers spearheaded by the demon Wayne Daniel. He was lucky that his able lieutenant, Gatting, was one of the most consistent county pillagers of all time. You can't make a silk purse out of a sow's ear.

But he made his own luck, too. A pipe appeared round the dressing-room door as we were tucking into the custard creams just before the start of the next match against Surrey. On the end of it was Fred Titmus, now fifty and taking a day off from his subpostmaster's duties to congratulate the lads on staying top of the championship table.

'Teddy, what marvellous timing,' Brearley said. 'Got your boots? We could do with you today, it's a good old Lord's bunsen – I don't think three seamers will be much good.' And before Titmus could say premium bonds, kit had been rustled up and he was trying on Radley's spare footwear. He hadn't played seriously for two years. Who do you think was relegated to twelfth man half an hour before play? I'll give you one guess.

Brearley couldn't possibly have foreseen that Edmonds would hobble off on the last afternoon of the match with a bad back, but he had taken a gamble and roped in an ageing accessory just in case, and it paid off. On Brearley's last appearance at Lord's he whistled up a man who had first played there in 1949, having set Surrey an outrageously easy target of 161. Titmus took three vital wickets and Middlesex won a remarkable victory in the final hour. You don't see captaincy of that instinctive genius any more.

The championship was there for the taking, but we had to wait until the last match to clinch it. In between times we lost at Hove, where Nepo made his long-awaited debut and began with two sparkling fifties. He was upstaged by the unknown Alan Wells, who clattered a bouncer from Daniel memorably over the scorebox in a match-winning innings.

So, arriving at Worcester on 11 September, we needed four points to secure the title. In front of the majestic cathedral, for once free of scaffolding, we hustled out the home side by mid-afternoon on the first day to become champions. As the youngest player in the team, Nepo was appointed champagne monitor and moved about topping up everyone's glasses. I was starting to get a taste for the stuff.

Winning the championship is the prime quest for every county player, but often it passes almost unnoticed to out-siders. There was only a sparse crowd at Worcester that Satur-day to witness our victory and a few cocked an ear when the England touring party to Australia was announced over the tannoy. Cowans was in; Gatting and Edmonds weren't, which was surprising news to all three. The diehards were re-immersed in their newspapers and their knitting by the time the decisive wicket fell. Even our celebrations were forcibly muted, because we were still in the middle of a match. Ten minutes after Brearley had sealed his last triumph, he had to go out and open the batting with his celebratory glass of Lanson only half drunk.

Still, we got down to the dregs on the Monday. Worcester's chairman and specialist bat-maker Duncan Fearnley had cordially invited the team round to his factory for a champagne breakfast before the second day's play. We wandered between the lathes and presses and stacks of timber, sipping buck's fizz, and I chatted with one of the old machinists greasing a piece of 1940s equipment originally used to make armaments. Well, cricket felt like combat when you were facing Sylvester Clarke or Wayne Daniel.

Edmonds picked up a piece of raw willow cut crudely in

the shape of a bat and waved it around a bit. 'I'll use this,' he said.

'OK, when?' Fearnley asked.

'Now. Today.'

'But it hasn't been pressed or treated yet. It weighs nearly four pounds.'

'It feels fine to me,' Edmonds went on adamantly. 'Just put a grip on it.'

In the afternoon he took out that unmarked clump of prime virgin willow with rough, bulging edges and a handle clad in unglued rubber and made a rumbustious 92. It was a magnificent display of clean hitting, witnessed perhaps by 200 people, and afterwards he returned the pock-marked, dented blade, peppered with red marks, to the factory where Fearnley proudly put it on display for several years. Inadvertently, Edmonds had demonstrated that premier first-class cricket and the rustic village variety were not so far apart.

Brearley scored the winning runs and came off, bat raised, for the last of a hundred goodbyes. In the course of his final three years, he had displayed the magical ability to extract the juice from the fruit and make it into a magic potion. He changed the bowling constantly and fiddled with the field, forever trying to make something happen. Teams seemed to visibly wilt as soon as they lost a couple of wickets and new batsmen succumbed to the feisty bowling and cacophony of sound round the bat which he orchestrated. The opposition disliked the urbane cockiness of this bunch of southern show ponies and bolted for the warmth and security of their dressing room.

I rode happily on the back of the steamroller, scooping cheap wickets and continuing to annoy my colleagues by wandering away from precise fielding positions. 'Go where I damn well put you!' Brearley yelled right across the field at Weston. He was studying to be a psychoanalyst and sometimes I thought he faked anger just to test our mettle. He could be sympathetic too, though, and made a point of always being available for a heart-to-heart in the hotel restaurant during away matches.

He wasn't afraid of being provocative to help our cause, either. He ordered the fast men to intimidate stubborn tail-enders, put novices like me on to bowl at crucial times, baited aggressive batsmen with daring field settings, laughed at abusive spectators. 'Brearley, you're a toffee-nosed wanker,' a fat Sussex supporter bellowed as we inspected the damp outfield before a tense Gillette Cup semi-final.

'You're not only very rude,' Brearley retorted, glaring at the man. 'You're very ugly as well.'

Not a peep was heard from the chap from then on.

His record as Middlesex captain spoke for itself. In seven seasons (1976–82), the county won four County Championship titles (one shared) and only once finished outside the top four. During that spell, 65 championship matches were won and only 25 lost. Ultimately, this gave Brearley the complete thumbs-up from the players. They may not have always seen eye to eye with him, rather an understatement in Edmonds' case: the following year, in an Australian questionnaire, Edmonds wrote under the heading Biggest Break in Cricket: 'The retirement of Mike Brearley', but to a man everyone believed in his conjuring finesse and total self-belief, and that bred irresistible confidence.

As the presentation of the trophy at Buckingham Palace wasn't until November, the season petered out and there was no grand farewell for our retiring captain. Players turned up to Lord's in dribs and drabs to collect their P45s and a last batch of travelling expenses. The holes in the Middlesex office floor were still visible (in spite of our on-field success, the club had made a loss of £14,617), and there was a new picture on the wall showing a few of the team gathered round their sponsored Volvos. 'Some of the Middlesex players' cars are available for sale now,' advised a slogan above. Little did would-be buyers know that Radley drove his under the influence of Emerson Fittipaldi, Selvey hammered back and forth from Newport Pagnell every day, Emburey regularly bumped up sump-savaging kerbs and Brearley's car was driven at enormous speeds by his otherwise delicate Indian wife.

Brearley's parting act was to advise me on my winter plans now that my pseudo-academic days were over. I had been approached by two overseas provinces and couldn't decide whether to sign for Wellington in New Zealand or Northern Transvaal, South Africa. 'Well, New Zealand's the nicer place, but the Currie Cup will be harder cricket,' he said. 'I'd plump for South Africa.' Like all good subjects, I did as I was told.

FROM POLLOCK TO PILLOCK

Thursday 21 October, Pretoria

A winter playing top-class provincial cricket in South Africa might sound like dying and going to heaven, but people had warned me that Pretoria wasn't the friendliest city in the world. I soon discovered that for myself. Despite being given quite a reception by the press as Northern Transvaal's first official overseas player, I didn't exactly get the red carpet as far as my accommodation was concerned. In fact, I didn't get a carpet at all.

The flat they had rented for me was little more than a large bedsit in an unattractive 1960s block, and it was uninhabitable for the first week because the bed hadn't been delivered. When it did arrive it only had three legs. There was no other furniture, no fridge, no rugs or mats to cover the bile-coloured vinyl floor; various lightbulbs were missing, there was no plug on the toaster (and no screwdriver), no pots or pans, and the kitchen sink was blocked. Rather like your average council flat in Toxteth, I guess. Worst of all, there was no phone. It's incredible how utterly isolated the absence of that basic appliance makes you feel.

The night I finally moved in, I cooked just about my first-ever meal – sausages and mash – using a large kettle to boil the potatoes. 'Being inexperienced, I made rather too much mash,' I wrote in my diary, 'and lobbed the leftovers out of the window straight on to a car bonnet.' Such a mature chap

I was. The occupants of the other flats were all Afrikaners or German so I didn't make many friends there. And the only English people I knew in Pretoria were the three Yorkshire fast bowlers Chris Old, Alan Ramage and Graham Stevenson, whose daily routine involved lounging around a motel pool swilling vast quantities of Castle lager. Practice was a dirty word.

Because the Currie Cup only had six teams, there were only two first-class matches a month and there was no coaching to do, so I was dead bored and quite homesick. At least I had a robust VW Golf to gad about in, and I visited everything there was to visit: the Union Buildings, the Voortrekker Monument, General Smuts' house, the snake park, the zoo, the Sanlam Shopping Center, the Sanlam Center again, the zoo again. I even fitted in a safari in the Kruger National Park and a two-day hike in the Drakensberg Mountains. Sometimes I went and talked to the blacks sitting under the trees in the park over the road from the flat, but then the government suddenly announced that all local parks were to be for whites only and they weren't allowed in any more.

As Brearley had predicted, the cricket was incredibly tough. Our local rivals, Transvaal, were like a Test team. They had Graeme Pollock, Clive Rice, Alvin Kallicharran, Jimmy Cook and several other internationals, including my ex-colleague Vince van der Bijl. Barry Richards and Mike Procter played against us for Natal until Procter fell off a balcony and concussed himself. Sunday was a rest day in Pretoria, and Richards spent it at Sun City, gambling in the casino until dawn. Four hours and a hundred-mile drive later he waltzed in to bat, blinked sleepily in the bright sunlight and then impossibly flicked a decent yorker from me way over square leg onto the pavilion roof.

We played exciting day–night matches at the Wanderers in Johannesburg, getting overcome by the smoke from the *braais* round the amphitheatre, which wafted across the field. And in a noisy football stadium in Cape Town (the only local arena that had floodlights), facing Garth le Roux on a dicey artificial pitch redefined masochism.

Third Degree: 1982

Our team always arrived at the venue the day before a match, had a strenuous work-out and a pep talk over dinner, then got totally legless on cane and Coke. All of this was new to me. Northerns had also hired as coach the legendary New Zealand batsman John Reid. He had a very down-to-earth approach ('After you've hit a four, try to push a single') and a cruel streak in catching practice: he positively wellied the ball at us from close range. It was easy to predict he would become a hard-line Test-match referee.

As an eleven, we weren't in the same league as the others (a sort of Glamorgan of South Africa), and regularly returned to Pretoria to vitriolic write-ups by the local cricket reporter, Trevor Chesterfield, who hobbled about around the country after us wearing disgusting fireproof trousers. I later discovered that this was because he had a wooden leg. But I learned masses from playing against men of the calibre of Richards and Pollock. I saw how even they were nervous and prone to self-doubt and played premeditated shots. Pollock could afford to, he had been given out lbw only six times in his Currie Cup career. This was probably one of the reasons why every South African schoolkid tried to emulate his rigid legs-akimbo stance. But I was generally less than devastating with the ball and after two months I escaped to a more hospitable place.

Disillusioned with her job prospects after university, my girlfriend Sally had done a bunk of her own to join her expat parents in Malaysia. This was the little matter of 8,000 miles away from Pretoria, but I was so depressed – with my bowling, my lifestyle, my alien surroundings – that I couldn't get there fast enough. Taking a fortnight's holiday in the middle of the season was a stupid, reckless thing to do, but, as with drinking and driving or relying on the withdrawal method, you don't give much thought to the possible consequences when you're young. On my return, neither the Northern Transvaal players nor the press gave my excuse – that I'd been ill up country for two weeks – much credence.

In a way it was true, though. Having left the warm

university pool I was now in a much bigger, chillier pond and I was disturbed by its size and murky uncertainty. There had been no easy transition period to prepare mind and body for the assault. My father, for instance, had had a decade in rep before he faced a nationwide TV audience in *Emergency Ward 10*, whereas I had been pitched in at the deep end to deal with the pressures and the expectations as well as hulking great South African batsmen who devoured 12oz sirloin steaks and floundering bowlers with the same greedy relish. I felt I was being forced to grow up too quickly and began having second thoughts about the direction my life was taking. I loved cricket itself, but it was a job now, not fun, it was making me nervous and ruining my love life. The exhilaration of going out on to the field in front of a large crowd was soon dampened by a loose over, a misfield on the boundary, a captain yelling at you, 'For the third time, *save the one*!', or a hopeless tail-ender connecting with a massive heave over mid-wicket. The complimentary write-ups were diminishing, and reporters couldn't now use the get-out clauses 'He's good but raw' or 'Has great potential'. It was time for results.

GROWING PAINS: 1983

full-time pro • Gatting in command • Clarke
the 'fat black git' • bluffs and double bluffs •
re-arranged faces • scholars and spivs •
northern time-warps • eating disorders

'Put Your Shoes at the Door, Sleep, Prepare for Life'
(T.S. Eliot)

One-year-old children are vulnerable but they have no fear. They'll try anything once and hang the consequences. There's a lot of giggling and the tears are short-lived. When they're five, they're still vulnerable, but they're much more aware of danger, and that makes them wary. I'd reached the five-year-old stage in my cricket career. I'd done the dumb things one-year-olds do – spilt my food, fumbled the ball, squandered good learning opportunities (e.g., South Africa), and people had been sympathetic and understanding. But their patience was close to exhausted now, and I was a proper, fully fledged professional cricketer, not some irresponsible junior let loose in a playpen. I needed to get on the fast track to Matureville.

At Middlesex Mike Brearley's measured, thoughtful attitude had been replaced by the brusque, orderly, ravenous Mike Gatting. In Brearley's mind Kipling was something to read; to Gatting it meant apple pie. His no-nonsense captaincy was typified by the last words of his first team talk. 'Don't forget, jeans are not allowed on match days or away trips,' he announced. 'And if you're going to get pissed or poke a girl, do it before midnight.'

As it happened, I wasn't in a state to do anything of the kind for a while, because during a five-a-side football match at pre-season training I'd been up-ended by the county's newest recruit, Winky Robins, and had dislocated my right elbow. So much for the attempts to get us fit in a dusty old gym. It was the single biggest mark Winky made in his career. The son of the cricket committee chairman, Charles Robins, he had been expelled from Eton, but had wangled himself a temporary pass on the county circuit.

Small, with an unruly red mop and facial hair reminiscent

of Oliver Cromwell, Winky was a pukka chap but an ordinary player who wouldn't even have commanded a regular place in a club team. He was quite irritating as he never had a helmet or a bat, and when you lent him your box it was always a bit clammy when he returned it. But as a relic of a bygone era, he was a source of great amusement, particularly when wearing his brightly striped public-school cap or riling opposing fast bowlers in the Second XI with his posh accent. 'I'll tonk you all over the place, you hairy blighter,' he said to the young Australian, Merv Hughes, who was turning out for Essex Seconds. He did, too, though most of his attempted hooks flew straight over the keeper's head.

My elbow healed sufficiently for me to play in late May for the second team at Harlow. Flouting my parents' wishes, I stayed at my girlfriend's a lot (they didn't think I got a proper night's rest there) and when I set off for the ground from her crummy flat in Crouch End I discovered my car had been broken into and all my gear had been stolen. I spent most of the morning traipsing round town trying to find a decent pair of boots.

'The tealeaves must've been pretty pissed off when they smelled your kit,' said Spikes, who'd just helped dismiss Essex Seconds for 53. 'It pen and inks. I'm surprised they didn't put it straight back where they found it.' Why do people assume that something merely crumpled inevitably reeks? I suppose the state of my gear did draw attention to my general lack of discipline. By contrast, Spikes, who was quite orderly in approach, made the most of what he had. The trouble was, his bits and pieces didn't quite fit anywhere in Middlesex's specialist jigsaw.

BOUNCERS

Saturday 11 June, Surrey v Middlesex, The Oval

The season took ages to get going because of an exceptionally wet spring. Once the wickets hardened up, everything seemed to revolve around the new sport of cranium-clattering, inadvertently pioneered by the West Indies. Nothing gave me a clearer indication of the gravity of this business than facing Sylvester Clarke at The Oval. He was an immense man, so strong he could lift dumb-bells I couldn't even roll. He had a reputation for taking it easy with the new ball, then terrorising the lower order later in the day. So my sanity was seriously questioned when I made to leave the dressing room without a helmet, thinking the wicket wasn't all that quick. When I reached the door Barlow plonked one on my head. 'Don't be an arsehole all your life,' he said touchingly.

I was eternally grateful. The strapping West Indian came pounding in to bowl, looking more menacing with every stride. The spectators were egging him on and I was hemmed in by close fielders. Some people might think this sounds exhilarating. It's not the word I would use. Fear is closer to the mark, less of the physical variety, more the potential mortification of being made to look totally incapable, flailing arms and legs around like a demented punk.

'Step back and across, back and across,' I repeated to myself as the ogre approached. 'Keep low and watch for the bouncer.' The first two balls were relatively straightforward and I played them OK. Well, they hit the bat, anyway. 'Let's polish 'em off, Silvers,' several fielders beckoned. 'D'you hear what he called you, Syl?' another player called out. 'A *fat black git!*' Christ, it's coming this time, I thought. Back and across, back and acr— I saw the third ball pitch short. Then it vanished from view. I was vaguely conscious of flailing my arms skywards and jerking my head sideways – just like a demented punk, in fact. Then there was a terrible clanging sound and the ball ballooned upwards and was caught at slip. It had crashed into my temple, and but for the helmet it would have scrambled my brain. Instead it left a menacing red autograph on the perspex side piece, a gory reminder of the time I had been 2mm of man-made fibre from death.

'HOWZAAAAT!' yelled Clarke jubilantly.

'That's not aaart,' said umpire Arthur Jepson, a charismatic Midlander, if that's not an oxymoron. He had a dome-shaped head and protruding ears that made him look like a human FA Cup, 'and that's enoof of that short stoof.'

'What is this, a ladies' game?' Clarke snorted. He stormed back to his mark and sent down another bouncer. I felt the wind displacement as it sailed 2ins over the nape of my neck. Then we declared.

You could say I was shaken and stirred. With a bit of whip-lash thrown in. Was the ancient game sacrificing its old-fashioned image of fair play and breaking out into trench warfare? I asked myself. Were the umpires losing the plot? Was I a hopeless batsman? The answer to all these questions was yes, and that was somewhat disturbing. Cricket's soul was being trampled on by a growing obsession with success, mirroring the rise of Thatcherism. Get rich quick and sod how you achieve it. No one was apparently strong enough to buck the trend. Asset-owners were all-powerful.

This was the subject of constant debate. In one corner we had the once dominant establishment – the old landlords, if you like – demanding respectability and a curb on short-pitched bowling. It was unethical and boring, they said, and sooner or later someone was going to get killed. In the other corner were the gazumpers, the ambitious county captains and nouveau team managers determined to use any malicious means to win their prize. 'Stick it up 'im,' they ordered. 'You can see he doesn't fancy it.' They didn't care one iota for the fast-bowling lackeys caught in the middle who did as they were told and were then pilloried by sections of the crowd and the media for unseemly conduct. The mind of the young fast bowler was being twisted first one way, then the other, tangling the conscience into knots. It was better to be stupid. Fortunately, a lot of them were. I acted as if I was.

Growing Pains: 1983

Why hide under a duvet, anyway? There's something quite addictive about setting off your own ammunition, especially on an explosive site. Uxbridge was the fastest, bounciest wicket in the country in 1983. We were there for the next match and I tried out most bits of the pitch against Hampshire, taking a few wickets and clonking Robin Smith on the head first ball with a hasty bumper. He sank to his knees in a combination of shock and annoyance.

Having played with the demon Daniel for three years, I'd learned that after nobbling someone with a bouncer the fast bowler has several options:

1. Pitch up the next ball – an old-fashioned ploy with the aim of nipping through the batsman's defences while he's still groggy.

2. Bowl another short one despite the ostentatious bluff of reinforcing the slip cordon, giving the impression you're going to try the tempting out-swinger.

3. The double bluff: another short one, telegraphed by putting men out for the attempted hook. The batsman thinks you've laid the bouncer trap so transparently that you're bound to try something else (i.e., a yorker), so, theoretically, another bouncer *is* a surprise.

Confused? So was I. I bowled another short one anyway, unsure whether it was intended to be the bluff or the double bluff. Maybe I thought I was Sylvester Clarke. Smith gave a pretty vigorous response in any event, as you might expect of a guy who'd just returned from a stint of South African army training and did 200 press-ups a day. He catapulted the ball off his nose end into a bush. The shot made a sound like a 12-bore rifle crack and there was quite a commotion as several crows rapidly exited the distant undergrowth. After a moment's stunned silence, all the fielders collapsed in hysterics, which wasn't very reassuring. But I suppose it taught me another salutary lesson. Never trust men with bulky physiques and bushy moustaches. And, if in doubt, pitch it up.

SHATTERED

Monday 18 July, Middlesex v Leicestershire, Lord's
The tension and pent-up ambition in professional sport makes the participants liable to break out in unsympathetic laughter when any misfortune befalls a colleague. Whether it's crashing into the cameraman at football, spreadeagling the corner flag in rugby, or taking a bash on the shins fielding at silly point, the titters and insensitive remarks are guaranteed. It's an emotional release. 'Give him an Oscar,' they whoop at someone draped across a flattened advertising board. When a batsman is hit in the cods – 'amidships', in polite cricket parlance – even the spectators chuckle. The only time the hilarity turns to grave concern is when a player sustains a head injury. There we were joking about the red blotches on David Graveney's torso, which he'd sustained fending off our bumpers, and about Jack Russell's helmet being knocked on to the stumps. Ha ha ha. It was cannons against peashooters, we said; if our pacemen didn't get you, our spinners would. But something seriously unfunny was lurking round the corner.

At the time Emburey and Edmonds were at their peak, teasing and tormenting, complementing each other brilliantly, one nagging and persistent, the other full of spite and variation. They preyed on cautious batsmen: Emburey exerting a mean stranglehold, placing his field meticulously, even in benefit matches; Edmonds constantly striving for the classic pitch-leg-hit-off delivery and yelling 'CATCHIT!' whenever the ball cannoned off the pad.

Though Gatting was in charge, Brearley's legacy was powerful and Middlesex were taking the country by storm. We were marching ahead in the championship and, having got to the Benson & Hedges final largely on the toss of a coin, had stolen a narrow victory from Essex. Norman Cowans clinched it in the final over by castling Neil Foster, and obliging Fred Trueman, who, at the beginning of the innings, had said on the radio, 'Well, I've seen Norman Cowans bool one ball this season and he's gone backwards,' to eat his words.

But success can go to people's heads, of course, and over-confidence can quickly turn into recklessness. Roland Butcher sauntered out helmetless to take on the explosive fast bowling of George Ferris, a young West Indian playing for Leicester-shire. As usual, when Butcher walked in to bat, the team balcony was crammed with players expecting some lavish Caribbean stroke play. No one told *him* to put a lid on, I noticed. For a while he obliged with some extravagant shots; then, as he tried to hook a lifting delivery from Ferris, there was a crack like hammer on wood, a yelp of anguish and Butcher crumpled to the ground. He lay there for several minutes, whimpering, holding his face and kicking his legs about. It seemed as if he might expire there beside the wicket until, at last, an ambulance came and took him away.

For a while we thought he'd come back a vegetable and the incident shackled the team like a lead weight. It is true that you never feel someone else's pain, but the sound of the impact had been so distinct and vivid it sent a tremor down the spine. We stopped dead in our tracks and hardly won a game after that. Butcher was sorely missed, particularly for his fielding. He had been a dynamic one-man slip cordon in the champion-ship, pulling off catches with the elasticity of an invertebrate, and cleaned up everything in the outfield on Sundays. He totally deserved the nickname Hoover.

Naturally, Butcher didn't play again that summer and he was never quite the same batsman again. The ball had shat-tered his cheekbone like an eggshell, and when he came out of hospital his face was all wired up to stop it becoming lopsided. He looked like Hannibal Lecter on parole. You would have thought the mere sight of him would have prompted everyone to start screwing visors on to their helmets, and to think twice about hooking fast bowlers. But, borrowing the philosophy of the man who continues to chain smoke as his mate dies of lung cancer, they didn't.

SCHOLARS AND SPIVS

13–14 August, Lancashire v Middlesex, Old Trafford
In fact Butcher's accident coincided with a spate of injuries to batsmen, and by August run-scoring reserves were stretched. This didn't help me (with a highest score of 18), and given our supreme bowling strength, I was constantly on tenterhooks as to whether I'd be playing. Luckily, there was plenty going on to keep life entertaining.

Two years at Oxford University had turned Nepo (Richard Ellis) into a potential nutcase, but his talent was still intact and he and two other recent Blues, John Carr and Andrew Miller, stood in. They were joined by an individual from the other end of the educational spectrum: Jamie Sykes, a seventeen-year-old all-rounder from Bow Comprehensive via the Lord's groundstaff. 'Cor there aren't 'alf some fick bastards 'ere,' he remarked on his debut at Old Trafford, when a waiter mistakenly served him stew for lunch instead of chicken and chips.

Even at that age Sykes was a classic Arthur Daley figure, a bumptious East-Ender with the gift of the gab, though this was somewhat marred by a tendency to shower people with spittle when he spoke. He was a dead ringer for the Roy Hattersley puppet in the appropriately named *Spitting Image*. This habit was mercilessly mocked by his peers, but Sykes usually won verbal jousts with comments like, 'Well, at least I haven't got a face like a burst arsehole.' Or he would come up to you after you bowled an expensive over to say, 'You better fackin' geddorf before someone sees yer.' He became a dominant figure in the dressing room even before he'd done anything on the field.

For some baffling reason, Brearley also played in the Old Trafford match. Middlesex were looking a bit short of batting experience, but this hardly justified sending out an SOS to a forty-one-year-old who'd retired almost a year earlier. But even that wasn't as incomprehensible as Brearley responding to it. With a shock of almost pure white hair emerging from beneath a floppy hat, he stood incongruously at first slip, and made a scratchy 17 going in at number 5. Instead of admiring the way Brearley had gamely tried to fill the breach, I felt he'd sullied the distinguished image he had departed with. We were reminded of most of his bad points – his stiff technique, slight irascibility and eccentric dress sense – and none of his good ones. This often happens when champion sportsmen hang on too long or make sudden post-retirement comebacks. Brearley was intelligent enough to know better. As he was studying to be a fully fledged psychoanalyst and had to acquire complete self-knowledge, I can only assume his participation was an active extension of the course.

The Lancashire team under Clive Lloyd were still a bit of a rabble. Most seemed to be either drinkers or neurotics, and virtually all of them batted left-handed. I don't know whether you can infer anything from that. They were inclined to sudden collapses, and one morning when the pavilion steward was closing the gate behind an outgoing batsman, a member muttered: 'Don't bother to shut it, there'll be another one through in a minute.' Their two spinners for that match couldn't have been more of a contrast. Flat Jack Simmons was approaching 16st and had a gargantuan appetite for fish and chips and a thick Accrington accent. He coughed intermittently before he bowled, which some people assumed was a signal for his quicker ball. Actually it was because he smoked forty a day. He only bowled quicker balls anyway.

At the other end was the wee young Pakistani leg-spinner Nasir Zaidi, whom everyone called Zebedee. He didn't make much impact, and in one innings got out to a nasty delivery from Emburey. I overheard him telling his parents about it on the pavilion payphone afterwards. 'Nicha vallum balla die punka wallah the ball turned and lifted delli pincha diccum,' he said. It sounded like a line from *It Ain't 'Alf Hot, Mum*.

The pavilion at Old Trafford was a relic of feudal segregation. The Lancashire team were divided into two rooms according to seniority and the captain had his own private chamber. Women weren't permitted anywhere near the building (there was a ladies' stand further round the ground, totally open to the elements) and any serious debate on allowing them in was always hampered by comments like, 'Eee, before we know it there'll be breast-feeding in the bar.' It was the kind of embedded misogyny even a platoon of radical feminists with castrating irons would have had trouble eradicating.

DAILY BREAD

Such attitudes were symptomatic of the time warp in which our game existed. Gatting insisted we got to the ground every morning at 9.30 a.m., but few players used the ninety minutes before the game productively. Usually they'd sit around with a cup of tea trying to digest huge fried breakfasts, bash a few half-volleys against the advertising hoardings at ten, have a bit of fairly gentle catching practice and be back in the dressing room for tea and biscuits (bacon sarnies in Gatting's case) before 10.30. By the start of play their muscles had stiffened up again.

Lunchtime saw the same feeding frenzy as breakfast. It was almost like a nervous release. Most of the cooks seemed to be under the impression they were preparing a stodgeathon. Steak and kidney pie was standard fodder, and they all somehow knew that Gatting was addicted to spotted dick and custard. Geoff Howarth of Surrey and New Zealand, who'd been reared on The Oval's more basic fare, was violently sick at mid-on soon after lunch at Lord's. The groundstaff had to come out and cover it with sawdust.

Then at 4.10 p.m. at most grounds, plates of Hovis sandwiches arrived, usually containing processed ham or that funny fish paste out of a jar, along with chocolate mini-rolls, Bakewell tarts and those cakes covered in stringy bits of coconut. The players, led by Gatting, attacked this offering like a pack of hyenas, tearing the meat from the bread, and less than sixty seconds later the tea tray was just a mass of discarded crusts and wrappers. You'd never eat this kind of thing in mid-afternoon at home. The tempo of cricket seems to stimulate the stomach: the spectators, too, got out their Tupperware and flasks when the players went off and munched their way through a small feast which four hours of sitting on their backsides hardly warranted. Even the sparrows began congregating expectantly around gaggles of spectators just before an interval.

For the away team's players, an evening in the hotel bar was commonly followed by a curry – a most inappropriate end to a sportsman's day, but it was cheap and it didn't matter how you behaved. Or else you had a burger to soak up the beer (and to save on expenses). At Cleethorpes, a sadly faded resort with rotting boats and 1950s tea rooms where Notts played the odd Sunday League match, there was nothing to do in the evenings but hang about dingy amusement arcades eating fish and chips. People there thought nutrition was a kind of warfare.

A 'controlled' diet meant you consumed three rather than four packets of chocolate bourbons before the match, rejected a second plate of cheese after a three-course lunch, and just ate the filling in the sandwiches. You played over 120 days' cricket a summer but, no matter how energetic you were or how many overs you'd bowled, by the end of it you had put on weight rather than lost it.

BANANAS

Wednesday 31 August, Yorkshire v Middlesex
But it was immensely enjoyable trawling round the country doing what you loved and getting paid for it. Walking out on to the field in front of a crowd did give you a buzz, and a surge of adrenaline and a feeling of importance that my university friends who assembled theodolites or folded maps for firms of chartered surveyors didn't have. They grudgingly

donned a jacket and tie to sit in a stuffy office each day while we cricketers roamed around, free-spirited, wearing V-necks and sponsored polo shirts.

Unless you played for Yorkshire. Now here was an archaic culture which had been clearly preserved since Queen Victoria's reign. You only have to remember their ludicrous rule about picking exclusively Yorkshire-born players to be aware of that. Immaculately dressed commissionaires with shiny peaked caps and tassled uniforms greeted you at the entrance to Headingley; ruddy-faced men in tweeds and flat 'ats milled about. Once play had begun, an old chap who was so lacking in expression he could have been an automaton plodded endlessly round the perimeter in a white coat and tie, completely oblivious to the game, crying 'Yorkshire Post!' every ten seconds throughout the day. At 3.30 he changed it to 'Evening Post!' You could set your watch by him.

Members of the team were ordered to wear the traditional Yorkshire cap (my Dad would've approved). Anybody taking the field in a trendy white sunhat was given a severe lecture. The same fate befell a player who didn't wear his Yorkshire blazer at the lunch table.

On the terraces neanderthals lucky to be allowed out by their keepers hurled abuse at any member of the Jackson Five within earshot. 'Throw him a banana,' they shouted. 'Get back to't trees.' I concluded that this sort of ignorance was restricted to a small group of retards, until one of the players' wives buttonholed me. 'How coom you've got all them overseas players?' she said, looking at our five black guys reclining on the balcony. I explained that most of them had been in Britain since primary school, but to some people colour is an indicator of everything from nationality to IQ.

In between dismissive yells of, 'Yorkshire, you're bloody roobish' (they were bottom of the table), the ground reverberated to the sound of wily old seamers crying for help. '*Owzat*?' they pleaded fruitlessly, merely confirming that York-shiremen can't pronounce their aitches. You can easily get lost in the Ridings because pronunciation of local place names bears little resemblance to what's written on the AA map: 'Edinli, 'Alifax, 'Ull, 'Uddasfild, Cleck'eton. Even 'Bratfort', for that matter.

Of an evening the home team minus Boycott retired to the Three Horseshoes up the Otley Road for a few pints of HDTs and a moan about Geoffrey. ('Why do people always take an instant dislike to me?' Boycott asked a colleague. 'Because it saves time,' the player replied.) Then they directed the visitors into Bryan's Fish Restaurant next door. It's only in the Roses counties that places like this exist. Something between a Berni Inn and a canteen, it was stacked with togged-up OAPs out for their Monday treat. They were served vast portions of crisply fried fish and chips, mushy peas, bread and butter and pots of tea. Even the baby haddock on the menu lapped over both sides of the plate. The batter was light and crisp, not that saturated, chewy cardboard you get in most places, and the chips were perfect. Despite the fact that it was the best fried meal I had ever tasted, I couldn't finish mine. Gatting polished it off.

PROFIT AND LOSS

The most poignant evidence that Yorkshire cricket remained in the dark ages came at the end of the season, when a friend of mine from their second team went down the road for a takeaway. He returned with two spam fritters wrapped in a two-day-old copy of the *Yorkshire Post*. On the back page beneath the grease was the headline 'YORKSHIRE RELEASE FIVE', and there, in the small print below, was his name. They just hadn't bothered to tell him.

By then Middlesex had narrowly failed to win the championship for a second successive year. We had had to take maximum points in the penultimate match against Northants and asked our landlords, MCC, if we could have a turning pitch at Lord's – Emburey and Edmonds had already taken

162 wickets between them that summer. MCC flatly refused, intimating that it was not in the spirit of the game (try telling that to Notts or Essex). Instead they produced a belter and Northants waltzed to a seven-wicket win. As I said earlier, property-owners were all-powerful.

Phil Edmonds was gradually becoming one himself, through various shrewd purchases, and his financial acumen was further underlined by an imaginative twist on the idea of benefit matches. Instead of organising umpteen exhibition games against local clubs and relying on spectators' generosity, he hired the Hounslow ground for a whole week in September to stage a sequence of corporate six-a-side competitions. The formula allowed each company to enter a team of five which would be augmented by a Middlesex player.

It was the first time a beneficiary had tapped into the business community in this way, and the company reps loved the participation and the chance to pit their skills against players from the top flight. What's more, they parted with tidy sums for the privilege, allowing Edmonds to pay us £100 for turning up, something previous beneficiaries had never done. Like pension plans, benefits are a vague and distant notion when you're twenty-three, but my immediate future was assured. Despite a patchy season, my occasional electric spells had won me another three-year contract, laying any early fears I had about the arrival of real life firmly to rest. I had also acquired a fan, a boy of twelve called Roy who wanted to sit with me at matches and wrote me infatuated letters. It made a change to get something personal rather than an envelope addressed to you containing a wad of pictures of everyone else which the sender wanted autographing.

The others from Group 4 were in a less happy position. Nepo got a few games in the first team but struggled to raise his game a grade and had one of those frustrating seasons when you're perpetually in the squad as an extra batsman, but they always play the extra bowler. He'd arrive hopefully at Lord's before the match and have a decent net, then the captain would wander over at 10.30 and deliver the fateful verdict: 'Sorry, mate, we've decided to play all three seamers. Keep going.' These last two words had an immediate relevance, since he was often expected to make straight for his car and belt headlong down the A217 to Banstead, where a Second XI match was just about to start.

Spikes wasn't quite sure whether batting or bowling was his best suit, though the terrible mauling his left-arm swingers received from Zaheer Abbas in the Sunday League might have been an indicator. He did have Zaheer dropped early on and came off muttering that he would have given his kid brother a good spanking if he'd shelled it. 'Good spankings run in the family, then,' said Nepo, surveying Spikes's figures of 8 overs for 67.

The Rat's spin bowling seemed to have gone down the drainpipe. Certainly it had in Gatting's eyes, and that was what counted. If the captain consistently thrashed you around in the nets and you spent half the time retrieving the ball from the car park, it was a fair indication he didn't rate you. The Rat did his best to compensate with lots of eager scuttling and scurrying about in the dressing room and during practice, but Gatting's mind was made up and he was given a free transfer. The security of Group 4 had been breached for the first time. And, as things transpired, not the last.

The enigmatic Winky had also failed to pass Go. But whereas the Rat was snapped up eagerly by Hampshire, there was no scramble at the Middlesex secretary's door for the signature of C.W.V. Robins Esq. So the red-haired, jazz-hatted, ramshackle Winky bid farewell with a cheery, 'Goodbye, chaps,' and headed off to Victoria Station to buy an Inter Rail pass. In a pair of *my* cricket socks.

Out Of Order: 1984

bowlers' anxiety • dressing-room silence • the office typist selects • a regimented approach • Fraser emerges • Radley nurdles victory • lone survivor

LOSING THE WAY

Who'd be a batsman? Nine possible ways of being dismissed (ten, if you count timed out), no second chance, the stress of knowing that the next ball could be your last and walking off on your tod stared at by everyone. Being out is so immediate, so final, like nothing else in sport, and yet batsmen have to suppress their exasperation for a good two minutes before letting it all hang out in the sanctity of the dressing room. The concentration of emotion released at such times reveals more about an individual than who he marries or what his sitting room looks like.

Middlesex's cultural mix guaranteed an interesting range of responses. Wilf Slack, a reserved Windward Islander who never betrayed any nerves despite the daily task of standing up to some of the fastest bowlers in the world, rarely said anything when he came back into the dressing room. He'd sit down, quietly unbuckle his pads and carefully lay them to rest in his case, then stare glumly into space for a while. He was deeply religious, which was possibly an explanation for such contemplation.

If Gatting was out for a low score it was best to keep well clear as he re-entered the room. He'd burst through the door, wielding his bat like a mini battering ram, send the blade flying then emit an agonised 'Bollocks! Gatt, you stupid fat cunt!' before ripping off his kit and slamming it into his coffin in annoyance. He hated failure, and found being confined to the dressing room watching lesser mortals eke out runs intensely frustrating.

Graham Barlow, a man with a slight inferiority complex, sometimes made an excuse of some kind. 'How can I make runs with this plank?' or, 'Bloody old farts moving about in front of the sightscreen again.' Paul Downton, self-effacing and diplomatic to the last, always said 'Sorry, chaps,' even if he'd just hammered 80. Clive Radley, a man of few words, grunted 'Aaargh,' and John Emburey generally blamed himself: 'Pissole shot. Should have tried to hit it over cover,' or whatever. When Edmonds came through the door he was often chuckling with a mixture of mild disbelief and perverse pleasure. The bowlers were annoyed at getting out, mainly because it meant the time for some serious work was imminent.

Regardless of who he was, the batsman was always received back in the dressing room with either sympathy or congratulation. If he'd made runs there was always a chorus of 'Well played,' or 'Great effort.' If he'd failed, people muttered 'Bad luck,' or 'Well tried,' in as reassuring a tone as they could muster. Run-making is an invidious job, and everyone understood what he was feeling. In the name of teamwork it was important to say something – anything, no matter how banal.

In my first game of 1984 – a Benson & Hedges group match – I was elevated to number 9 in an effort to help knock off the 20 or so needed to win. Radley was running strong the other end, but the game was going to the wire. Gatting was a bad watcher and his tense pacing up and down the dressing room had made me nervous. I blocked one ball, then drove at the second and set off for an improbable single to mid-off, where it just so happened that Paul Parker, probably the best fielder in the world at the time, was stationed. I was run out by a mile, plunging the side into unnecessary trouble with only two unreliable tail-enders left.

There was no comforting 'Bad luck,' or 'Well tried,' when I returned to the dressing room. Just dead silence. Eventually Gatting let out an anguished 'Oh, *Yozzer*!' – pretty cast-iron evidence that I'd made a major cock-up. God knows what he'd said when it actually happened. I sat in an armchair I had temporarily inherited since Brearley's retirement and felt useless and a liability. It affected my whole season.

I'd come to the conclusion that my unpunctuality, clumsiness and inconsistency were becoming an irritant. I now had fewer pros than cons and they were looking to ease me out. The seeds of my paranoia had been sown the previous year, when I'd been dropped soon after taking a rather streaky six wickets against Gloucester. From then on I'd felt extremely insecure. Overhearing a cigarette card-collecting kid trying in vain after the Sussex match to swap six Simon Hugheses for one Mike Gatting didn't help.

Confidence is an intangible and elusive thing, triggered by minute details such as a word of praise from an unusual quarter (father, wife, bank manager), a small moral victory over a dangerous opponent or being artificially immune (drunk, for example) to fear of failure. Stoned or inebriated people who jump off buildings actually believe they'll survive. Loss of confidence sends talent off to hide under a large obstacle.

My game went to pieces. The overstepping disease which had always plagued me worsened. One no-ball, which should have dismissed Boycott for nought, brought a lopsided smile to his face as he took a fresh guard and left my father tearing out what bit of hair he had left. Perhaps his shiny pate helped him that week to clinch the part of the P & O officer in the award-winning film *A Passage to India*.

I had no rhythm or accuracy and against the West Indies tourists I couldn't stop delivering full tosses, as if someone had suddenly shortened the pitch overnight. Bowling seems such a simple operation when everything's working smoothly and it becomes virtually second nature. As soon as one part of your method goes on the blink you begin to analyse it, examining your approach and tinkering with every little part of your technique. Before long you're standing stupidly at the beginning of your run-up trying to remember which foot to start with.

This is when bowlers wish they were batsmen. One decent ball puts struggling number 3s swiftly out of their misery. They can even run themselves out if the worst comes to the worst. But a wayward bowler whose nervous first delivery has just been deposited ten rows back has got to get through a whole over, and sometimes another one after that, in the vain hope that things might improve. There's no immediate escape.

Bowlers frequently suffer from neurosis, and tragically there's really no one to turn to for help. You daren't go up to the captain and say, 'Er, actually, Skip, I can't guarantee being able to hit the cut strip this over – could you put someone else on?' though that's more or less what you feel like. And when you do send down a load of dross the usual response is 'Come on, *concentrate*,' when your whole body is already so taut with determination that you can hardly let go of the ball. Later, the well-meaning coach takes you into the nets where, away from the pressure of a real contest, your ability miraculously returns. Then he'll say, 'Well, what's the problem?' But when you go back into a match it returns with a vengeance.

Most of it's in the mind, of course, like impotence or fear of spiders, but in those days sports psychologists were regarded as weirdos needed only by serious headcases like Hurricane Higgins or John McEnroe, and I couldn't see that sitting on a couch with some shrink charging £70 an hour could help me bowl an in-swinging yorker. So the apprehension lurks and festers like a cancer, feeding off every subsequent failure. You try to hide in the outfield, but inevitably the ball follows you, and, totally preoccupied with your bowling difficulties, you can't field, either.

Even when I was invited to chuck a few close range half-volleys for one of the batsmen to crack into the advertising boards there were mishaps. My throws kept swinging into Barlow's legs, rapping him painfully on the shins (batsmen didn't wear pads for this kind of practice), and one to Gatting popped slightly causing him to welly it straight at an old man in the stand pouring tea for his wife. The antique china teapot disintegrated on impact, but miraculously the couple survived unscathed.

Whether this was the last straw for Gatting I don't know,

but in the end he obviously decided that enough was enough. Unfortunately, he didn't get round to actually telling me himself. I found out from Val, the office typist, who mumbled, 'Bad luck about not playing,' as I popped in to collect my mail on the morning of the next match, against Surrey.

'Uh?' I said articulately.

'Well, you're not in the team I've just read out to the scoreboard operators,' she explained.

Sure enough, when I got into the dressing room Spikes was in my seat and Edmonds said, 'Hey twelfth, I've got an important business client coming later, can you ask Nancy to send down a bottle of claret and two glasses at lunchtime?'

The relentless piss-taking in the dressing room – hilarious unless you're the butt of it – just reinforced the feeling of swimming against the tide, and in this respect Spikes suffered worse than me. His tendency to bite when the bait was cast encouraged ridicule which he couldn't silence with runs and wickets. He lasted only one game in the first team and his confidence slid to a low ebb.

He tried to disguise it by offering to bowl at a rampant Essex batsman in the next Second XI game, at Westcliff. 'The wind's perfect for me now,' he said having battled unsuccessfully against it earlier. But his first two deliveries were clobbered into a nearby pond, and he then lost his wicket to a terrible slow long hop after grafting magnanimously for two hours. His second-team colleagues christened him Mareman after that, far more brutal and demeaning than the inoffensive Spikes. He never fully recovered his composure and asked to be released at the end of the season so that he could escape to more sympathetic surroundings. He joined Hampshire. It wasn't long before 'Jamesy' became 'Spikes' there, too.

The Grey, Grey Morass of Home

The Spurs footballer Steve Archibald once said: 'Team spirit is an illusion you only glimpse when you win.' In a way, though, the sadistic internal sniping that was the trademark of the Middlesex team was actually the secret of its success. The quirks of each character were kept in check rather than being allowed to run amok and they fuelled a sort of collective drive. Strong personalities cancelled each other out and mutiny was never seriously on the agenda. Anyone who started mouthing off about something was quickly accused of having just pebble-dashed the toilet or having been spotted chatting up a dragon and their ranting subsided. Barlow still had the occasional moan, but he had developed a slightly lopsided walk on account of an arthritic hip, and use of the nickname Dougie (after Douglas Bader) soon shut him up.

The disparate elements needed strong leadership to give them direction. In this sense Gatting was ideal. A vigorous captain, he waved his arms a lot, yelling encouragement from the slips, glaring at upstarty opponents and battering bowlers everywhere into complete submission. His 258 at Bath was a marvel of footwork, bravado and withering power. Even mishits sailed into the hospitality tents which dominated the little ground on two sides, perhaps the first sign of the corporate muscle that was to become a lifeline for our little summer jamboree. Gatting made the art of batting, fielding, even bowling look humiliatingly simple. A rare lapse was cursed then instantly forgotten, and he'd disappear off to the squash court to release his surplus energy on some unsuspecting victim (only Nepo could give him a decent game). He was never hampered by the mental contortions that accompany frequent failure.

Meanwhile, my insecurity was compounded by the emergence of a tall, stripling fast bowler called Angus Fraser who made the thing I was incapable of doing – landing the ball consistently in the same place – look as easy as hanging out the washing. Though essentially good-natured, he had that vital weapon in the fast-bowler's armoury, grumpiness, and he was soon welcomed into the fold as 'a Long Streak of Piss'.

Fraser had no frills. He stuck to the basics and he was, I realised, just the sort of player the new hierarchy had been looking for. Reliable, consistent, unadventurous and, above all, accurate. Gatting hated his own hard-earned runs being haemorrhaged in the field and Emburey seemed more satisfied to have bowled a maiden than to have taken a wicket. They begrudged the opposition every half-volley, and if one slipped out they pulled long faces and adopted the bristling hands-on-hips pose we called the double teapot. It made the contest into a long drawn-out struggle rather than an entertaining game, which the stipulated 117 overs a day did nothing to help. (We were still on the field at 8.10 p.m. trying to suffocate Glamorgan.)

In retrospect, I think this approach, which had percolated into the national psyche, had a lot to answer for. In true British political style, it put a dampener on ideas and retarded progress. Instead of encouraging freedom of speech and self-expression, the main objective was to stifle the opposition (or snub it) until it capitulated. Our game stagnated, and as a bowler you became afraid to try anything that didn't conform to the rigid master plan. Essex won the championship two years running on the back of this philosophy. No wonder crowds at county games were dwindling. It was all so formulaic.

People still flocked to Test matches, of course, but England's colourless sloop was literally blown out of the water by the West Indian guns, whose flamboyant individualism called all the shots. They swept up the Test series 5–0 (the least emphatic victory was by 8 wickets) on a tidal wave of runs from Green-idge, Gomes and Richards, while Marshall, Garner and Hold-ing consigned a sequence of ordinary batsmen to the hutch or occasionally to the local infirmary. Courtney Walsh, on his first tour, was surplus to requirements.

The dourness of our county game was further shown up

by the Sri Lankans in their first Test at Lord's. England took only one wicket the whole of the second day and conceded a first-innings lead, and Botham resorted to bowling off-breaks (he still took five wickets). Mike Turner, secretary of Leicestershire, called for English cricket to 'put its house in order' and the TCCB set up a nine-man working party to investigate the standard and quality at all levels of the game. Sound familiar?

It was so demoralising seeing our approach stuck in a grey morass of inadequacy with no solution but to turn inwards. In the real capitalist world outside consumers were responding to the similarly dull British fare in the car and electronics industry by buying cool German or Japanese models instead. But English cricket had no cheap competitor, so the sponsors kept sponsoring, and, at Test level, anyway, the turnstiles kept turning.

A Spicy Finale

Saturday 1 September, NatWest Final, Lord's
The showpiece of the domestic season, the NatWest final between Middlesex and Kent, rejuvenated the depressed mood. It was high-scoring, pulsating and went to the very last ball. The night before I was told I'd be playing (by Gatting, rather than by some office dogsbody), which wasn't a good idea as I slept fitfully and had a terrible dream that I was fielding on the boundary when the ball became lost among people's legs. The batsmen were still running and I was being discredited by everyone, including my father.

I enjoyed big matches and conquered my nerves sufficiently to bowl a decent first spell. It resulted in some good banter with the crowd in front of the Tavern, who kept singing '*Dur*ham, *dur*ham, durram durram durram,' to the tune of the *Pink Panther* music. This was modified to 'Eeyore' when I slightly misfielded one and turned into hysterical cheering when Chris Cowdrey launched into my last few overs. Maybe I should have been on the stage; at least there you know the plot beforehand.

A canny innings from Clive Radley took us to the threshold of victory, diffusing Derek Underwood's stranglehold in the middle of the innings. It was a mesmerising old-fashioned sort of duel between two virtuosos who had the utmost respect for each other. Underwood shuffled up to the wicket, varying his flight to a man who weaved giddily up and down the pitch trying to upset his rhythm. Radley won this particular contest and had become a sort of Bobby Moore figure – always there when it counts with a cool head and a positional sense second to none. He seemed to subconsciously know exactly where the fielders stood and was brilliant at nurdling shots between them, often from some rarified place on the crease. Sometimes he appeared to be giving the bowler an extravagant view of the stumps, but just as the ball was destined to crash into them, down came his bat to glide it to some unlikely quarter, followed by a blaring, '*Yeess*. Easy run.' People who may be concerned that this man is now MCC head coach needn't worry. There will never be any Radley clones – his method is completely uncopyable.

The seventh-wicket pair came together with Middlesex needing 16 to win, which meant I was next man in. The tension mounted on the balcony as the final over approached and Gatting couldn't watch until the terrifying sight of me in my pads standing in the doorway prompted him to turn back to the game. With one needed off the final ball, Emburey clipped a full toss to the boundary and the wave of relief that engulfed the dressing room was orgasmic.

You might have thought the committee would roll over and take us in a post-coital embrace, but you'd be wrong. After the initial champagne surge, players were left to their own devices and the evening petered out in the Akash Tandoori on the Edgware Road. The nucleus of the team were in predictably high spirits, and when the plates were removed at the end of various food games it looked as though someone had tried to force another meal up through the table. But then, isn't that always the case in Indian restaurants?

Though he didn't play in the final, Nepo joined us during this skirmish, ostensibly to say goodbye. His summer had been miserable. After an argument with his father, he'd been shown the door and had finished up with nowhere to live. He'd spent the summer literally living out of the back of his car. He parked his Volvo 323 on the boundary edge at many Second XI grounds, shoving all his worldly belongings in the boot and sleeping on the back seat.

It didn't do his game much good, but at least it gave him the shortest journey to bed after the pavilion bar closed. His resultant drinking habit spawned quite a temper, however, and eventually he was released by the club. Concerned about his volatility but more captivated by his natural ability, Gloucestershire took him on.

Four seasons after assembling, Group 4 had only one survivor. Me. It wasn't that I had much greater talent: the Rat had proved that during the season by winkling out seven Middlesex batsmen in an innings for his new county, Hampshire, including the prized scalp of Gatting for a duck. That had settled an old score. What had given me a kick start was the extrovert streak and relish for performance I'd gleaned from a showbusiness upbringing. Without that I'd have been tossed back in the lucky dip like the others.

Ray Illingworth was also binned at the end of the season. As Yorkshire manager he'd taken the rap for failing to revive the county's fortunes. Fred Trueman, welcoming Illingworth into the Courage Old England XI, said: 'Ray will find it rather strange joining us after all he's been through in recent years. In this team all the players talk and actually like each other.'

Illingworth was one of the last people to do the double of 1,000 runs and 100 wickets before the championship programme was reduced to twenty-four matches, but remarkably Richard Hadlee managed it in 1984 before the end of August. He carried a briefcase around all season containing specified targets for each match: how many runs and wickets he would get against Glamorgan at Trent Bridge; how many maidens he could bowl against Essex at Chelmsford. Probably even what pair of socks he would wear at Bournemouth.

It betrayed an obsessive mind, a characteristic emphasised by his house in New Zealand. It is a shrine to himself, stashed with balls, bats, scorecards and statues commemorating his every achievement. He suffered severe bouts of loneliness and depression during the season – which was hardly surprising, since no one could relate to him – but he stuck to his plan and achieved his goal. People described him as egocentric and statistically motivated, but in my book he was a nutter. If that sort of self-denial was necessary to get to the top, I felt I'd rather live life to the full and do without the accolades.

COCKSURE: 1985

Spanish lessons • physical damage • Daniel v Greenidge • the speed machine and the Master Blaster • bouncer wars • bumptious champions

WELCOME TO THE PLEASURE DOME

April, Costa del Sol

Although the calendar tells you the year begins on 1 January, people measure the twelve-month cycle in different ways. For schoolkids it starts in September and is mercifully over by July; professional misers align their activities with the tax year; Eric Clapton fans structure their whole existence round his annual concerts at the Royal Albert Hall. By the mid-1980s, the football season had encroached into summer to such an extent that the players probably felt one year more or less merged into another.

This was not the case in cricket. County players virtually went into hibernation (or disappeared abroad) from October to March, almost forgotten by their employers apart from the odd perfunctory letter about winter nets. In autumn the salary cheques dried up, the sponsored car was handed back (though people hung on to them as long as the dealer's patience lasted), the kit was packed up and knackered bats given away. You read in the paper about additions to the squad or minuscule rises in the minimum wage, and you developed a split personality where money was concerned. You'd be liberal in summer, particularly after the fortnightly expenses hand-out, but accused of having short arms and long pockets when you were reluctant to buy a large round in winter.

The communications from the club suddenly quadruple in early April, when it's time to report back. Memos, dates, itineraries, contracts; questionnaires to fill in, photocalls and committee receptions to attend, measurements for the new team blazers to send back. Equipment sponsors send out standard letters advising you that in respect of your performances last year they would be delighted to supply you with a couple of short-sleeved casual shirts in addition to your complimentary bats and pads.

Cricket is not often compared to sex, but there is a parallel between the arrival of the cricket season and the start of a new relationship. Freshly cut outfields have the same seductive smell as the scent of a chase. The stimulation and excitement obscures potential problems, urge banishes doubt. Abandoned optimism masks the old gripes about always being asked to bowl into the wind or girlfriends habitually using your razor to shave their legs. Regardless of previous heartache, we keep coming back for more.

The welcome to the pleasure dome was enriched at the start of the 1985 season when Middlesex decided to take the playing staff to La Manga, a golf resort and leisure centre on the Costa del Sol, for pre-season training. Spain? Had the committee lost their marbles or become punch-drunk? Or been duped by a shady package-holiday agent? In fact we'd been invited on a promotional basis and were given an additional helping hand by the chairman of Tesco, Ian McClaurin, whose son had just been taken on the staff.

The one proviso was that we played three limited-overs matches on the resort's artificial pitch against Lancashire for the La Manga Trophy – a sort of duel between the two cup-winners of the previous season. No gentle practice against Slough CC, or a scratch Bucks XI now. Pre-season warm-ups were getting serious. Still, it was a marvellous refreshing change from sweating buckets in that grimy old Ealing gym, and despite the fact that I was hobbling about after minor knee surgery, they even let me go.

I'd better explain. Using cricket as a means to travel and discover myself, I'd spent a third winter abroad, this time playing for a club in New Zealand. My previously healthy knee gave me gip as soon as I'd bowled in the first match, but the standard was so bad I took wickets almost on one leg. I didn't know what the problem was and neither did the guy with whom I was sharing a flat, which was a pretty poor show considering he was the New Zealand team physio. But he was more interested in examining frustrated divorcees on his couch than itinerant cricketers. So I sat around in midweek with a packet of frozen peas clasped to my leg to ease the swelling, played golf instead of going to nets and hobbled in to bowl on Saturdays.

By the time I flew back to England in late March, my handicap was down to 16 but my knee was up like a pumpkin. I got an instant upgrade to business class, but a severe reprimand from Middlesex. Why had I not got proper treatment in New Zealand, they asked, or better still come home? I had to earn my living, I countered (though I'd spent more than I'd accumulated), and surely the playing experience was valuable? Not if you're crocked when you return, they retorted understandably, and packed me off to the clinic. The surgeon said he'd hardly ever seen a knee joint in a worse state. 'It looks like you've dragged it across a rugged hillside, through a forest and over a cliff,' he remarked accusingly.

'I did on the back nine at Wanganui Country Club,' I replied.

Using a tiny implement called an arthroscope – a sort of miniature dentist's drill – he cleaned up the joint and said I shouldn't do anything strenuous on it for a month. So in La Manga I umpired in the nets, took the odd fielding routine and looked after the dressing-room key, which I soon lost, causing a practice match to be held up while a replacement was found.

The Spanish trip was a great success socially, but whether it did our cricket any good was a moot point. Quite apart from the boozy nights, by day Lancashire's West Indian speed merchant Patrick Patterson turned the artificial pitch into a terror track and several batsmen went home with battered hands. The nearest Edmonds got to the cricket was the golf driving range next door and he took great delight in trying to pepper the fielders with 180-degree hooks. And Daniel had a fixation on the resident physio, a buxom northern wench. Saying he needed treatment for a twinge, he was excused fielding practice one morning but then didn't turn up to bowl. I was sent off as a search party and discovered him in the physio's apartment. The huge, rippling West Indian was face down on the floor, wearing only a jockstrap; the girl in a little white tunic, was astride him administering a full massage. All he had was an injured thumb.

A Clash of Titans

Wednesday 12 June, Hampshire v Middlesex, Bournemouth
Apart from working his bollocks off on both sides of the boundary, Daniel had an innate talent for avoiding unnecessary work. Once, in an early-season match against Cambridge University, he was late on the field after lunch. His whereabouts were eventually given away by the telltale sight of his huge boots visible under the toilet door, and he was left alone to finish what he was doing. But when he still hadn't emerged twenty minutes later the door was pushed open to reveal – a pair of boots. Daniel was catching forty winks in the dressing room.

Middlesex, aware of this sort of temptation and under-standably wanting their pound of flesh, had offered him only a one-year contract in 1985. This effort to concentrate his mind worked a treat. He tore in to bowl with the same zest and enthusiasm as he showed when pursuing women, which took quite some doing, and by mid-June at Bournemouth, when I was able to return to action, he was positively flying.

This was the contest the punters wanted. Not the top-of-the-table skirmish between Hampshire and Middlesex, but the clash of the Bajan Titans, Wayne Daniel and Gordon Greenidge, which had all the other participants clasping their hands tightly to their ears in anticipation of a loud explosion. Intense pride and inter-island rivalry guaranteed West Indians always tried that bit harder against each other, and there was definitely no love lost between these two.

Daniel marked out his run as Greenidge swaggered to the wicket with the aura of a man who had caned the England attack to all parts the previous year, often on one leg. For once he wasn't limping. He cast a cursory glance round the field and settled into a slightly hunched stance, fiery-eyed, ready to pounce. As Daniel generally bowled two lengths – short and very short – he knew what to expect.

The first ball was short and exploratory, the proverbial loosener. Normally an opening batsman has a careful look at the first delivery or two in a match, gauging the pace and bounce of the wicket, the light and the speed of the bowler. Greenidge flogged the offering to the boundary in front of square and twirled his bat with satisfaction. Four off one. Slightly taken aback, Daniel lengthened his run-up, came pounding in and sent down a quick bouncer. Greenidge swayed back and hooked it savagely one bounce into a marquee. Eight off two. He smiled contentedly to himself. It was an astounding stroke that had already elevated this little conflict way above the actual match in terms of importance. As if two feuding gods had just popped in for a scrap, though in normal circumstances Bournemouth would not be high on their list of chosen meeting places.

Seething with rage at Greenidge's disrespect, Daniel made a great thing of placing a man at deep square leg for the mishit hook, getting him in exactly the right place with elaborate hand movements. He tore in a third time and unleashed a furious yorker of landmine potential, hoping to catch his man unawares on the back foot. With staggering speed and reflexes, Greenidge jammed his bat on to the ball and rifled it past the bowler's despairing boot and into the sightscreen for another four. Twelve off three. Greenidge broke the stunned silence. 'Hey, it's 1985 now,' he uttered triumphantly to his compatriot. 'Don't try those 1920s tactics on me.'

This humiliation was galling enough for Daniel, one of the most feared fast bowlers in the world, so imagine how it made an honest county trundler feel, playing his first game for nine months. Agitated is putting it mildly. In common with many journeymen players, part of me wanted to hide behind our overseas hulk until his fearsome opposite number had been dispatched.

A Lot of Hard Yakka

I needn't have worried. When a sportsman is trying to settle an old personal score, he often loses concentration. Sure enough, after two more sumptuous boundaries, Greenidge attempted a wild drive at Neil Williams and was bowled all over the place. I immediately understood why the Hampshire guys had mixed feelings about playing with Greenidge. The main requirement of the numbers 3 and 4 to follow an opening partnership of Greenidge and Barry Richards was a phlegmatic acceptance that they could be together at 5–2 or 205–2.

Just to underline the extraordinary cricketing prowess of the island of Barbados, at twenty-one miles long and fourteen wide, of a similar size to the Isle of Wight, another Bajan dominated the rest of the game. Sprinting in, arms pumping like pistons, Malcolm Marshall twice bulldozed through our batting and had such amazing control he even nominated some dismissals. In our second innings he moved a silly point in for Radley and had him caught there the very next ball; then he announced he'd give Edmonds the three-card trick – out-swinger, out-swinger, in-swinger – and trap him lbw. He got it spot on, leaving us 82–8 and still 180 behind with a whole session left for play, more or less dead and buried.

The Middlesex team were disconsolately packing their bags as I walked to the wicket, as unnerving as the sight of the groundsman starting up the roller when the number 11 isn't even halfway to the centre. But some tail-enders are adept at missing everything off line and locating straight balls with the middle of the bat. I stuck around for 15 overs.

The last hour had arrived and Marshall's desperation to get the match finished was showing. He tried longer runs, shorter runs, charging up behind the umpire so that all you could see was his elbows, then popping out at the last moment to let you have it from round the wicket. You kept watching for signs that he was about to have a breather – the way he took off his sweater, his body language during a confab with the captain, the sight of someone else loosening up. But it was all a con, and he'd stay on for another over.

Which was all the more honourable considering the pitch

was like an old mattress. No spring or bounce to it whatever. It sagged under anything that made contact with it, to such an extent that Jamie Sykes, my Cockney partner, said, 'I'll take Marshall if you like, I could play him with my cock.' And on the day he did. We survived until close of play, drawing the match and depriving Hampshire of sixteen points. It turned out to be the decisive moment of the season. Eventually we topped the championship table, and Hampshire finished second. By sixteen points.

FOLLOW THAT

Saturday 13 July, Middlesex v Somerset, Lord's
Neither this gesture of defiance nor frequent Test calls kept me regularly in the team. The departure of Gatting, Emburey, Downton and Edmonds to the 1985 Ashes series left no gaps a fast bowler could fill, and besides, my form was slapdash. One weekend we'd all be playing together for Middlesex, then sometimes while the big four headed off up the ladder into the lofty eyrie of the England Test team, I slipped down the pole into the Second XI. It was like being invited to a slap-up lunch with the boss one day, failing to impress him and reverting to pie and chips on a park bench the next.

To reinforce the feeling of anonymity, when the home Tests are in full swing – particularly in series against Australia – county cricket becomes almost invisible to the casual observer, as if it has gone into temporary hibernation. But it is still there, ebbing and flowing like the sea at Lowestoft, and in each match there are dramas and subplots and champagne moments that published scorecards never reveal.

On Live Aid day, at about the time U2's 'Sunday, Bloody Sunday' was assaulting 70,000 sets of eardrums at Wembley, the master blaster himself, Viv Richards, sauntered out to the middle at Lord's to play a tune for Somerset. Chewing furiously, maroon cap positioned defiantly askew, bat brandished across his rippling torso, he exuded a formidable aura. 'Gimme two legs, please,' he grunted at the umpire, and surveyed the field, still masticating. He seemed particularly interested in the area around mid-wicket and beyond. Not many people were in the ground though, and it looked unlikely that he'd be sufficiently motivated to hang about for long.

The delight of sport is its unpredictability. Nobodies might rise to the occasion when star performers have buckled under the burden of expectation. That's partly why we journeymen return year after year, addicted to the lure of upstaging the greats just for one day. Sometimes, however, there's a sign – a sublime stroke, a searing leg-cutter – that tells you the mighty are about to deliver, and that there's nothing you will be able to do to stop it.

The ball to Richards was straight, slightly short of a length, bowled from the Pavilion End with all the speed I could muster, and climbed up towards chest height with the aid of the notorious Lord's ridge. Many batsmen of Test standard would have fended it down, or even gloved it, and poked suspiciously at a spot on the pitch afterwards. None would have been quick enough to attack it, especially so soon after taking guard. I got many wickets with similar deliveries and was quite proud when I produced one, accidentally or on purpose.

Richards eased forward as usual, then laid back and, with almost casual indifference, flipped the pesky ball away from under his ribs, over an incredulous square-leg fielder and into the twelfth row of the Mound Stand. It was an astonishing stroke born of fantastic reflexes, marvellous timing and outrageous arrogance. It was the most brilliant shot I have ever seen, better than Botham's sixes at Headingley or Kapil Dev's to save the follow-on at Lord's or anything by Clive Lloyd, because it was so effortless. We knew at once that he was going to get a hundred, and he did.

In a way I relished the experience. You knew you hadn't the power to resist his advance, so you had nothing to lose and might as well lie back and enjoy it. This was a master at work, and it was fabulous entertainment for the crowd. That, for me, was of utmost importance. Professional cricket is ultimately an arm of the entertainment industry, and if the players neglect that fact, they're not doing their job.

Mindful of that the next day, and wanting to exhibit my own little repertoire of strokes following Richards' display, I had a huge swipe after blocking for a while and was bowled all over the place for 0. 'I always said Hughes was a hopeless batsman,' an MCC member groaned within earshot of my father, who always encouraged me to take my batting seriously and used to record my innings on the scorecard, ball by ball. He was so mortified he hardly spoke to me for a week.

Another case of unlikely melodrama was the drawn match between Middlesex and Leicestershire. It looked a pretty unremarkable game on the face of it, with various scores of 200-ish and the odd individual highlight all being vastly overshadowed by England trouncing the Aussies at Headingley (where Tim Robinson made 175). But there was always naked aggression in these encounters, perhaps because both counties were rather mouthy in the field.

Jon Agnew lit the fuse with an unprovoked bumper barrage at Wayne Daniel, still our resident number 11. One struck him on the shoulder and another he hooked at ferociously, and with a remarkable combination of brute strength and terrible footwork, swatted it over cover for six. This, coupled with his humiliation by Greenidge a few days earlier, made his blood boil, and he embarked on the most terrifying spell of bowling I have ever witnessed.

Staring into the batsmen's eyes from short leg, I saw the kind of fear that is usually confined to the besieged ground forces in films like *Apocalypse Now* and *Platoon*. With only a thin blade and a bit of skimpy padding to protect them from this onslaught, the Leicester batsmen clearly didn't want to be out in the middle, and not many of them were for very long. Five were bowled or lbw in the space of four overs, James Whittaker had his arm broken, and Russell Cobb was struck so forcibly on the helmet that one of his visor's screws was catapulted back over the bowler's head and halfway to the boundary. A photo of Gordon Parsons' dismissal in the paper next day put the events into perspective. It showed a bowler's-eye view of the stumps being shattered, but there was no sign of the bat or the batsman. He had retreated out of the way as fast as a millionaire on Skid Row.

This carnage was perpetrated by the same guy who would softly chat up your girlfriend in the bar afterwards, plying her with drinks and compliments before coming out with such toe-curling lines as, 'Do I make your juices flow?' On Sundays he also generously brought in for the players armfuls of foil-wrapped spicy chicken rotis made by a lady in Ladbroke Grove, hoping the gesture might persuade Gatting to give him the day off. It seldom worked.

SMART ALECS

August–September

Daniel worshipped the ground Edmonds walked on, and this possibly brought out his fiery streak. 'Any chance of a bit of pace, Diamond?' Edmonds would challenge from his position in the gully, often with the desired effect. The two were almost inseparable. It was an odd pairing – sort of Frank Bruno meets Michael Heseltine. They always travelled together, usually very late at night – their nocturnal habits ensured they both got a single room.

Despite his dated flared trousers and 1960s moccasins, Edmonds was in many ways an avant-garde cricketer. He was never without his briefcase when most players didn't even possess a diary, and ran his property business from an office in Marylebone. Finding the county routine rather tedious, he occasionally decamped there during home matches if Middlesex were batting, saying 'Ring me if we lose a few wickets.' His wife was as bright and ambitious and ostentatious as he was, not at all the sort of obedient Dorothy Perkins-type the others married.

'Well, I suppose I'm going to bowl immaculately again today,' he would say loudly, with un-English arrogance, as the team took the field. He'd be visibly upset if he wasn't bowling by midday. He took painkillers for a lingering back problem and, to counteract the drowsiness they could cause, he often swigged brandy during the day, which only made his fuse even shorter. He should have had 'Handle With Care' daubed across his forehead.

Gatting did his best to channel Edmonds' contrariness in the right direction, with significant results. But when a person is really determined to draw attention to himself, there's nothing you can do about it. At Hove, towards the end of the season, some minor kerfuffle about field settings got Edmonds' goat and when Gatting asked for responsible batting from the lower order to hold out for a draw on the last afternoon, he did the opposite. Going in at the fall of the sixth wicket with at least an hour to negotiate, Edmonds waltzed up the wicket to his first ball and smote it over the sightscreen. He mowed his second over mid-wicket, was dropped off the third and bowled by the fourth.

We lost by a wide margin and Gatting's face was puffed up and purple when he ordered everyone into the dressing room afterwards. But before he could explode with invective, Edmonds, trying hard to hide a smirk, said candidly, 'Well, you'll just have to fine me, Skip, that's all there is to it. You can't do things like that and expect to get away with it. Couple of hundred quid be all right?'

'Very fucking clever, Henri,' Gatting retorted, attempting to retain his composure, but the sombre mood had been destroyed and soon we were all sniggering like errant children.

Edmonds might have occasionally ridden roughshod over the all-for-one-and-one-for-all principle (he drove away in a huff at 11 a.m. when he was relegated to twelfth man the next game), but it was behaviour like this that helped the players retain a sense of perspective. His antics jettisoned any lingering feelings of disappointment after a lousy performance. It's over, history, he was saying metaphorically; don't dwell on it. Focus positively on the next challenge. This was very much a trademark of the Middlesex sides of the 1980s. With such a broad range of personalities, there was plenty of cut and thrust and you could always rely on someone to alleviate the pain of defeat with a personally directed wisecrack or wind-up. The collective bubble didn't take long to resurface.

Other teams hated this aspect of Middlesex – that we were so cocksure and unfazed and so bloody noisy. The strutting and jabbering got on their nerves, but they were powerless to do anything about it. Warwickshire had seven international players, but subsided meekly to an innings defeat in the last match of the season – Edmonds taking four wickets and Daniel blasting out the tail – to give us our first championship title under Gatting's leadership.

A posse of cameramen attended Gatting's post-victory speech when he admitted that we'd won the title against the odds. There had been an element of luck – second-placed Hampshire lost their penultimate match by one wicket off the last ball. Middlesex's monopoly on that particular commodity infuriated the other counties most of all. A mishap always seemed to befall the opposition whenever they managed to temporarily regain the initiative. But the assertion of Geoff Boycott as he left the Yorkshire dressing room to the usual accompaniment of 'Good luck, Boycs,' could have equally applied to Middlesex. 'It's not good luck,' he'd say tersely, 'it's good skill.'

PRIME TIME: 1986

toughened-up Down Under • dressing-room hullaballoo • Tufnell's feline impressions • Boycott's rabbit • final tension • chauvinists and lesbians • hiring and firing

IT'S GREAT OUTDOORS

A crunch summer. Andrew and Fergie were getting married, the City was gearing up for Big Bang and it was the last year of my contract. To harden my resolve and leg muscles, I signed up with a premier club in Perth for the winter. Having lost 3–1 to David Gower's team in 1985, the Aussies still had a healthy respect for county players. I'd heard they played a merciless brand of league cricket in Western Australia – no prisoners taken – and that plenty of English pros went out there to get knocked into shape.

I didn't realise this meant bump-starting a 2-ton 1971 Falcon several times a week to get to the club, or being obliged to complete a mini triathlon on the beach after bowling flat out in the nets for two hours. For once I was abiding by my dad's passion to 'build up your strength, it's the only way'. At least the reward for a swim/run relay was reclining in the sand guzzling a case of Swan lager as the sun sank gently into the sea on the horizon. It was still 85°F at 10 p.m.

Australia is always depicted as the great outdoors and the land of opportunity. In practice this means if you manufacture sunblock or insect-repellent you're quids in; otherwise, you're in the rat race like everybody else. Look at all those luxurious scenes in holiday brochures for the Gold Coast or the Barrier Reef. Is there any sign of a wasp or a fly or people wincing as they rub cream into their burnt shoulders? It's all an illusion. As it happens, there is a higher incidence of skin cancer Down Under, and there are more stinging, biting, life-threatening organisms there than on any other continent. And that's before you set foot on the cricket field.

The bushflies! Buzzing round your ear, up your nose, in your eyes, between your toes; guzzling your beer, all over your steak. God's sick joke, I suppose – creating paradise, and then tossing in some trivial irritation which ends up driving you nuts. He might have thought it would keep out the riff-raff, but it's had the opposite effect. There's only one solution: buy one of those hats with dangling corks. They get rid of the flies instantly. Unfortunately, they frighten away the Sheilas as well.

The Perth experience also banished another myth: that Aussie women respond favourably to English chivalry. Live there for a couple of months and you realise that the cliché 'Australian women like being treated badly, and Australian men always oblige' hits the nail squarely on the head. I was too polite or too sarcastic or too clumsy to open an account with any of them. I did go out with one girl, the delectably named Bronwen Shmack, but she was German.

Dermot Reeve, who I shared a house with, was the type of self-flagellating bloke who could have scored every week, but he was so self-obsessed he didn't notice anyone else. Even on the local nudist beach he only admired himself. I must say I hadn't expected Australian beaches to be populated by wobbling women playing volleyball and Fat-Bellied Gutbuckets lying on their backs with their Factor 20-tipped willies dangling to the side like soggy ice-cream cornets. That isn't in the brochures either.

Australians are unsophisticated by nature and that may be the secret of their athletic prowess. Their minds are uncluttered and the men really do have only three things on their agenda: sport, beer and their dongers. Sometimes all at the same time. Stand behind the goal at an Aussie rules match, and you'll see clumps of lager-swilling males all waiting eagerly for the moment when the umpire below the posts signals a score in that funny semaphore they use. A nanosecond before he brings his hands abruptly in front of himself about eighteen inches apart, they all shout, 'How big's your dick?'

Puerile the locals may be, but when all's said and done, a winter's cricket in Australia is a beneficial exercise. Every club team contained at least two Test players (Kim Hughes and

Terry Alderman regularly turned out for one, for instance), the wickets were hard and reliable and the matches were two-day examinations rather than afternoon frolics. You didn't earn much, but the serious attitude to twice-a-week practice, the lengthy team talks, the total commitment to win and the unbelievable levels of sledging definitely left their mark. Many English players had their best county season after a winter in Australia. They were lucky they had the chance. Now they wouldn't want us even if we paid 'em.

LOOK, NO CITROËN!

April, London

Whether spending the winter playing on dry, bouncy tracks with the hot wind off the Nullarbor Plain blowing in your face was good preparation for running into a damp sou'wester at Bristol is a moot point, but Australian cricket is an attitude thing, and you do return with just a little extra swagger, as well as a tendency to use words like 'bonza' and 'ripper' in everyday conversation. There's nothing like a bit of English disparagement to put you back in your place, though. A letter from Slazenger, my kit sponsor, did that easily.

I had written to them assuming that, as part of the championship-winning team, I'd get an improved deal. People like Gooch, Gatting and Gower were being paid £5,000 to use a certain make of equipment, in addition to receiving apparently unlimited quantities of casual gear and more than enough bats for a small regiment, so surely they could afford to lob me a few bob? Er, no, they couldn't, actually. In addition to my regulation bat, pads and gloves, they fobbed me off with two T-shirts and a pair of tennis shorts.

There was some consolation on the first day back at Lord's. I got a sponsored car, if only by default. Wayne Daniel arrived from the Caribbean in early April announcing that he'd passed his driving test. He was immediately allocated a Peugeot 309 estate, which came as a great relief to the players who regularly had to wait until after closing time to pick him up for away trips, and then jolt themselves awake every few minutes during the long, dark drive to Manchester while he lay slumped and snoring in the passenger seat.

The cars were presented on the forecourt inside the Grace Gates after which the selected drivers were free to take their gleaming new vehicles away. Daniel eased his gingerly into St John's Wood Road, took one look at the streams of taxis, vans and cars shooting by and reversed back into the ground, nearly colliding with a wall. 'Man,' he exclaimed, 'they don't drive like that in Barbados!' and handed the keys back. The only two first-team players without cars who could actually drive were the reserve batsman Keith Tomlins and me, so we shared it. It had Middlesex County Cricket Club written on the side in large silver lettering, which made me feel quite self-satisfied driving round town. Except when I stalled.

"'Ere, when am I going to get a sponsored jam jar?' Jamie Sykes inquired after training.

'When your bat makes as much racket as your mouth, maybe,' Barlow ventured.

'Fanks a bunch, Dougie,' Sykes retorted, and let out a loud, deliberate fart. It dawned on me how lucky I'd been to have risen to company-car status at twenty-six when some people twice my age were still clanking around in old jalopies. It made a change from listing round corners in the tin-can Citroën 2CV my girlfriend drove.

But it was a status with responsibility. It meant I was an official away-trip driver and carried the assumption that I was a secure member of the side. Someone who was consistent and reliable. If I didn't establish that this summer, I might not be granted many more chances. Middlesex were intolerant of people who failed to live up to their early promise. You could ride on the bandwagon for a while, but eventually, if your game stuttered, you fell off. Life was too much fun to risk that happening.

I began by trying to be more punctual. Gatting wanted us in by 9.30, and for a month I made it. But then I started getting slack. Lateness is an addiction, you can't do without it for long – all that attention you're not getting. And there are so many ways of making yourself late if you really want to.

1. Assuming your journey will take the minimum time – in *London*. Dumb!

2. Going back for something you left behind in a rush. (Batsmen regularly have anxiety dreams about being unable to find their pads or gloves as the crowd and fielders wait expectantly.)

3. Deciding to have a shower or shave fifteen minutes before leaving.

4. Finding the shirt you want to wear is unironed.

5. Staying to watch that programme for just another five minutes.

6. Leaving the packing to the last minute.

7. Answering the phone on your way out.

8. Losing the car keys.

9. Finding you have an empty wallet or petrol tank, necessitating a detour to the cashpoint or garage.

10. Faffing about.

In a way, I suppose my unpunctuality was a statement against the time I felt cricketers wasted in the morning. As I mentioned before, they all arrived like sheep at 9.30 but then mostly just hung around idly doing crosswords or reading a tabloid until someone goaded them into action. Rarely did anyone make it to the nets before ten.

I soon evolved a method for giving myself a bit more time. I kept my kit in the back seat and if the traffic was bad I'd change in the car and drive round to the Nursery End, emerging from some distant part of the practice area with a ball as if I'd just been to retrieve a big hit. When this happened several days in a row, Gatting – looking up from his daily net diet of gentle half-volleys fed by the coach – said drily: 'Afternoon. Forget to set the alarm again?' I realised my cover was blown.

THE HUSTLER

We were now into our fourth season post-Brearley, and the dressing-room atmosphere was markedly different. Where before there had been respectable noise levels – people chatting, playing backgammon or quietly reading – now it was utter mayhem. Indoor ball games, light-hearted wrestling bouts or flick football always incited a commotion. Instead of Brears, Rad and Smudge, there was Filthy (Needham), Lardy Arse (Fraser) and Zorro the Fat Geordie (Roseberry), and as I had a receding hairline my nickname had evolved from the respectable Yozzer to the brutal Spamhead. In addition to the copies of the *Sun* strewn about the place there was, for the more risqué, *Hustler*, which was not, of course, about snooker, but did occasionally feature a voluptuous bottle-blonde spreadeagled across a billiard table. The rhyming slang of anatomy was now the dominant language, especially when the players were poring over page three.

'Linda Lusardi's got great thrup'nys.'

'Give us a butcher's.'

'Phwoooar, she must be minging. S'pose she's shafted by an egg'un?'

'Nah, their whoopers'd fall out.'

'Yeah, but they've always got the biggest Hamptons.'

Observance of the rules about Second XI players being allowed in had become lax and Sykes, a larger-than-life character in all senses, ruled the roost. Commanding a captive audience, he tossed blunt insults this way and that, which were generally returned in good humour.

'You're fackin' GNATS,' he said to Angus Fraser, a comment on his perceived lack of pace. 'Goochy'll be going for your JUG today!'

'Hark at Don Bradman,' Fraser retorted, a reference to Sykes' colossal career aggregate of 279 first-class runs. 'I bet all the bowlers are really quaking in their boots when you come in.'

Those who couldn't take Sykes' confrontational approach eventually left the club.

He was accompanied everywhere he went by another young spinner, Philip Tufnell, a pseudo-Cockney (in fact he went to Highgate School), who always had a fag drooping from his mouth and wore a leopard-print G-string, baggy pants and winkle-pickers. At nights they careered around in Tufnell's old Rover, visiting pubs and clubs in the Mile End Road and doing what lads do. They usually had a Tracey or a Sharon in tow.

If you couldn't smell tobacco in the dressing room it probably meant Tufnell was asleep (he was nicknamed the Cat for this reason, not for his stealthiness in the covers), but if you went near him and said '*Aciiiiid*!' quite loudly, he woke with a start. These two mischievous fly-by-nights were the understudies to Emburey and Edmonds. The England spin twins were often away on Test duty and eventually Tufnell, who had a funny hopping run-up but had been taking wickets in the Second XI, got his chance in the first team at Worcester. I must admit I didn't think he had much hope of success, and neither, clearly, did some of the Worcester players. Seeing this dishevelled figure shuffling out nervously at number 11 for his first innings, helmet wobbling on his head, feet at ten to two, bat dragging behind him, David Smith, the burly left-hander who took bouncers on the body as though they were paper darts, stood aghast at silly point.

As Tufnell sheepishly took guard, Smith could contain himself no longer. 'Who's this fucking *muppet*?' he said severely, causing Tufnell to practically faint with shock. He managed to pull himself together to nudge a few singles off the spinners, but as soon as the pacy Neal Radford was brought back, he ran himself out. Later his bowling was collared to all parts and he was summarily sent back whence he came.

Things went better for me. Since Emburey and Edmonds were constantly with England, and the Jackson Five usually dominated the queue for the physio's room, there was no competition for bowling places. This reduced the intensity of our performances (and therefore the return on them), but at least I got to play every game instead of being often omitted on some selectorial whim.

Feeling secure and confident, I recorded my career best in early June, taking 7–35 on a damp day at The Oval as the ball swung and seamed. Dickie Bird was umpiring at my end, and when I beat the bat he kept saying, 'Ooh, well booled, lad – joost a bit straighter.' But when it was and rapped someone on the pad, he said 'Not art,' with a big grin. So I got everyone caught at slip.

I was lucky to be alive to achieve it. In the Sunday League the previous day I'd been inches from death as Sylvester Clarke, taking umbrage because I had just slogged him for four, sent down the most ferocious delivery it was ever my fortune to have avoided. Seeing me taking a couple of steps to leg, he aimed at my retreating rib cage, but the ball finished up whizzing head high 3yds wide of the stumps and shot straight to the boundary unimpeded. In darts terms, it was a bullseye attempt that ended up embedded in the blackboard. As we needed four to win, this attempt on my wellbeing finished the match. He never had another chance to get his own back. Shame.

One minute you're the rooster, the next a feather duster. Two days after bowling like a demon, I went off for a celebratory meal with the Worcester opening batsman Tim Curtis, a good friend from university days. Whether the steak in Malvern was infected or the beer was off I don't know, but the following day I had violent diarrhoea. In fact it was gushing from both ends. We were in the field on the second day of the match at Worcester but I was too nauseous to do the warm-ups and lay prostrate in the dressing room praying for it to rain.

It didn't. I staggered out on to the field at eleven o'clock, buttocks clenched, and stood at mid-on, where I knew I'd be safe because nothing ever went there off Wayne Daniel. Second ball of the day he dished up a juicy half-volley which Curtis punched to my left and there was nothing to do but set off in pursuit. Four steps into a jog I lost bowel control and had to dash straight to the toilet, ignoring the ball completely. 'That's the only time you'll get any runs at Worcester,' a spectator crooned. I'd recovered by the afternoon but my bowling was hit for a hundred.

The same fate apparently once befell the old fast bowler Alf Gover playing for England in India. He ran in to bowl, felt an unsavoury explosion downstairs as he prepared to deliver and just kept on going past the batsman and straight to the pavilion. He disappeared to the toilet, pursued by Jardine who called out, 'Take your time, Gover, but could we have the ball back?'

BOYCOTT'S VISION

Saturday 14 June, Middlesex v Yorkshire, Lord's
My accident was only a temporary blip, and I was still bowling well enough to consistently beat Geoff Boycott outside the off stump during an innings for Yorkshire which, he kept reminding us, was his 1,000th in first-class 'crickit'. He didn't practise with the Yorkshire team but warmed up on the boundary edge, gratefully hitting a few balls I threw at him into the hoardings.

Angus Fraser bowled superbly in the match and got so frustrated with Boycott's playing and missing that he finally emitted an agonised 'D'you want a bell in it, Grandad?'

'If tha can see so well, why doesn't tha bool at stoomps?' came the triumphant reply. Boycott had reason to be cheerful. Yorkshire won the match comfortably, consigning us to second from bottom.

There are as many Boycott stories as he's played forward defensives, but my favourite had a similar resonance. Mike Hendrick had been bowling some dastardly leg-cutters at our Geoffrey, none of which he could lay a bat on, but he kept up a gibing banter for most of the morning.

Hendrick (after an edge had gone between the slips): 'How many great bowlers *are* there in the world?'

Boycott (defiant): 'One less than tha thinks there are. Now, get back and bool.'

Hendrick (later, beating the bat): 'Has that bat got 'ole in it?'

Boycott: 'I'd put thee in mook and nettles if tha give me woon to reach.'

At length the mischievous umpire, Arthur Jepson, had had enough of this incessant rabbit and when Hendrick nipped one back into Boycott's pads and let out a half-hearted appeal, Jepson gave him out. Stunned and appalled by what appeared to be an outrageous injustice, Boycott marched off, muttering to the umpire as he passed, 'Hey, Arthur, what's happened to your guide dog?'

'I sacked it for yapping, same as I'm doing to you,' Jepson replied. 'Now, piss off!'

These weren't the exact words used by the Yorkshire committee at the end of the 1986 season, but the message was the same. After twenty-five years, they'd had enough of Boycott's foibles and wouldn't renew his contract. So ended the remarkable career of a dedicated, bloody-minded, fastidious, outspoken, immaculately turned out egocentric who could still inspire a loyalty most politicians would die for. He had a reputation for being selfish and blunt, and I dare say he was. Dickie Bird was certainly under no illusions. 'That man Boycott,' he said, seeing the maestro on the dressing-room balcony. 'E's got millions but he keeps it all to 'imself, y'know. When 'e dies, they'll bury t'money with 'im. An' I'll be t'first to go an' dig it oop!'

I always found Boycott polite and good company, and sometimes his altercations with Emburey and Edmonds actually enlivened a tedious day. Most surprising of all, he did have a wide range of strokes and wasn't afraid to use them, advancing down the pitch to the spinners, gliding the ball smoothly into gaps, cutting and even pulling the pacemen. Edmonds once berated him with a suggestion that people who just patted back half-volleys were a waste of space. 'He won't die of a stroke, anyway,' he grunted good-humouredly after one rigid block.

Boycott rose to the bait. 'I've got over forty-eight thousand first-class roons, average fifty-six,' he retorted. 'I moost've played soom shots soomwhere, else all the booling's roobish.'

There's no answer to that.

FIVE TO WIN

Saturday 12 July, Benson & Hedges Cup Final, Lord's
We had a rotten season in the championship, and Gatting, who had to divide his attentions between England, the Middlesex captaincy, his family and various other distractions, began to despair. Before the start of one match he implored the senior players to take more responsibility. Half an hour later he walked in at 10–2 and made 158, an innings given an authentic stamp of approval by Harry Sharp, our sixty-nine-year-old scorer. 'Brutal, bloody brutal,' he exclaimed in admiration when he returned to the dressing room for his whisky at the end of the day. From a man who played the triangle to Compton and Edrich's timpani in the glorious summer of '47, it was the highest praise.

To compensate for being stuck at the bottom of the table, we sailed through to the final of the Benson & Hedges Cup without a hitch. Youth and overexcitement rendered the previous Lord's extravaganzas in which I'd played a bit of a blur. This one was brought into sharp focus by the dying moments. My apparent nonchalance and ability to bowl the yorker had earned me the role of Middlesex's Death Bowler (so described because you operated 'at the death' rather than because you were capable of causing it). I liked this job because everyone was watching the climax and things happened. Major crowd reactions were guaranteed, and they gave me a buzz. You weren't just trying to sneak through a few cheap overs unnoticed. An added bonus was the fact that in the slog period of an innings you were expected to go for runs, so couldn't get a bollocking if you did.

On this occasion Kent needed 14 from the final over, and despite outward signs of confidence I was jangling inside from the stress of the responsibility. To make matters worse, it was raining. Hard. The ball was like a bar of soap. After two singles, it slipped out of my hand third ball and arrived pleasantly at thigh height to the Kent wicketkeeper, Steve Marsh, who swung it delightedly into the grandstand. Six! People in the thick of big sporting events often claim they weren't aware of the enormity of their contribution to the outcome at the time. The yelping, whooping, chanting Kent supporters, bonding together on all sides, made sure that I was. The penetrating gaze of 30,000 pairs of eyes went right to the bone.

They now needed only six from three balls – one hit if I offered up another such tasty morsel. I was nearly choking with fear; my legs felt about to buckle and the other players were bracing themselves for the worst. 'Save the two,' Gatting reminded boundary fielders hopefully. I fixed my eyes firmly on the base of middle stump, held my nerve and, with the rain bucketing down, conceded only a single off the next two, which meant Graham Dilley had to hit the last ball for five (effectively six) to win the cup.

This was the most important delivery of my career. My heart beat as loudly and rapidly as a road drill and, as I paused at the beginning of my run, images of permanent ignominy and deep, dark recesses passed through my mind. I would be tarred and blackballed for life if I blew it. 'Good luck, Yozzer, you can do it,' Gatting mumbled from mid-wicket without real conviction. The rain was beating down, the crowd were hysterical. 'Don't bowl a no-ball or a wide,' I repeated to myself as I ran in, trying to focus on the bowling crease. I served up another full toss. Dilley swiped hugely but could only toe it gently to deep square leg. We had won by 2 runs. I was engulfed by fielders and supporters whooping with delight.

We ran off the field, our weary legs powered by elation, but it was only sitting dripping in my corner of the dressing room with the team after the presentations had finished and all the champagne had been sprayed or drunk and the well-wishers had vanished back into the woodwork that the wave of satisfaction rolled over me. The moment of winning had been a climax, a thrill, but the warm glow of achievement, of earning the respect and gratitude of your colleagues, was a deeper sensation. Now I understood why women usually preferred the post-coital embrace to initial penetration.

This, I realised, is what true sportsmen seek. To reach heights they thought were unattainable and to be regarded as an equal, not some bit-part also-ran. To feel wanted and prized rather than used and excused. You play all your career to become accepted as part of the fabric, to be mentioned in the same breath as all the others, not be the subject of embarrassed whispers and glances. The desire to belong is in everyone. To achieve it, not to mention a win bonus of £2,300 is very special.

Be quick to enjoy it, though – the euphoria doesn't last long. And something always comes along to take the gloss off it. Emerging from the pavilion at 9 p.m., I discovered that after the match my mother had been treated as a second-class citizen by the MCC. Sheltering from the weather under the pavilion overhang to watch the presentations, she was confronted by a supercilious steward who ordered her away from the area. 'Women aren't allowed on the pavilion steps,' he said uncompromisingly, and sent her out into the rain. As if that wasn't bad enough, I then remembered I had half an hour to drag Wayne Daniel away from a scrum of admiring females, out of the pub and into my car for the journey to Leicester, where we were playing a Sunday League match the next day. Getting Naomi Campbell into the Lord's pavilion would have been easier.

DANGEROUS LIAISONS

August, Manchester and Leeds

'Good sportsmen have sex appeal.' Not my assertion – I read it in *Vogue* magazine. It's not the athleticism, the healthy looks or the money girls are particularly attracted to, nor the prospect of a free ticket to sit on a hard bench for several hours. It's the confidence that comes with success, the magnetism of fame, however minor, and the physical electricity generated by an exciting win, that is alluring. These are the main reasons why some ordinary-looking cricketers gad about with tasty women.

Suddenly and unconsciously and regrettably, I was sucked into this malarky. For the next few weeks I was brimming with noisy self-belief, and had a series of brief liaisons with nubile brunettes, mostly physios or nurses. But then, as we all know, there are only two certainties in life – death and nurses. Eventually I got so carried away I went back to a flat in Belsize Park shared by two well-presented girls who, I naïvely imagined, were up for a threesome, something I'd read about in a Dutch porn mag lying around the dressing room.

The slimmer, prettier girl gave me a beer when she'd removed her leather jacket, then disappeared into the bedroom. The other one, also dressed in leather and admittedly rather butch, followed and locked the door. It soon became clear that men weren't on their horizontal menu so I quietly let myself out.

Northern cricketers had considerably fewer delusions of grandeur when it came to the fairer sex. A week later on a dank Monday in Manchester, a friend invited me to sample the luscious wares of his local nightspot: the Lady Bar in Milnrow. As Milnrow is a sad annexe to Rochdale, itself not the most salubrious of towns, this sounded like an oxymoron, especially on a Monday. When we arrived, the place, a converted barn about 200yds from an instantly missable turn-off on the M62, was deserted.

We had an overcooked fish supper and I was just getting ready to leave when car loads of dolled-up females began filing in. By 9.30 the place was heaving with girls of every shape, appearance and denomination. Most had squeezed themselves into black leggings and tight white jackets and wore frosty pink lipstick, but some were quite presentable. A number of well-known West Indian cricketers loitered around salivating. If you hear overseas Test players saying they come over to play in the Lancashire League because of the quality of cricket, don't believe a word of it. What they mean to say is quantity of crumpet.

Later in August during a three-day match at Headingley, we were invited en masse to something that sounded even more incongruous, an event which rejoiced in the name of Arnie's Stagarama. This was a benefit function for Yorkshire's ruddy-faced seam bowler Arnie Sidebottom, held at a workingmen's club in some obscure part of Leeds. The place was like an oversized church hall full of leering, belching men sitting in nicotine clouds. There was a stage at one end on which lumpy girls were gyrating, and a bar at the other. Tickets were £3, for which you were promised three comedians, six strippers and a free pint of Webster's. We got in free.

Needless to say, the standard of everything was atrocious and several of our black players visibly balked at some of the crude racist jokes. The best part, by a mile, came at the end of a sleazy lesbian act when the two performers invited a member of the audience to come up and join them. Sykes, only twenty-two but boasting a rapidly expanding waistline, bolted head-long to the front with much greater verve than he ever mustered chasing a ball to the boundary, climbed up onstage, took off all his clothes and lay down. The girls began massaging him with oils, but as the show built up to a climax one spoilsport, either fed up with foreplay or finding the sight of Sykes' naked body distinctly unappetising, lobbed a plastic chair at the performers. They immediately gathered up their accessories and quit and the show was instantly abandoned.

How Sidebottom benefited from this I couldn't fathom.

There couldn't have been much change out of three quid a head once he'd stumped up for the entertainment and the free beer. At least it spared us a listless night cooped up in our hotel, one of those ill-equipped prefabs hugging the A1 which you drive past thinking that no one in his right mind could possibly want to stay there. It wouldn't have been fit for a herd of Leeds supporters. When I lay down in the room my head was precisely 25yds from the grinding juggernauts in the inside lane.

HIRING AND FIRING

September

All this larking about alleviated the guilt that accompanies a losing streak. We knew we were playing pitiful championship cricket, and that heads might roll, but we were powerless to do anything about it. A downward spiral is self-perpetuating in the same way as a winning streak, and, trapped in a vortex of poor results, teams turn up expecting to lose and actually become quite rooted to the experience. Gatting might have pulled us into line on the field, but he was mostly away with England, and nobody else seemed prepared to take on any real responsibility. It becomes a case of self-preservation, looking after number one, making sure your performance is up to scratch and sod what happens to the team. The results, of course, go from bad to worse.

I didn't like this selfish attitude, but there wasn't really a lot I could do. You can't fight a one-man battle. Anyway, the contracts meeting was in August and mine was up for renewal. Fortunately, at about that time I was top of the national bowling averages (they were printed weekly in the *Daily Telegraph*, though some players already knew theirs by heart to the second decimal point). To my great relief, I was offered another three-year extension, and in September I was mentioned in some dispatches as an outsider for the England tour of

Australia. It was flattering, but I wasn't holding my breath.

I was also named Middlesex Player of the Year by our sponsors, Austin Reed. Receiving the trophy, an engraved solid silver ball, ranked as one of the proudest moments of my career. It was slightly blemished by the fact that the presentation took place after-hours amid the racks of suits and coats on the first floor of their Regent Street store. Passers-by might have assumed it was the launch of the shop's annual sale rather than a prestigious awards ceremony. One or two of our number took the opportunity to slip an expensive leather belt into their pockets on the way out.

Some of my old university mates weren't so lucky. Our last match of the season was at Edgbaston, and on the second day, while we were batting, the entire Warwickshire Second XI was summoned, one by one, to the manager's office. Some came out smirking but others had visibly aged by the time they emerged. The committee were having a clear-out, and nine young players had got the bullet. One was told cryptically it was 'because your arms are too short'. That evening I went to the pub with some of the victims. It was a miserable experience. Most sat staring glumly into their beers or gazing into space, and for a long time hardly a word was spoken. Not one of them had expected the sack and none had made any provision for their future.

Some reproached their second-team coach, Neil Abberley, accusing him of being stubborn and short-sighted and denying people proper opportunities. In truth he was only trying to do his job. The crime many of these governors commit is not that of wrongful dismissal, it's negligence, pure and simple. They hire young striplings, making promises and predictions, use them and abuse them, then unceremoniously lop them down as younger versions bear tastier fruit. The only career advice they've ever offered is: 'You are to take adequate measures to ensure you stay fit during the winter months.'

Now these poor, numb twenty-five-year-olds were contemplating the end of life as they knew it. Most had nothing else to offer and feared thirty years of stacking shelves or sorting mail or working in the complaints department at Carlsberg. Even an HGV licence would have been something. But an addiction to the cricketing drug precludes young men from peering outside their cocoon. While other lads of similar age were ascending the ladder in their working environment, repping or broking, and were building up valuable experience and a bulging contacts book, this bunch had devoted their healthiest, most energetic years, their eyes, ears and mouths, to cricket, cricket and more cricket. Cricket was their identity, their raison d'être, and what good was that to IBM or Shell or Unilever?

TOTALLY INDEPENDENT

October

This experience, though depressing, was of immense value to me. In short, it was a wake-up call. It made me aware for the first time what a dicey existence this was, and of the necessity to make some kind of contingency plans. I had a new three-year contract but I realised that nothing was carved in stone, and a BA in general arts from Durham wasn't a passport to a dream job, either.

The late Peter Smith, then about to become the TCCB press officer, came up with the solution. He knew I wrote a monthly column for *The Cricketer* magazine and, as a former tabloid cricket correspondent himself, he followed the media world avidly. He told me about a new newspaper launching in the autumn. The *Independent*. Go and see them, he said.

I arranged a visit and was somewhat taken aback by the computerised office and the laminated desks and the smartly dressed yuppies behind them. This was nothing like the chaotic assemblage of dishevelled hacks and harassed editors running around with reams of inky Xeroxes that I had been expecting.

The outside of the building, a dowdy office block near Old Street tube station, was unappealing. But inside it was positively space-age compared to the dilapidated headquarters of the *West Australian*, where I had worked as 'world news editor' for a few weeks the previous winter. (This job actually entailed wading through rolls of paper in the telex room for anything that might remotely interest people in Perth, who rivalled Yorkshiremen for the title of xenophobic champions of the universe. Then I cut the selected stories into little pieces with blunt scissors. The best part was that I knocked off at midday, and got straight down the beach just in time to catch all the secretaries stripping off for their lunch-hour top-ups.)

'Can you write on anything other than cricket?' The *Independent*'s newly appointed sports editor asked me. 'Rugby, for instance?'

'Oh, yes,' I lied. My knowledge extended to a couple of games of touch as a fourteen-year-old. Still, they had me in to work on dummy versions of the paper while they tried out layouts and typefaces and I trained on the VDUs as a sub-editor. It was all very exciting, and I enjoyed writing articles about players I knew (Spikes and the Rat had just been offered new good contracts after helping Hampshire to win the John Player League), and seeing them appear on the page.

I remember the day of the *Independent*'s launch well. It was 7 October, and I was in Exeter trying to temporarily revive a flagging relationship with an old girlfriend so that I had some-one to go on holiday with. Why kill it off now when you could do it after a fortnight in Turkey? I stood outside W.H. Smith and watched folk going in, picking up their usual rag from the stack and heading straight for the till. Occasionally someone noticed the new title, fingered it suspiciously, then put it back. I was there for half an hour and saw two copies sold. We're such creatures of habit.

The following Saturday the sports editor asked me to cover Harlequins v Rosslyn Park. I accepted the job, despite the fact that I was working for a small sports news agency in the morning at the hockey World Cup semi-final. To complicate matters, I had never actually been to a senior rugby match before, so I arranged for my uncle, a sports fanatic and a member of Quins, to meet me there and talk me through it.

The sports editor rang the following Monday to say that my piece was so good it almost seemed as if it'd been written by someone else. Which in fact it had. The hockey had gone into extra time (England eventually beat West Germany) and then the traffic was appalling getting away from the Willesden stadium, so by the time I got to Twickenham, the rugby was half over. My uncle had been keeping random notes on the back of his chequebook between swigs of Beamish. As my knowledge of the sport was restricted to the contents of the *Duffer's Guide to Rugby*, his observations made up the bulk of my report.

THE MALLET FALLS

Saturday 8 November

I did manage full comprehension of my next assignment, but it took place somewhere I'd never been before nor expect to go again. At Shepton Mallet, in the depths of the West Country, ruddy-faced farmers looked on in amazement as 2,000 cars snaked their way down leafy lanes to a hall normally reserved for cattle auctions and lectures on animal husbandry. Somerset were holding a special general meeting to debate the club's rejection of their old life force, Viv Richards and Joel Garner. Ian Botham had resigned in sympathy.

The members were at full strength and backed the club's decision. People trying to get the great West Indies pair re-instated made emotive speeches which sometimes approached pure pantomime as they ripped up their notes to symbolise the rape and pillage of the club. The former Somerset player Nigel Popplewell, son of Judge Popplewell, scuppered the rebels' rudderless arguments. Popplewell Junior was a man of no mean intelligence, despite undermining his credibility by tending to dress like a tramp. 'In my last season,' he said rolling up the sleeves of an exceptionally tatty jumper. 'Viv and Joel only tried when it suited them, while expecting everyone else to contribute a hundred and ten per cent all the time. As a result, the county only won seven championship games in their last three seasons.'

Garner was at the back of the hall and bowed his head in shame when he heard this. In truth his fitness record had not been particularly convincing – 87 games in nine years, compared with, say, Wayne Daniel's 170 in the same period. He was a gentle, affable man (without the ball) who spent a lot of time asleep. His knees were beginning to give way and he was ready to retire from county cricket. He would wallow in a Lancashire League contract like a pig in the proverbial.

Richards was more the villain of the piece. Proud and haughty, he could be difficult if he got out of bed on the wrong side. He would flounce around if captain's decisions irked him and indulge in irresponsible bouts of slogging. You have to give your star players some leeway, but they must pull their weight too. For the previous few years, Richards palpably hadn't. Although he was unrepentant at the time, the episode probably did him good. When he came back to play for Glamorgan several years later he was a much more rounded, good-natured person who was inspirational rather than conspiratorial.

With my immediate future taken care of and something in the pipeline for later, there was just one other thing I had to do. Buy somewhere to live. I had sponged off my parents for too long and everyone else was climbing the property ladder. I toured banks and building societies looking for competitive loans but it was umpire John Hampshire who gave me the best advice. 'Borrow as much as you can,' he said. Well, you wouldn't really expect a Yorkshireman to advocate digging into your own pockets.

So I mortgaged myself to the hilt to buy a terraced 'cottage' in Brentford, where a hapless football team was singularly failing to eradicate the curse of the nylons factory. It was far enough from my parents' home to give me my independence but close enough for my dad to pop round and weed the garden (he didn't have much work on at the time apart from an episode of *Howard's Way*). The previous owner was a fragile old lady and the interior was in a real state. So after I'd bought it, I moved in some impecunious New Zealand friends, armed them with paint and brushes and buggered off to Australia.

SATURATION POINT: 1987

Ashes triumph • EJ the DJ • Botham and Hick United • Ramprakash dash • Emburey and Gooch • in reverse • following the Ball • Edmonds flips • Scarborough fare • rusty engines

CROCODILE ROCK

New Year, Australia

I arrived in Sydney in early January on the eve of the fifth Test. England, captained by Gatting, had already retained the Ashes, and the players were strutting about town like contented peacocks. I was sitting having a meal in their smart hotel with John Emburey when Elton John, himself on tour in Australia, wandered over from a nearby table. He is a cricket fanatic – he once travelled all the way out to Oz just for a day/night game and flew back to the UK again next morning. Still suffering the after-effects of a throat operation, he couldn't speak. Instead he presented Emburey with a bottle of $100 Dom Perignon and wrote a note on a paper napkin: 'To J.E. Well played. Love E.J.' Then he went back to his table.

There were lots of familiar faces in town for the Test – in fact I recognised more people in the Sydney Cricket Ground pavilion than I usually did at Lord's. English pros on holiday, *Test Match Special* commentators hosting supporters' tours, prominent committeemen from the shires who'd slyly told their wives they'd gone to London for a TCCB conference.

I also found the gatemen a good deal more helpful. Having bluffed my way into the ground on the premise that I was an England net bowler, I was then hailed by various Australian spongers I knew seeking my assistance to get them in the same way. The old stewards were easily convinced – even that a scrawny student wearing pebble glasses, board shorts and carrying a tatty rucksack was some vital accessory to the touring party. But then, nobodies could get into the Australian team, too; remember all the kerfuffle over the off-spinner Peter Who?

Gatting was accompanied everywhere he went by the industrial jar of Branston he had brought from England, and he conspired to send the Australians into a right pickle. Their game was in a mess. Their batsmen had become bloated on an endless diet of one-day cricket, and their bowling, apart from that of Bruce Reid, was innocuous. The anxious post-mortems and Hunt the Scapegoat campaigns were being conducted in the local press even before the Tests had ended. 'Place more emphasis on four-day cricket' (which in Australia means the Sheffield Shield) was the general consensus. Funny how cricketing fraternities 12,000 miles apart tend to come to the same conclusions.

I spent some time in the England dressing room at the SCG as they sought a draw on the last day of the series. Over lunch the players exchanged good-natured gibes and match discussions. Nothing new there, then.

'Is it turning out there, Bill?' Lamb asked Athey.

'Yep, and Sleep's hardly bowled a loose one.'

'How's Taylor bowling, Lubo [David Gower]?'

'A bit loose, I'd say he was sloggable.'

'What's the steak like, Gatt?' inquired Botham.

'Two were underdone but I enjoyed the third.'

As usual, Edmonds sat on his own in a corner with a cheese salad. Gower sent for more Stilton. This was his ninety-first Test.

'Could be playing your hundredth next winter, Lubo,' Edmonds observed.

'But it's Pakistan next winter, Henri, and I'll let you into a little secret . . .'

Gatting's Test captaincy was no different from the type of brawny leadership Middlesex players were used to. An honest mixture of logic and earthy competitiveness. British bulldog, people called it. And he was still reluctant to explain tricky decisions to touchy players. Emburey and Mickey Stewart dealt with his dirty work. But he was good at tub-thumping.

As England crumbled in the last hour of the fifth Test, he watched impatiently, pacing anxiously up and down the room, wanting to finish the tour on a high note. It was not to be. 'Well tried, Gladstone,' he said to Small, dismissed three overs from the end. 'Great effort, Embers,' last man out with only six balls remaining. 'Bad luck, chaps. We deserve a drink tonight.' And, as it turned out, into the next morning, at a private bash in the penthouse of their exclusive apartment block. They partied till dawn, predominantly to the strains of Elton John. Mainly because the man on DJ duty was, er, Elton John.

Even though Australia had won the final Test, the inquests into the state of their game continued unabated. But during a week-long tour of the outback, I found that cricket was thriving in some pretty inhospitable environments. Bradman was brought up in country cricket at Cootamundra in central New South Wales, where the sun bakes the skin the texture of crocodile hide, vipers lie somnolent in the long grass and one club plays on red ant-ridden dirt in the middle of a greyhound track. The hare is put through its paces in the tea interval. The temperature soars – 38 degrees C, 39, 40 – flies irritate, the changing room is the back of a truck, the drinks break means queueing for a rusty tap, the shower afterwards is a nearby swimming pool ('Not that you Poms ever bother washing,' they scoffed).

Yet they wouldn't miss it for the world. Players regularly travel for several hours to get there. One farmer's son had driven 700km – yes, 700km – mostly on untarred roads through Friday night for Saturday's match. The farm needed him back again on Sunday. And we complain about two hours of weaving between bollards on the M1.

A stocky man with bristling orange hair and a ginger beard strides out. Bushfire, they call him. He deposits each of his first three deliveries over mid-wicket with a resonant thwack. His partner is a crimson-faced man called Blood Clot, a bee-keeper. He nudges balls into gaps, calling for sneaky singles, giving Bushfire a wide berth. Then Stumpy, the keeper, runs him out.

The batting is aggressive, the bowling miserly, the fielding predatory. Everyone seems to have an arm like a missile-launcher. County cricket seems rather forgiving in comparison.

A Lot of Hard Yakka

There is no guile here – the game is built on naked commitment. Nobody gets one off the mark; reputations are irrelevant. It is all a matter of attitude. Cricket is the lifeblood of the outback, a place to test your heart and soul before going back to work. It is the source of the Australian river of pride.

SURVIVAL OF THE FLITTEST

Monday 6 April, First Day of Training

For a minion in county cricket, pride is smothered somewhat by the need for self-preservation. Our living depended on it. Cynically, you looked down the list of fixtures and worked out which pitches you most fancied and when various fearsome opponents would be away on Test duty. In this dicey profession, it was vital to plot a secure path and have emergency escape routes ready.

Some matches we labelled with a black mark. The prospect of going to Worcester to bowl at Graeme Hick was inhibiting enough: the fact that he would now be followed in to bat by Ian Botham made you want to run away and hide. Bowlers everywhere were contemplating their fate and campaigning for boundaries to be extended beyond 100yds.

At least Hick and Botham came in down the order, which meant that getting rid of the openers was about as sane as pitching base camp in the path of a giant avalanche. Keeping numbers 3 and 4 in the hut as long as possible was far more sensible. You didn't want the poor old ball suffering too much at the hands of two of the game's strongest men wielding two of the game's biggest bats. If one ball lasted the distance, that is. The River Severn at Worcester wasn't within normal range, like the Tone is at Taunton, but these men weren't normal. Even the twelfth-century stained glass in the cathedral was vulnerable if the wind was right.

I worked out some possible strategies.

1. Pull up the ladder. Declare yourself gone in the hamstring

before the match – the safest option. A few bowlers had this down to a fine art. A solution high in common sense, but low in fibre.

2. Bowl innocuously and keep the openers in. This could backfire, though, because you might get taken off, and reintroduced later just when the fireworks have been ignited and are ready to spark.

3. Bowl a long, exhausting spell of containment, then retire spent to the outfield or, better still, the dressing room, for a grandstand view of the onslaught.

4. Be a masochist. Offer to bowl at 2.45 p.m. when the wicket is flat, the guns are blazing and the ball has just been returned covered in essence of cow pat. You might go for ten an over but you'll get the George medal for being so brave.

Selfish and feeble as it may sound, all these tactics have been used, perhaps subconsciously, in county cricket as journeymen players look after number one. And we wonder why our game stagnates and no one watches.

LABOURING

Monday 13 April, On the Nursery
After a rank performance in the 1986 championship, Middlesex were denied the pre-season Spanish lark and endured a few days of physical conditioning at a sophisticated gym near Paddington instead. The treadmills and modern machinery gave our preparation a totally new emphasis. Sergeant Barlow had retired with a crippling hip injury that had reduced him to an undignified waddle. Having been such a superb athlete he cut a sad figure, and when he popped in for a visit we spared him the Dougie Bader references. Paul Downton took over training command with our new physio, Big Jim. The veteran Johnny Miller was poorly and it was time for a change.

Then we were back at headquarters. It's a funny feeling returning to Lord's after a winter away – a bit like going back to school after the summer holidays. Everything looks different, though the changes are only cosmetic. Polished floors, a touch of paint here and there, new white lines in the car park, the smell of bleach in the toilets, the grass lush and manicured. One or two players almost unrecognisable, having shaved off their beards.

The pristine scene was broken by the rough tones of Gatting, barking with the authority that came with his extended territory. 'You look like a couple of labourers,' he said to two players in denims. Wayne Daniel arrived late. 'Ahem, Diamond, I can see we'll have to get you a new alarm clock.'

'Pity you didn't have one in Australia,' a smart alec piped up from the corner, reminding Gatting of his well-publicised late arrival at a match in Melbourne.

As England captain he had to be seen to be doing the right thing and instilling a bit of discipline. But his credibility was eroded when he sent us all off on a run while he 'attended to some business'. He missed out on half an hour's limbering up, strategically sited near a group of schoolgirls playing tennis. We grabbed the chance for a collective moan about him. Too inflexible, too many distractions, too fat, etc., etc.

Unpopular leaders are usually good ones, though. They don't shy away from tough decisions, or pussyfoot around after poor performances, or get too pally-pally with the players. Sometimes they lose their tempers, but at least it shows they care and have the inner strength to take action. Most people come home from work at some time or other complaining about their overbearing boss. It's a mark of respect, really.

Clive Radley was never one to complain about the days of pre-season sprints into a biting north-east wind, even though he was doing them for the twenty-fifth successive year. His presence in the team was as predictable as April showers and double parking in St John's Wood High Street. 'Never gets any easier,' he said laconically, gazing at a new bat as if it were a present from Santa Claus. Once described as having a complexion like the north wall of the Eiger, his face would have looked a good deal less lived-in if he hadn't treated the drive home like a stage in the RAC Rally, barely slowing down to negotiate those fiendishly narrow 6ft 6 barriers on suburban rat runs to be home in time to mash the potatoes. He had made a career out of avoiding obstacles (i.e., fielders), and considering he'd already made 25,000 runs and been married for fourteen years, he obviously knew what he was doing.

Which was more than you could say for me. After a winter of relative inactivity and some ropy spells in practice matches, I was flailing around both professionally and privately, and my prospects of ever playing for England or finding a wife were receding as fast as my hairline (I was now known as Yul or Brynner as well as Spamhead). 'Behind every under-performing man is a chaotic private life' might have been a relevant reversal of the old motto.

Most of the other players had presentable, if slightly one-dimensional wives – prettier, more worldly versions of the girl-next-door. They were called Steph or Jacqui, slightly less common than Sharon or Debbie. They'd turn up on Sundays wearing tight blue and white stripey trousers, duty-free gold chains advertising suntanned necks. They carried fake Vuitton handbags and drank white-wine spritzers. There was a steadiness and predictability and straightforward attractiveness about them that I found alternately alluring and irritating. Like any twenty-seven-year-old, I didn't know what I wanted – stable and unchallenging or wayward and stimulating.

NOISES OFF (AND ON)

Saturday 25 April, Middlesex v Yorkshire, Lord's
I used my Player of the Year 1986 status to try to get a pay rise before the season began in earnest, copying Phil Edmonds' ploy and deliberately withholding my signature on the contract until the last possible moment. After a meeting with our secretary, the Honourable Tim Lamb, Middlesex fobbed me off with £500, taking my salary to £11,000. The

evening-meal allowance on away trips was now a princely £9.50. This was the high-spending 1980s. After two rounds at the bar we could only afford a bag of chips (except people like Tufnell, who had a strange aversion to buying anyone a drink). The affliction wasn't allowed to fester: misers were ruthlessly persecuted.

The first match was at Lord's, where the new Mound Stand now stood impressively at deep square leg. It was still a bit of a construction site, with workmen adding the finishing touches and black bin-liners covering the plastic bucket seats. It was described as 'a pagoda in St John's Wood Road' in one paper, and 'an elongated spaceship' in another. Today it was totally deserted, which deprived that side of the ground of any atmosphere. Fielding on the boundary nearby, I kept getting showered with builders' dust.

Gatting, Radley and Butcher were all injured, though Gatting was still there to give the vital first team talk. 'Right, this is where it all starts,' he said. 'Forget last year – we're good enough to challenge for top spot this time. Let's begin as we mean to go on. Good luck to all of you, and remember you're all good enough, else you wouldn't be here.' Then he made a beeline for the TV remote-control and was soon immersed in a rerun of *How the West Was Won*. He always turned the volume up during cowboy films and sometimes you could hear the *pop-pop-peeeoooww!* right out on the field.

The injuries meant a call-up for Mark Ramprakash, a precocious seventeen-year-old who had squeezed in a few matches for the seconds between classwork the previous year. There were whispers that he was a bit good. I hadn't really seen him before and was struck by his composure and audacity. Still a schoolboy but no whippersnapper, he batted without a helmet against Paul Jarvis, and though he got out hooking in the first innings he made an eloquent fifty in the second. 'That lad'll play for England,' Arnie Sidebottom said afterwards.

Apart from Ramprakash, the most noticeable feature of this match was the incessant noise, even without Gatting. On the field, Emburey and Downton clapped their hands, constantly urging commitment. Younger players like Mike Roseberry and Andy Miller added vociferous encouragement which was amplified by the acoustics of the empty stands.

And then there was David Bairstow, possibly the loudest wicketkeeper ever to play for Yorkshire. Certainly the largest. When keeping wicket he was on at the bowlers all the time. 'Coom on, Shandy, keep goin' ... Pitch it oop, Jarvo.' The fielders weren't spared either 'Froggy, wider, WIDER! Oh, Shimon, keep the throws OOOP! Don't be a cooont. Keep it TIDY!' That was all very well, until he started rabbiting when he was batting. 'You'll not be giving that big black lad another, will yer? I can take my helmet off can't I?' he exclaimed to no one in particular. Daniel was off, I was on.

'Embers, can I have square leg a bit deeper for Bluey?' I asked. ''Ey,' Bairstow chipped in. 'If I get 'old of it, you'll need 'im a lot fookin' deeper.' The silence was deafening when he was out for 5.

Saturday 9 May, Southampton
Playing for Hampshire against Combined Universities at Oxford a few days earlier, Gordon Greenidge had clocked up a century before lunch which included two huge straight sixes off successive balls, the second of which struck the pavilion clock, altering the time from 11.40 to 11.36 – surely the first time a batsman has hit another six before the previous one has landed.

Hearing this did not put us in the best of heart when we played Hampshire and sure enough the old-fashioned military medium of Tim 'Trooper' Tremlett and Spikes' left-arm swingers – now more consistent in a settled environment at Southampton – brought us to our knees. Greenidge's blade finished us off. Our weak demeanour and dozy fielding incensed Edmonds, who trolleyed by hurling the ball in my direction at long-off. 'Can't someone get this annoying man into position?' he ranted.

'Where would you like him?' Gatting enquired.

'As far away as possible,' Edmonds growled.

MORK AND MINDY

Tuesday 12 May, Chelmsford

There's something about visiting Chelmsford that's patently unfair. There are only crappy boarding houses to stay in, one of which has sheets thicker than its walls and provides a garden sprinkler in each bathroom which is advertised as a Jacuzzi. The sounds of next door's farting and snoring are relayed to everyone during a restless night; then we're sardined nose to backside with the culprits the next morning getting changed in the smallest dressing rooms outside Toytown. To make matters worse, Keith Fletcher, an expert fisherman, used to have a large, oppressive cloud on a string, which he reined in whenever Essex won the toss in a home B&H group match causing the ball to swing and seam all over the place.

He was a cunning bugger, Fletch. He had a mental image of every opponent and a special field for each batsman preprogrammed. He knew exactly which bowler to put on when and what his strategy should be. He stood in the gully cackling at Gooch's jokes while he plotted each batsman's downfall. It's very disconcerting if you're that batsman.

Essex must have primed the umpires, too, because after four overs we were 3–3, all lbw. The chance of cashing in against Essex's new overseas player, the South African Hugh Page, who we all reckoned would struggle to get a game for South Woodford Third XI, was also dashed. Page took three cheap wickets and in sudden bright sunshine Essex knocked off the required runs speedily. It was a relief in a way, because no one wants these round-robin games to drag on, and if this had gone into a second day we'd have had another night of prefab turmoil.

Emburey wouldn't have minded staying behind, though. He could have escaped for another twelve hours chez Gooch, a place he seemed almost magnetically attracted to. Emburey and Gooch had been virtually inseparable ever since they roomed together on the London Schools tour of East Africa in 1969. They shared many characteristics – a working-class discipline, a phlegmatic temperament, an affection for South Africa, and a slightly thin speech habitually laced with expletives.

Mork and Mindy, Ian Botham called them, because of their unique friendship and the strange, unintelligible language they spoke. Gooch affectionately referred to Emburey as 'Ern' or 'Knuckle' (a South London version of 'mate'); Emburey called Gooch 'Gray' or 'Zap' (alluding to his Mexican moustache). Emburey spent so much time in the Essex dressing room playing bridge or chatting with his old mate that we actually dumped his gear in there on one occasion.

They were diametrically opposite in physical terms, however. Gooch only had to look at a cream bun to put on weight, so he adhered to a rigorous fitness routine. He was mystified by Emburey's apparent lack of enthusiasm for practice and training, and on one of their early tours together he asked him, 'Well, how d'you keep fit, then?'

'I go bed early,' (sic) Emburey replied.

They mimicked each other relentlessly in benefit matches. Gooch would bowl round-arm with a towel stuffed down his front; Emburey stood at the crease with an exaggerated backlift and wobbling head. Their laconic exchanges at slip in charity games were priceless.

'Anything lined up for this winter, Ern?' Gooch asked during their ban from Test cricket.

'Oh, I think I might work in computers,' Emburey mused.

'What you gonna do, paint them?'

Gooch, it always seemed, was the dominant partner in the relationship, and the more dedicated, and although there was mutual admiration, he usually milked Emburey's bowling with such ease that it was pointless putting him on. Emburey had even tried one year to get Gooch plastered on red wine so that he couldn't bat the next day. The plan misfired. Set an unlikely 214 to win after tea, Essex cantered to victory in 31 overs, and Gooch, playing almost in a trance, lashed a brilliant century despite Emburey inciting Daniel into a ferocious spell of bowling.

What they recognised and respected in each other was an unshakeable resolve and consummate professionalism on the pitch and a wonderfully phlegmatic temperament. They were both indefatigable in a crisis, and could disperse tension as effectively with a funny comment as with an influential act. Gooch used his wit to great advantage. He had an infuriating ability to laugh and joke with the bowler while he was non-striker, sympathising with the footholds or the strong headwind or the pernickety umpire, then ruthlessly larrup the poor, unsuspecting chap all over the park when he was back at the business end.

A similar thing happened when you played against West Indian pacemen. It didn't matter how polite or complimentary you were towards them between balls, observing how much their out-swinger was moving or how crummy the run-ups were today, you still got an unpleasant going-over if you hung around. It was definitely a mistake to say sympathetically: 'Cor, hard yakka this old circuit, isn't it?' It just made them want to get rid of you all the quicker and make a beeline for the dressing room. Their talent and desire raised them on to a level above the journeymen, but they were as eager to recline in a hot bath as the next man.

> *Friday 22 May, Cambridge*
> *Saturday, Hove*
> *Sunday, Canterbury*
> *Monday, Hove*

A sequence that illustrates how absurd our itineraries could be. It mightn't look too taxing, but this was over spring bank holiday, which meant two hours' queuing for the Dartford Tunnel trying to get to Brighton on the Friday evening and crawling behind caravans on the Sunday-morning meander to Canterbury. Post-match gossip between opposing players resembled a highway-maintenance engineer's checklist.

'Where are you tomorrow?'

'Taunton.'

'Ooh, that'll be three hours plus. Watch out for the

contraflow near Andover, and there's a detour on the 303 by Ilminster. We're at Canterbury.'

'The A27's down to one lane near Eastbourne. You might be better off on the 267.'

'OK, cheers. See you Monday.'

It was like being part of an elite club whose one common denominator was the experience of weaving from Scarborough to Cardiff through Friday-night traffic in less than four hours thirty-seven minutes. The politicians' excuse, that motorways were only built to last twenty years, cut no ice with us, and the news that a British manufacturer was making a handsome profit selling 25,000 road cones a week just served to bond us more tightly in our frustration.

Gatting spent less time than most on the road, mainly because he drove at incredible speeds. He wrecked his white sponsored BMW, accidentally ramming into some ponderous Fiesta driver at a roundabout, and would always beat you down the motorway, even if you had a head start. I travelled in his Vauxhall Carlton once, and on a clear bit of the M1 the digital speedometer read 148mph. Harry Sharp, the seventy-year-old scorer, was cowering in the back. 'I've had *my* life,' he muttered, shaking his head, 'he's still got 'alf of his left.'

It Swings the Other Way

Saturday 30 May, Middlesex v Pakistan, Lord's
The day I discovered reverse swing, that phenomenon commentators keep going on about without ever enlarging upon or properly explaining. Bowlers walk back to their mark polishing the ball, picking little bits out of the seam, looking as if they know what they're doing. It's just habit. Not one has successfully explained to me why a ball moves a particular way in the air or off the wicket, or how to accurately predict that movement. The only reassuring thing is that even if the

batsman knows what's coming – bouncer, in-swinging yorker, whatever – he still has to play it.

On one of his regular visits to the Lord's nets from his flat off Sloane Square, Imran Khan had captivated some of the Middlesex lads by making an old ball that appeared to have been savaged by a Rottweiler suddenly bend all over the place. I had been elsewhere at the time, but his methods at practice that day, which it was thought involved some sort of manipulation of the quarter seam, were eagerly discussed.

I was sceptical, since the only previous trade secret to which I'd been party was a method of transferring a bit of sunscreen from arm to ball and then rubbing it in without the umpire seeing. In my experience it just made the ball smell of Ambre Solaire and had no effect on its behaviour whatsoever.

The Pakistan–Middlesex match was played on a very dry Lord's pitch and the ball soon got scuffed from landing on the cracks or being rifled into the boundary boards by Mansoor Akhtar and Salim Malik. When I came back for a second spell it was the texture of a Brillo pad, and almost the same shape. There was still a hint of shine, but when I held the ball for an attempted out-swinger, with the shiny side positioned to the right, facing the leg side, it kept curving the opposite way. And vice versa.

Rather than trying to fight the ball's natural inclinations, I played along with it, and sent down a number of deliveries ducking this way and that, which well-set batsmen had difficulty negotiating. 'Blimey, you're bowling bananas,' Javed Miandad exclaimed after a lucky edge through the slips. The other fast bowlers had trouble believing my claims (I kept having to remind Neil Williams to hold the ball with the shine facing the opposite way) but eventually it worked for them, too.

My only explanation is that the rougher side of the ball had become so badly ripped that it was practically weightless, and therefore the normal tendency for shine to guide movement was overridden. It was now a matter of weight distribution and the ball would veer *with* the heavy (moist and polished) side, rather like in lawn bowls. Hence the term reverse swing. A slingy type of action and a fast arm seemed to help. But if the Pakistanis are good at purveying various types of swing, they're equally accomplished at assaulting it. They lost only three wickets and got well past 300.

STRANGE APPETITES

Saturday 13 June, Somerset v Middlesex, Bath
The notice was already pinned up in our dressing room when we arrived at the tarted-up Bath Recreation Ground. Mike Guttin: Order of the Branston Empire. It was a reaction to the news that Gatting had been awarded the OBE. The Somerset miscreant who'd penned the slogan soon regretted it. Gatting clubbed 196 before tea, tucking into all comers with the sort of relish he normally reserved for steak and kidney pudding followed by spotted dick and custard.

There was even more for him to eat this year, since Edmonds had gone on the Cambridge Diet (I bet he wouldn't have bothered if it had been called the Loughborough Diet or the LSE Diet), closely followed by Emburey and Downton, and there were lots of leftovers. It made for a strange lunchtime. While eight of us indulged in the usual cholesterol loading, the other three sat at the end glumly stirring coloured powder into glasses of water. It didn't even taste nice.

The diet might have helped Edmonds lose weight, but lack of nourishment also made him lose his temper. He was becoming more and more involved in the business world, his property empire was growing rapidly, and he was understandably miffed that the club refused to allow him to pick his games. His irritation, combined with the stress of doing deals and the repercussions of his wife's book, *Another Bloody Tour* made him prone to violent mood swings. 'Come on, Hughesy!' he would bawl at me as I dozed in the critical position at backward point allowing a quick single. 'Jesus, why is this chap so annoying?' When I then pulled off a brilliant diving stop in the next over, he'd clap while muttering to another fielder, 'Even that annoys me.'

In the Bath match he asked to leave the field after bowling several good overs. 'What for?' Gatting asked.

'I've got to make a very important phone call,' he replied.

Gatting went ballistic and forbade him to go off in any circumstances, but two overs later Edmonds told the umpire he had to change his boot and discharged himself. Within twenty minutes he was back, but something had inflamed his mood. Simmering at third man, he went to field a ball with one hand, missed, then ambled after it. 'Come on, Henri, get it in!' Gatting shouted, puce with rage, as the batsmen stole a second run. The pot boiled over and Edmonds hurled the ball in Gatting's direction at slip instead of returning it to the keeper. His aim was poor, and the batsmen ran two over-throws. Gatting was livid, and play was held up for several minutes while they had a slanging match.

As the unfortunate bowler, I should have been spewing too, but the game was going nowhere and instead I found it quite funny. It wasn't so amusing for Edmonds. The committee took a dim view of his antics and, blanching at his requests to continue his career as an amateur, didn't renew his terms. He was still playing for England late that summer, but after the Bath incident Middlesex gradually eased him out.

ANOTHER PARTY TO GO TO

Sunday 14 June, Worcestershire v Middlesex, Worcester
Edmonds already had a contract excusing him on Sundays so that he could commentate for BBC2. As it happened, the cameras were covering our match at Worcester the next day. The sensible members of the team decided to stay in Bath overnight, then travel up the M5 in the morning for the 1.30 p.m. start.

I had other ideas. There were half a dozen Test players in our side and they were always being invited to interesting-sounding functions at the Café Royal or the Dorchester, where they were fawned over by flirty PRs. There would be much innuendo and whey-heying during pre-match stretching the next day as various players embellished accounts of their exploits. The only event I'd attended recently was the annual sports day of the North Paddington Boys' Club on a ropy concrete paddock beside the Edgware Road. So, having been asked to join the same table as a girl I had my eye on at the Rosslyn Park Rugby Club Ball, I wasn't going to miss out. It was my petty way of showing I was important, too.

The evening went even better than I'd anticipated and I overslept the following morning. Then, having left west London later than I should have, I got a flat tyre on the M40. It took me ages to find the jack (if only car manufacturers would standardise where they hide it), after which the A44 around Chipping Norton was clogged by ponderous Sunday drivers gazing wistfully at twee cottages. By the time I got to Broadway, I was battling to make Worcester in time for the start, and nearly mowed down a troupe of morris-dancers performing around the village green.

The upshot was that I arrived at 1.20 p.m., ten minutes before the scheduled start, to be met by a fuming, foaming Gatting, still dressed in his civvies. He looked as if he was about to burst. Well, he often looked like that. It was only then that I realised the entire contents of his and Emburey's kit was in my car. Gatting had had to toss up in a pair of grey strides and his golf sweater. He was not a happy camper.

And this was my preamble to the dreaded confrontation with Hick and Botham that I'd been fretting about for three months. If anyone is looking for ways of whipping themselves into a frenzy before a key sporting contest, then try this method: party food, beer, wine, jiving, sex, four hours' sleep, sex, no breakfast or lunch, groping about under a Peugeot 405 for twenty-five minutes, and swerving round rural B roads at 85mph to get the captain's bat and pads to him a couple of minutes before he is due at the wicket.

I was still in a whirl by the time it was my turn to bowl, but surges of adrenaline are useless if they're not channelled. I was turbo-powered by anxiety but my aim was like a scattergun, and most of the stuff I sent down was savaged by Botham and Hick. After I'd been clobbered for an eighth boundary, Edmonds said on TV: 'Well, that's another terrible over from Simon Hughes, but he won't worry – he's probably got another party to go to tonight.' As it transpired, through a combination of humiliation and exhaustion I skulked off to my room at 8.30.

The combined effects of a complacent environment, an aversion to going to bed early and a surplus of able bowlers stopped me from taking wickets and the uncertainty in my game returned. It didn't help that we weren't rolling teams over as we had in the past, and if you hadn't grabbed a wicket after five overs you were taken off.

Our various captains that summer had different ways of removing you from the attack. When Gatting was in charge you knew an expensive over meant curtains; he didn't really have to say anything except, 'OK, Yoz, thanks.' Sometimes he just grimaced. He had a lot on his mind with the England captaincy as well. John Emburey took more time to carefully explain a situation, but he was constantly away with England, too, leaving Downton at the helm. Downton's diplomacy went a bit overboard. Trying to be sympathetic after a lousy over which had just been carted for fourteen, he would come down and say, 'Ooh, *bad* luck, Yozzer. Well tried. Have a little blow . . . Maybe come back later.' I think a comment like 'That was crap, piss off down to fine leg' might have been more appropriate, but he was too nice to say anything as blunt as that. He had also played twenty-five Tests, and was universally respected, so who was I to criticise?

GETTING NOWHERE

Saturday 20 June, Hampshire v Middlesex, Southampton
No one thought Maggie Thatcher would ever get back in, but then no one thought Charles would ever divorce Di, either. The Conservatives made a big rallying call to sportsmen the day before the general election and various England cricketers, notably John Emburey and Bill Athey, turned up on a podium to support her. You could probably count the socialist cricketers on the fingers of one hand. After a couple had been amputated.

On the day itself Athey's new team, Gloucester, were playing in Harrogate, so he and Jack Russell, who lived in the same constituency, drove south that night to complete their ballot papers. But as Athey voted Tory and Russell was an isolated Kinnock supporter, they cancelled each other out. Another pointless journey.

The same could be said for my 80yd stroll to the middle at Southampton a day later. Malcolm Marshall put our limp attack into perspective with a blistering spell and I came in after a bouncer put Neil Williams flat on his back and then a wicked in-swinger trapped him lbw next ball. As I took guard, I looked at Marshall waving his arms and ordering his field into position. 'Jamesy, Jamesy, closer, round a bit. STOP, STOP! Kippy, squarer. Third slip, please, captain. Rat – up, up, UP.' Two of the original members of Group 4 (James and Maru) were eyeing me pityingly from their predatory catching positions.

I tried to work out what Marshall was going to bowl. Bouncer? No, too nice a bloke to do that first ball to a number 10. Yorker? Too obvious. Out-swinger? In-swinger? Slower ball? Even that was quicker than most. I thought of looking to see how he was holding the ball, but he was too far away and in any case he used a weird two-fingered grip, with his right thumb pressed against his palm. All sorts of things go through your mind. Does he dislike me? Might he be getting tired? Will my arm guard stay in place? Is the physio ready with the cold spray?

A Lot of Hard Yakka

Ultimately, the most important thing is not to do anything premeditated: just watch the ball like you're taught to do at school. 'Move your foot across, head over the line,' the games master says irritably for the seventy-second time. But when someone of Marshall's calibre comes raging towards you, instinct takes over. I automatically shuffled back, peered for the red lump, and somewhere between it leaving his hand and extracting my off stump, I did see something. I was vaguely conscious of a seam homing towards me at one point, and that's all. It was all over before I'd even begun to feel nervous, the first golden duck of my career. At least I didn't suffer it to the bowling of Spikes or the Rat. I'd have never heard the end of it. 'Did you bat today?' asked Robin Smith, trying to stifle a laugh, in the bar afterwards.

Heavy rain delayed the start of play on the Monday and the umpires, Dickie Bird and John Harris, decided there would be no play before lunch. Southampton is one of the better places to be stuck if it's raining – there are squash courts, a health club and bevies of attractive waitresses to-ing and fro-ing to exchange small-talk with. Dickie and I took the chance to try out the leisure facilities, ambling between the sauna, steam room and finally the Jacuzzi – something he clearly hadn't experienced before. At first he tried to get in wearing his long johns. Eventually he stripped down to his war-issue Y-fronts and dozed in the warm, frothy water. I knew he must have temporarily nodded off because he stopped talking for about three and a half minutes.

A strong wind dried the ground and when play began, I was given the new ball and was soon confronted by the Smith brothers, hungry for runs. With his bristling pectorals and iron wrists, Robin, particularly, is quite inhibiting to bowl at. As I ran in to begin my third over, Dickie suddenly stuck his arm out. I assumed there was debris blowing across the pitch, or movement behind the arm, or that he'd dropped one of the six miniature beer barrels he used as counters. I came to a halt beside him. Beaming with satisfaction, he exclaimed, 'Eee, it were grand in that booble bath, wannit?'

SUNDAY REVERENCE

July

A monsoon arrived in midsummer, which didn't enhance our position close to the bottom of the championship. The break wasn't refreshing, either. One weekend, the central fixture computer had us playing Nottinghamshire in a three-day match at Lord's on a Saturday, Monday and Tuesday, but crazily scheduled the Sunday match between the same two teams at Trent Bridge. This of course meant twenty-two players shuttling up and down the M1 and covering a combined total of 4,300 miles. And the weather was so atrocious that not a ball was bowled on any of the four days.

After that I was dropped to the second team. Presumably my driving had been too wayward. On the first day of the Second XI match at Bedford School it was still raining and play was called off by 2 p.m. The following morning it was called off as soon as most of us had arrived. The forecast was terrible for the third day as well, so some of the players retired to the hotel bar, ordered the beers and got out the cards. 'Come into my lair,' Jamie Sykes growled, and like sheep, we filed in. It was 11.15 a.m.

We were still there ten hours later, when Angus Fraser, who could hardly speak and was a good few pounds poorer, challenged several others to a race across the river that flowed beneath the hotel. The Great Ouse, I think it's called, though it is more of a gush than an ouse. Barefoot and down to their boxers, everyone dived in only to find it was barely 4ft deep. Keith Brown's brother banged his head, and the Frasers, Angus and Alistair, suffered cut feet from broken bottles on the bottom. The race fizzled out as everyone staggered back to the bank.

Bright sunshine greeted the walking wounded the next morning and for a moment it looked as if we might have to take the field with nine men – neither Fraser could get his boot on. Luckily, the Yorkshire all-rounder Graham Stevenson, now touting his wares with Northants, and a man who invariably put his golf clubs and snooker cue into the car before his cricket kit, talked sense into the umpires and the match was abandoned. Bear that story in mind when you next read in the paper: 'Studley: Warwickshire II v Somerset II, no play yesterday.'

My first-team appearances had become largely restricted to Sundays. People even started calling me the Reverend. Most normal citizens regard the Sabbath as the time for a holy lie-in, a perusal of their weekend bible, the *News of the World*, and the taking of modern-day bread and wine (a steak sandwich and two pints of Marston Pedigree down the Bull and Bush at lunchtime), avoiding the sinking feeling of it's-Monday-tomorrow for as long as possible.

But for me Sunday became the highlight of the week. There was adrenaline and expectation in the air, and people in the ground. Real people. They even watched us practising our fielding, which, as a result, achieved rare heights of commitment and ostentatiousness. The presence of a crowd gave the event meaning and importance and made county players feel like performers rather than machinists. There would be a fight in the dressing room over complimentary tickets (officially two each) because someone had their entire extended family waiting at the gate, and quite often an attendant had to forge the date on used passes.

On the field there would be big hitting, sprawling stops and flying stumps, each greeted with cheers and applause, which was all the more invigorating if you spent most of your days treading the boards to an empty house. Matches veered alarmingly one way and then the other, the course altered by an inspired cameo or a brilliant catch or a surprising bowling change. It was the kind of environment in which, to corrupt Andy Warhol's observation, everyone was famous for fifteen balls.

And the euphoria if you featured significantly in a narrow victory beat anything. It was better than meeting royalty (too impersonal), winning money at gambling (too fortuitous), or sex (too short and predictable). Your body swelled with satisfaction and pleasure; players slapped you on the back and the dressing room gushed with congratulations. Sometimes the twelfth man even ran you a bath.

Yet Sundays were always criticised and pilloried for doing untold damage to the game, ruining technique and encouraging bits-and-pieces players. In fact these skirmishes brought cricketers out of their shell, and the climaxes were a far better test of mettle and temperament than any sluggish first-class match. Both players and spectators loved the topsy-turvy nature of the contests, and it would have been an act of vandalism to scrap them.

There were downsides, of course. The matches tended to finish at 6.00ish, which meant you had to hang about outside pubs until 7 p.m., our licensing laws were fatuous, before you could continue your celebrations. And the euphoria was short-lived. By Monday morning the heroics were forgotten and we were back at the ground, sometimes a different one, to continue a three-day game (in my case often for the second team) in front of the usual gaggle of diehards and pensioners discussing their varicose veins. A pre-lunch duck or an iffy spell or a dropped catch was a quick reminder that love and hate are two sides of the same coin.

YOU DON'T GET OWT FOR NOWT

Sunday 12 July, Yorkshire v Middlesex, Scarborough
The atmospheric Scarborough ground was crammed to the rafters for our Sunday League game there in mid-season. It was nothing to do with our collection of famous names: Yorkshire had won the Benson & Hedges Cup at Lord's the day before and most of the town seemed to have turned out to celebrate. There were still a few oblivious families sheltering behind windbreakers on the beach leafing through the *Sunday Sport*, and men walking their mongrels on the promenade or queuing up for tickets to Showaddywaddy at the Pavilion

Theatre, but Marine Drive was besieged by well-wishers as the bleary-eyed team went walkabout on their way to the ground. Once inside they made an emotional appearance on the balcony, followed by a lap of honour with the trophy. Gatting looked equally the worse for wear, having travelled up through the night on the Yorkshire coach.

The scene was wonderfully old-fashioned. Spectators had put on their Sunday best in honour of their heroes; single white roses, stems clothed in tinfoil, were being sold by the bucketload; ladies with big hair and heavy foundation sat brandishing G&Ts next to the mayor in all his finery. Even the beered-up louts on the open terraces were respectably dressed, although they soon launched into a chorus of 'He's fat, he's round, he bounces on the ground, Mike Gattiiiing . . .' when the teams warmed up.

The individual men in the crowd seemed to fit the familiar Yorkshire caricatures. Burly gents with square heads and high blood pressure who probably took their Dorises down the local once a month; others in flat 'ats eating their own sandwiches because the chip butties were 'sixty pence, bloody 'eck!'; broad-beamed representatives of rural enclaves who seemed to be under the impression that Yorkshire people were the only pure species left. 'We woon t'coop without any of them niggers,' said one. There wasn't a single black face among them.

On the boundary the accents and the banter were so diverting I could hardly concentrate on the game, and I got several bollockings from Gatting, which only made that section of the crowd noisier. They starting chanting, 'Who ate all the pies? Who ate all the pies?' and 'On Ikley Moor bar t'at, oh why is Gatt so fat?' and Jim Love stuck a towel down his shirt to look like an expanded stomach when Gatting was batting, which our skipper took in good humour.

By the time it was my turn to bat, the match was out of our reach, so, attempting to join in the festive spirit, I came in wearing a large red nose I'd bought that morning in a joke shop. Unfortunately, I was out second ball. 'You lot don't need to dress up to look like clowns,' a gloating spectator commented as I walked off.

The match was a microcosm of our season. We were a bit of a rabble, really. Test calls meant we played under three different captains, and when Gatting was present he often had to come in to bat lower down the order owing to urgent phone calls or important discussions with the England manager, Mickey Stewart, on the balcony. We couldn't find a settled batting line-up or a consistent bowling attack. The coach, meanwhile, seemed to be spending even more time throwing balls for Gatting to drill into the nets.

After years of great service, parts of the fearsome Middlesex engine were wearing out or not in tune – Radley, Edmonds, Daniel, the latter a battered, burned-out hull of a once-gleaming machine – and it was time for younger people to take over. Some weren't quite ready; others never would be. Maru and James, who, in different circumstances, would have still been with us, had had storming seasons with Hampshire (though Nepo had achieved nothing at Gloucester but a down-in-one record at the boozer). The Rat had taken a stack of wickets and Spikes finished the highest English batsman in the national averages. How we could have done with them now.

To really ram home the message of mediocrity, we had to play the last match of the season at blustery, cheerless Derby and lost by a mile to a hotchpotch of a team drawn from the outer limits of the cricketing empire and spearheaded by the great Dane Ole Mortensen, a devout Christian, who howled, 'God hell fire!' if he was hit for four. The lunch was stewed gristle followed by cartons of Ski yoghurt, the showers were a cold trickle and the airless visitors' dressing room smelled of five-month-old sweat and badly needed fumigating. A bit like our team.

GRIDLOCK: *1988*

Gatting in and out • Fraser on the spot •
quaint venues • lads on tour • roommates in
the dark • corporate invasion • down the
wrong lane • teenage saviour • jobsworths

BLEEPS AND SNOOPS

June, Rothley Court

Poor old Gatt. He wasn't exactly flavour of the month at the beginning of the 1988 season, his benefit year. He'd had a public spat with umpire Shakoor Rana which had almost led to war with Pakistan, then defended some petulant behaviour from other players during the New Zealand tour, which didn't meet with universal approval.

In early summer he did his best to compensate. He made 210 in Middlesex's opening match, the first four-day county game ever played at Lord's, and we kicked off with five wins out of five in all competitions. And at Denis Compton's sumptuous seventieth birthday dinner at the Hilton, he picked out the name of the TCCB chief executive, A.C. Smith, as winner of a major prize in the raffle. He received a pair of tickets to Gatting's own benefit ball at the same venue.

He shepherded England to three one-day victories against the West Indies, and seemed to have got the make-up of the team right – except for the inclusion of Monte Lynch, who made 0, 2 and 6. Rumour had it that in the selection meeting Gatting had nodded approval when Lynch's name was raised because he thought they'd said 'Lunch?'

Actually, he was now on a diet, spurred on by Jim the physio, who'd reacted to the game's growing fitness trends by monitoring our heart rates and body fat and putting us all through a 'bleep test', which entailed sprinting back and forth between two markers literally until you dropped, in time to quickening electronic pulses. The longer a person lasted, the higher he scored. Gatting, who didn't last very long, was skipping the bacon sarnies in the morning and pointedly ordering chicken salads with Lite mayonnaise from Nancy in the players' dining room, though he still couldn't resist pigging out in the evenings. All the piss-taking had finally got to him and he was trying to watch his weight. Unfortunately he wasn't watching his back.

The day after England valiantly drew the first Test at Trent Bridge (Gooch batted nearly seven hours for 146), the *Sun* proclaimed that there had been a 'sex orgy' at the England team hotel, and that Gatting had been involved. He was alleged to have cavorted with a girl in his room. I met him wandering the Lord's corridors the following morning, moments after he'd been sacked as England captain. 'I've been stitched up,' he muttered, looking thoroughly downcast.

'Did you do it?' I asked.

'What d'you think?' he snapped.

Ian Botham was adamant. 'It couldn't have been Gatt,' he said. 'Anything he takes up to his room after nine o'clock he eats.'

Gatting had become the victim of a modern type of war – the circulation kind. A Midlands news agency had homed in on a barmaid with loose morals and even looser knicker elastic who worked at a pub the England team were known to frequent. The agency offered her money if she could bed a player then spill the beans. Once asked back to the team hotel, and having performed whatever was her particular pleasure, she had recounted her version of events as agreed and the agency had auctioned the story on the open market. The *Sun* were the highest bidders. The figure bandied about was £10,000.

It brought into sharp relief the fact that various disruptive elements had crept into professional sport as it advanced into the media mainstream. There were now stump mikes picking up players uttering expletives on the field, longer and longer lenses probing deeper and deeper into people's personalities, and the team milieu had been infiltrated by newshounds and nymphos.

All to satisfy Joe Public's apparently insatiable appetite for salacious gossip and sadistic desire to see the stars of sport in a murky light. It all made the man in the street, still weighed down by the inferiority complexes of Britain's grim, glum, glam-free 70s, feel a tad better about himself. Many perceived the sporting world as an extension of the TV soap-opera society through which they vicariously lived their lives. In many ways they were probably right.

The most infuriating aspect was the generally accepted myth that moral standards were slipping from cricket's 'halcyon days' when it was such 'a gentlemanly game' played in a country idyll. That in the past, cricketers had been above sledging and arguing with umpires and sexual misdemeanours. The it-didn't-happen-in-my-days, the reminiscing over-fifties, had become downright smug.

Oh, so I suppose Dr W.G. Grace was a paragon of virtue, was he? He never claimed he wasn't out, that a gust of wind must have blown the bails off, or that 'they've come to see me bat, not you bowl'. No, of course he didn't. Cheating and byplay only arrived in the laissez-faire 1980s. Why, then, did the former England captain Gubby Allen admit he was not averse to the odd oath, particularly if he'd just gone past Bradman's outside edge, and the 1950s England player and current MCC president J.J. Warr claim, 'If Fred Trueman had been fined £500 every time he swore on the field, he'd have financed the national debt'?

From its origins, cricket was rooted in political manoeuvring, exploitation and philandering at exclusive men-only clubs where vast wagers were exchanged on the sidelines. Gatting and his cohorts were more or less like any other generation of English cricketers – tempted to enjoy the spin-offs of their international fame. Geoff Humpage, the chunky Warwickshire wicketkeeper who'd had a taste of the big time in a few one-day internationals, admitted, 'In county cricket you chase the women. In Test cricket they chase you.'

But after decades of cover-ups and blind eyes, the era of the exposé had arrived. Just to rub salt into Gatting's wounds, his replacement as England captain, our very own John Emburey, was dubbed 'Mr Clean' by the tabloids, a description that made us double up in mirth. There wasn't anyone with a muckier sense of humour, particularly when walking around the dressing room in the altogether. 'Hey! That's a black man's cock!' the West Indian George Ferris exclaimed when he popped in after one match.

Shakoor Rana was standing incongruously by the entrance to Worcester's ground later in the summer as Middlesex arrived for a Sunday match. He waved airily as Gatting drove into the ground, but Gatting didn't really see him. The next day there was a big picture of this near-miss in the *Sun*. Above it yelled the headline: 'GATTING TREATED ME LIKE DIRT', and underneath were some pathetic quotes from the umpire, saying he'd paid his way over specially to make the peace. In fact the whole thing had been set up by the paper, and they'd captured just the reaction they'd dreamed of to keep the original incident simmering.

BAG O'NERVES

Gatting wasn't receiving much consolation from some old colleagues, either. In the first round of the NatWest Trophy, Middlesex played Hertfordshire, whose opening batsman was our erstwhile team-mate Andy Miller. When Gatting put himself on for a gentle bowl, Miller, predominantly a defensive player, nudged one behind square for two. 'Haven't you got any other shots?' Gatting mocked.

Miller sauntered up the pitch and smeared the next one over cover for six. 'Yes, thanks,' he replied delightedly.

Events were conspiring to turn Gatting into a nervous wreck, and I wasn't far behind. Entering my ninth season, I very much identified with what the entrepreneur Peter de Savary said when he looked back at his early business career. 'The fact of being a few years older and having suffered a number of embarrassments and losses during the eighties, obviously tempers you on the side of conservatism and caution.'

The innocence and confidence of youth had gone completely,

to be replaced by trepidation. I couldn't work out whether to run in and bowl as quickly as possible or to settle for line and length. In the end I fell between two stools, and was neither accurate nor fast. 'Simon – what*ever*'s happened to your bowling?' a spectator I'd never met blurted out to me one morning. The very idea that I'd been thought of as potential England material little more than twelve months before seemed ludicrous. Now the task of just trying to get the ball acceptably down the other end was absurdly stressful. My earlier career problems were minor blips compared to this complete seizure.

The situation was exacerbated by an energy-sapping relationship with my new girlfriend, Jan (the one from the rugby-club ball). She liked late nights, a bewildering mix of soft rock and loud punk (I spent hours making her a compilation tape of Santana and Steely Dan interspersed with Billy Idol and Eddie and the Hot Rods), and was a convert to the Mediterranean cuisine offered by *nouveau* delis. After a long day in the field I was being refuelled with stuffed vine leaves, taramasalata and marinated olives. I kept having to get up at 4 a.m. for a bowl of cornflakes.

Maybe I should have complained, but you daren't in new relationships, and anyway, many women take criticism to heart. They store it away and bring it out as ammunition weeks later when they discover that your fridge contains only a piece of old cheese and twelve cans of Löwenbrau.

The sound of Angus Fraser's advancing hooves added further to my problems. Tall, youthful and dedicated, with a grisly demeanour if he conceded any runs (including a violent feigned left-foot volley into the top corner), he was now coming on to bowl ahead of me, getting the downwind end if he wanted it and taking stacks of wickets. He deserved them, too, and it was not long before he attracted the attention of the England selectors. His 'sponsorship' of a free pint per wicket by his local pub, the Seven Balls – always referred to as 'The Three-And-A-Half Men' – which he generously shared out.

Fraser had also developed a dry wit and an amusing

cut-and-thrust relationship with Emburey. They would take it in turns to ruck at each other over some triviality, like over rates or practice regimes, and sometimes it spilled over on to the field. 'Bollocks, I should have kept my legs together,' Emburey winced at slip as a Fraser-induced edge fell out of his lap on to the ground.

'Wish your mother had,' the dismayed bowler countered. Their verbal jousts alleviated the tedium of four-day cricket, which I found indescribably dull, especially standing abandoned at long leg for hours on end. When I was asked to bowl it was generally as a last resort, making me feel like a spare part which didn't help my confidence or attitude. I tried to get myself noticed by running back to my mark (to improve the over rate) or bowling a succession of bouncers from round the wicket. They were enthusiastically seized upon by batsmen that Fraser, Cowans and co. had previously shackled.

Predictably, I wasn't getting much of the action, and I killed time on the boundary composing columns in my head for the *Independent*. Then I'd jot down my ideas over lunch, usually with bored players who'd wolfed their food in three minutes flat, peering over my shoulder. They found my *Roget's Thesaurus* intriguing and sometimes tampered with it when I wasn't looking. Beneath 'parsimony' someone wrote 'Philip Tufnell', and next to 'odour', simply 'Sykes'. Alternatives for obesity had the inevitable 'Gatt' daubed across them in felt pen.

Some of my articles started out quite fruity, but I had to show them to the committee before they were published and they usually wanted them watered down. It was an infuriating aspect of the dib-dib-dib mentality which pervaded professional cricket and made the players resentful of authority. Supporters sometimes came up and kindly said they liked my writing. They never mentioned my bowling. I still got picked because no one else stayed fit.

I tried to make amends by taking my batting seriously, and in my ninth season, I finally realised one of my childhood ambitions: raising my bat to the crowd having reached a half-century. Admittedly it was only against Cambridge University, and mostly off Mike Atherton's occasional leg-spin, but it was a first-class fifty none the less, and no one could take it away from me, so I milked the applause from a sprinkling of coffin-dodgers. Imran put my 'achievement' in perspective when he twice clattered me on the head with bouncers in the next championship match. The gap between undergraduate class and world class wasn't so much a gulley as a canyon.

LADS ON TOUR

June, Away Trips

One-day cricket was more fun despite some odd venues. We played Derbyshire at Repton School, a wonky-shaped ground with a ruined priory, a fives court laid out like the inside of a chapel and a thatched pavilion stashed with memorabilia. There were photos of the legendary sprinter Harold Abrahams, the 1932 Wimbledon finalist Bunny Austin and C.B. Fry, the England batsman who at the turn of century won a major poetry prize, was offered the throne of Albania and, the story goes, put down his cigar momentarily at some athletics meeting to break the world record long-jump.

The voice of a local newspaper-seller reverberated round the Repton ground: 'Derbyshire in full colour, coom 'n get it!' This was an appropriate description as the team contained two West Indians, a Dane, a Zimbabwean, a South African and an Australian. The unexpected figure of Brian Johnston was perched on the pavilion balcony surveying the scene through ancient binoculars. What was he doing there? I asked. 'Getting accustomed to the Derbyshire players before I commentate on the Benson & Hedges final next weekend,' Johnners replied gaily. 'Batsmen wear so much protection these days I mostly identify them by their posteriors.'

Another Sunday we were at Blackpool. It was a glorious morning, so we climbed the tower and visited the funfair.

Going on the Train of Death – a precipitous ride which plummets from a 100ft tower and through a loop the loop, and then repeats the route backwards – was probably not the ideal way to prepare for a hectic forty-over skirmish. We lost in front of a packed house.

The intimate little ground is a cricket haven where the corpulent off-spinner Jack Simmons first played as a £3-a-week pro. The impressive wooden clubhouse atop a small mound, looks unchanged from the 1880s – about when it felt like Simmons started playing. They're so obsessed with sport in these parts that at a sportsmen's dinner the previous night, a local vicar said grace brandishing a copy of *Wisden*.

The flipside to these away trips was the assortment of hotel room-mates. Either they kept you awake half the night with their snoring (Keith Brown), or they went to bed at 9.30 (Neil Williams) forcing you to creep in at twelve and get undressed in the dark. Feeling around my sponge bag in one unlit bathroom I squirted what I thought was Macleans on my toothbrush, finding out too late that it was actually Raljex. My breath smelled like a football changing room for several days. Settling down to watch a favourite TV programme in the room always seemed to be the cue for a colleague to 'clock in'. In the case of the young batsman Ian Hutchinson, this meant phone foreplay with his wife. Forty minutes of mwah-mwahs and 'I love you, darlings' is not only highly embarrassing but thoroughly distracting when an episode of *The Professionals* is reaching its climax.

Apart from my early experiences with Phil Edmonds, the West Indian-born batsman Roland Butcher was the worst person to share with. He never remembered to leave the key in the door when he went to bed and turned the light out at 10 p.m., having dumped the leftovers of his room-service chicken Kiev on the floor for me to tread in. He booked an alarm call at 6.45 a.m., and then spent an hour noisily sploshing about in the bath and clearing his nasal passages with loud snorts. When I eventually got into the bathroom it would be flooded and all the towels sopping.

Gridlock: 1988

There was one break in this sequence of sleepless nights. Gatting had organised a benefit match with the Society of Chartered Surveyors at Imber Court, just off the King's Road. The event attracted a number of corporate bigwigs who politely ignored the fact that one of the players, Collis King, was so inebriated by lunchtime that he was almost unable to stand up. He fielded for several overs lying down and giggling hysterically, but still managed to bowl.

One young tycoon took some of us out for a Chinese afterwards and then invited Greg Thomas, Derek Pringle and me to his penthouse in the swanky new Chelsea Harbour complex, all glass and chrome. The views across the Thames and into the private marina were stupendous. As soon as we had plonked ourselves down with a drink on the leather sofas, he said, 'I'm going for a line of charlie at my girlfriend's place. Make yourselves at home.' We each had a luxury bedroom to ourselves with electrically operated curtains.

Middlesex were at Trent Bridge in midsummer but it rained the whole of the previous Saturday and most of the Monday, so when we arrived on the Tuesday the pitch and outfield were even lusher than usual. This prompted the public announcer overlooking the green baize to declare just before the start of the match, 'Ladies and gentlemen, Middlesex have won the toss and will break.'

Derek Randall made a typically eccentric fifty, full of admonishments and exclamations of 'Coom on, Rags' every ball, and absurd running. In a one-innings match our run machines failed to spark, but a draw seemed a possibility. With a few overs to play out from the Barbadian fast bowler Franklyn Stephenson, I walked in at number 9 to discover halfway to the middle that a condom had been stretched over my bat handle. I handed it to a rather startled umpire, but then found I couldn't hold the bat because of the residue of lubricant. I swapped bats with Emburey, but was soon out: the solution was still on my gloves. Two balls later Emburey was bowled. Holding my bat had made his gloves slippery,

207

too. Shortly afterwards we were dismissed to lose the match by 40 runs.

There was a bit of a scene in the dressing room. Emburey reserved most of his venom for Fraser, the culprit. 'That's pissole, so unprofessional,' he kept saying. It probably taught Fraser a lesson, but nevertheless I still couldn't get my head round this 'total commitment' concept. After Monday's deluge we had enjoyed a very civilised round of golf with the gangling Stephenson who, it must be said, was a bit good with a 1-iron. Twenty-four hours later he was charging down the hill like a demented bull trying to knock all our heads off.

That's the root of county cricket's ills. A jovial, lads-on-tour approach helps you to cope with the endless travelling and nights in miscellaneous town centres – English cricket is, after all, wedded to socialising and beer. Yet a dedicated single-mindedness needs to be switched on for the gladiatorial confrontations on the pitch. Gradually, as the season wears on and the years go by, the two mentalities merge into one and the direct focus fades. You end up with teams of Des O'Connors: amiable, decent repertory performers who don't excel at anything. Australians are tougher and their game has an extra intensity and edge because the gradients are steeper: if you slip up in the Sheffield Shield you can topple out of sight. County cricket exists on a comfy plateau.

A Tortuous Business

Wednesday 10 August, Surrey v Middlesex, The Oval
One of the penalties of batting down the order was an obligatory visit to the sponsor's hospitality suite at home matches. The coach selected players to pop into chosen boxes after lunch on batting days, and it was uncanny how most of his nominations had disappeared into thin air come the appointed time. Admittedly, it was a chore. Our sponsor in 1988 was a German computer company, Siemens Nixdorf, and

few of their employees and even fewer of their customers understood the game. One, sporting a large cigar and a ghastly beer gut, turned to me during a match and said: 'By the way, do they still have sixes in cricket?'

That comment symbolised the corporate invasion of the first-class game. A day at county cricket was recognised as a cheap, undemanding environment in which to woo clients, getting them tipsy without embarrassing other diners in a restaurant or having to explain the huey in the golf clubhouse toilets. The economic boom had spawned a million reps and salesmen who more or less expected to be taken out on a binge once in a while. It didn't matter that none of them had a clue what was going on between the wickets. Give them a good lunch and they were anybody's.

The counties, meanwhile, saw this as an easy way to make money, sometimes at the expense of the enthusiast. At Cheltenham, for instance, the college ground was almost completely surrounded by striped hospitality marquees, while the paying public were squashed into a little stand at deep square leg. It made the atmosphere at such matches surreal. There were very few spectators at the ground before twelve; then the crowd swelled as scores of chaps in cheap suits arrived from their offices for pre-lunch drinks. The game continued for several hours to the hum of chatter inside the tents which turned to inebriated jeering when the guests finally emerged just before tea. By the close they were either asleep or gambling with their livelihoods by driving home under the influence. If the fuzz had hung about outside the ground after tea they could have arrested half the insurance salesmen of Gloucestershire.

Potential beneficiaries fearlessly waded into these corporate shindigs, grabbing any opportunity to advertise their forthcoming events or collect business cards. The practice made benefits more commercially orientated but it also raised questions as to why they were necessary at all. Why, if county cricket was becoming more profitable, was an ageing player required to chase around for twelve months organising fundraising dinners and ferret-racing evenings to supplement his income? Why didn't the counties get properly into bed with big companies, rather than just entertaining them at the door? Because they were worried it would prostitute the game, and jeopardise its soul, that's why.

The media were also giving county cricket much more attention now. Newspapers were developing sports pull-outs and separate sports sections, the BBC launched a fifth radio station to expand its sports coverage and British Telecom began ball-by-ball feeds from each first-class match. As these 0898 numbers were charged at premium rates, listening to an entire over from a West Indian fast bowler could often cost in excess of £2.

The evolution of all these extra services was helping to make even average sportsmen into household names, but my own career had taken a turn for the worse. At times I was an embarrassment. Going in as nightwatchman against Gloucester, I survived to the close, then arrived at the ground early the next morning to prepare for the bumper barrage I was bound to get from Hissing Syd Lawrence.

Syd was the sort of uncompromising hulk who would have bounced his mother in a charity game. This wasn't because he was especially malicious, just that he knew nothing else. I spent forty minutes in a net wearing full regalia while the Fraser brothers hurled balls at my head from close range. I survived more or less unscathed and felt confident walking out to the middle. Lawrence's loosener was an easy leg-stump half-volley which I somehow plonked into short leg's lap.

OK, that was a laughing matter, but my subsequent plight in the NatWest semi-final against Surrey at The Oval most certainly wasn't. In the dressing room we hatched a plan to concentrate on a leg-stump line to the potentially destructive Alec Stewart. 'Don't give him *any* width,' Gatting stressed.

Stewart had just arrived at the wicket when I was put on. Conscious the match was live on BBC TV, and having bowled poorly throughout the summer, I was very nervous, but determined to get through the ordeal without straying from our objectives. The result was a perpetual stream of legside wides: I just couldn't stop bowling them. One was so wild it travelled unimpeded straight to the boundary at fine leg.

The feeling of utter helplessness when this happens in a big match I wouldn't wish on anyone. It's like those dreams children have when a burglar breaks into their bedroom and they try to scream but can't manage anything more than a hoarse whisper. The loneliness is suffocating and your body is gripped in total spasm. Batsmen who suffer this sort of anxiety are normally out before neurosis sets in. Bowlers have to finish their over. In this match Gatting saved me further humiliation by removing me from the attack. Usually he signalled the end of a spell with a 'Well bowled' or 'Great effort.' This time he just said, 'Oh, Yozzer!' and shook his head sadly. We won the match, but in the pub afterwards with some friends who'd been watching, I was so choked I couldn't speak.

Sport is that cruel sometimes. And failure plays such havoc with your senses that you doubt your ability to perform even the most basic of tasks. I mean, there I was, a professional fast bowler for nine years who'd dismissed many of the world's greatest batsmen (some for under a hundred), and now I was apparently incapable of pitching it on the cut strip. At the beginning of my run-up I felt as if I didn't know my arse from my elbow. It was disturbing and frightening, and now we were in a big final, so there was the prospect of a major foul-up in front of the entire nation. *Help*!

Beware Ramps!

3 September, Middlesex v Worcestershire, NatWest Final, Lord's
The Middlesex selectors had more confidence in my big-match aptitude than I did at that time, and I was chosen to play in the final. I desperately needed something to distract me from the potential trauma, to bypass the burden of apprehension.

Inadvertently, on the morning of the match, I found it. Roadworks on the A40(M). In the Year of the Contraflow, how could it have been anything else? Gatting had wanted us in at 8.45 for a 10.30 start, but, having waited to give a friend a lift to Lord's, I left late and then encountered gridlock at White City. Nothing was moving, and once we were on the motorway there was no way out. My anxiety was heightened by my Asian friend, oblivious to my plight, jabbering away relentlessly about Rajiv Gandhi's policies and Kapil Dev's captaincy.

I eventually arrived at 9.45, midway through fielding practice and only fifteen minutes before the toss. Net practice had finished ages before. Gatting had spent his irritation on a number of other latecomers and was in any case resigned to my unpunctuality by this stage. I was so relieved to have got there just in time, and to have avoided a severe bollocking, that I completely forgot to be nervous, even though I hadn't warmed up properly. It was straight out onto the field, where we all bowled superbly on a damp wicket and, mixing slower balls with yorkers, I took 4–30, hastening Worcester's decline to 161–9. At the halfway point I was the potential Man of the Match.

I was massively upstaged, however, by the boy Ramprakash. Coming in when we were a perilous 25–4, he guided us to victory with an innings of such composure, selectivity and consummate skill that it was hard to believe he was still only eighteen. How could he know what to do at such a critical time, when to take a calculated risk? Why was he not affected by the enormity of the situation? Simply talent and the instinct of innocence. Know no pain, feel no pain. The very same combination that had clinched me a match-winner's medal at the outset of my own career. If only you could bottle that invigorating cocktail for sampling when life has chewed you up and spat you out a quivering wreck. Ramprakash would have killed for it himself after getting a pair in the Lord's Test seven years later.

This is one of the reasons why we English underperform at Test level. Instead of pitching uninhibited teenagers into the fray to take on all and sundry, no holds barred, we keep them back until they've been put through the county mangle to re-emerge with their natural exuberance and youthful enthusiasm crushed. Alec Stewart made his Test debut at 26, Kim Barnett 28, John Morris 26, Martyn Moxon 26, Wayne Larkins 26, Devon Malcolm 26. The list is endless. Dominic Cork and Graham Thorpe scraped in at 24, lucky lads.

We don't shove them in because we lack initiative. It takes one person to carry out an adventurous idea, but in cricket everything is done by committee. A lone dissenting voice and the whole proposal comes unstuck. An infrastructure based on committees is actually a sign of massive disorganisation. English cricket's governing body is split into twenty camps, each with about twenty minions. That's about 400 people to consult for every decision. No one's prepared to stick his neck out and take a gamble. Sport in this country, whether it is cricket, soccer, rugby or tennis, lags behind the rest of the world because it is ruled by well-meaning but ultimately useless jobsworths.

BOOM AND BUST: 1989

batsmen's graveyard • new balls please • the young ones • Haynes explosions • Gatting rebels • to walk or not to walk • seaside skirmishes • ten to win

No More Slacking

Winter 1988–9, New Zealand

Despite the upbeat ending to 1988, I had had a dreadful season, finishing 115th in the national bowling averages with only 27 wickets. My contract was again approaching its final year, and I couldn't face the prospect of relocating to another county or, worse, being forced to work in an office. Positive action was required. I offered my services to a lowly club in Auckland who were in no position to pay me anything, but agreed to subsidise my air fare, lend me a car and help me find some journalistic work.

They were a casual club with a hopelessly run-down pavilion next to a motorway flyover, nomadic happy-go-lucky players and a wicket more suited to growing potatoes. Or marijuana. Some of them certainly smoked a lot of it during the lunch and tea intervals. Sometimes the dressing-room air was so clogged up I must have become a victim of passive doping. But, as it turned out, the season was therapeutic and undemanding, with only moderate weekend cricket. I spent most of my days swimming, running or writing articles.

Jan, my girlfriend, took six months off from her law work and came too. We argued quite a lot, mainly because our lifestyle was rather makeshift and we didn't have enough to do. But, having received a thousandth admonishing letter from my father berating me about my perpetual no-ball problem, I found her presence invaluable. I spent several mornings trying out different run-ups in a park, setting off from various arbitrary points and getting her to mark where I started and finished. Gradually, a pattern emerged and we made careful measurements.

The sight of a bloke charging about on open ground pursued by a girl with a ruler must have been decidedly odd, but after several test runs and a couple of matches, my bowling was transformed. I was beginning from the same place each ball, and lo and behold, landing in the same place, not once overstepping. My consistency improved dramatically, and so did my confidence. Mission accomplished. It had taken me nearly ten years of trial and error and resistance to fatherly advice to realise that a proper run-up was a fast bowler's number one priority.

After the Christmas break, I wrote some articles for the *New Zealand Herald* on a crappy old typewriter, using so much Tipp-Ex that the keys got all gummed up. The paper's offices were reminiscent of 1950s Reigate and so was much of the copy. I also covered the New Zealand–Pakistan Tests for the *Independent*. As I phoned through a piece in mid-January, a sub-editor gave me the shocking news that Wilf Slack, Middlesex's cherished opening batsman, had just dropped dead during a tour match in Gambia. Slack was a popular figure in Auckland, where he'd spent a number of winters, and many of his friends were at that moment watching a game at Eden Park, a stone's throw from where I was living. I circulated the news there, reducing a busy members' bar to aghast silence.

Alas, poor Wilf, I knew him well. We practised together constantly. He would tinker with his technique, always asking questions – 'Am I moving my feet properly? Was that wide enough to cut?' – but was still unselfish enough to throw me a few in the nets when all the others had buggered off. Together we were Gatting's whipping boys in the field, often castigated for fumbling at backward point or failing to hear his instructions because we were chatting to spectators on the boundary. In the dressing room, we discussed the game, something people were doing less and less, or talked about the classy-looking 'snitch' we had spotted in the Tavern Stand.

He loved batting, and people said he probably took his bat to bed. He certainly cosseted it like a favourite pet. Aside from a peerless prowess against the fastest bowlers (he could play bouncers virtually with a straight bat, always showing the maker's name) and unflappable concentration, he stood fearlessly for hours under the helmet at short leg, bowled vital overs in one-day matches and willingly repaired people's damaged bats or faulty dressing-room TVs. An essentially fit man, he had nonetheless suffered a number of mysterious black-outs during the previous twelve months, fainting several times before going out to bat. Stress, high blood pressure and West Indian flu were all offered as possible causes, but no one accurately diagnosed the problem, a partially blocked artery, until it was too late. He was hugely missed.

So too was umpire Peter Plumley-Walker from the New Zealand cricket scene. An ex-British army major, he cut quite a dash with his smart attire, handlebar moustache and pukka accent, and was always punctual and polite. He led a quiet middle-aged life which revolved around officiating in the Auckland League. Or so we thought. His non-appearance on the second day of one of our games was therefore baffling. There was neither sight nor sound of him all weekend.

Three days later his naked body was found bound hand and foot at the bottom of the Huka Falls, a North Island beauty spot. He had certainly aroused the ire of a few batters with some dodgy lbw decisions, people said, but this was a bit of an overreaction. It later emerged that his secret regular S&M session with a leather-clad young dominatrix had gone seriously wrong and he had accidentally been strangled. I suppose there are worse ways to go.

Tragedies such as this merely gave my Auckland playing colleagues even more of an excuse to get stoned. Incredibly, though, it coincided with an upturn in the team's form and we ended up winning our division. This success, coupled with my sprightly physical condition (not too much bowling and valuable fitness work, even if I was regularly lapped in the swimming pool by a man with no legs), put me in a good frame of mind to approach the last season of my three-year contract.

TALKING BALLS

Thursday 18 May, Lord's

The only blot on the horizon was Middlesex's recruitment of another fast bowler. Ricardo Ellcock, the strapping paceman from Barbados via Malvern College, had joined us from Worcester, where exciting early promise had been stunted by injury. His signing was a metaphorical kick up the arse for the other Middlesex fast bowlers. Not only did it have the desired effect, but with the signing of the prolific West Indian Desmond Haynes as the county's overseas player, it restored the Jackson Five, which had recently lost the retired Daniel and the deceased Slack, to full strength.

The deep friendship between Ellcock and Haynes went back some years to their days drinking rum beside a Caribbean village pitch and their rich banter galvanised everyone. It was jab and counter-jab augmented with constant attempts at one-upmanship in the nets. 'Come on Buddha,' Haynes chimed at the shiny bonce and protruding ears of his mate. 'I'm gonna give you some *drives*.' He twirled his bat in feverish anticipation.

'You want drives, you better buy a Peugeot,' Ellcock retorted, and sent down a humdinging bouncer. I lost count of the number of top edges that flew out of the nets and on to the roof of the groundsman's house.

Now, with Cowans, Williams, Fraser, Ellcock and myself, there were five quick bowlers we could rotate. As soon as anyone showed signs of fatigue he was rested, though for one simple reason no one wanted to be. The TCCB had recommended the Reader ball for use that season because it kept its shape better. It was a ruling well received by the fast men, since the Reader had a huge, thick seam so proud you almost cut your fingers on it. The ball looked like a miniature of the planet Saturn. It zigged and zagged off any grassy surface, and the right-angled break-back, a delivery which had become extinct with the advent of lifeless, covered pitches, was reborn. I had never moved the ball about as much as this.

It was great while it lasted. Unfortunately, a few teams got bowled out for under 60 (including us) and soon the powers that be, who were mostly former batsmen, were expressing their concern. The press followed suit. True, by mid-June there was a score of bowlers taking their wickets at less than 20 apiece – I was one of them – but I also noted that there were still plenty of batsmen averaging 50-plus.

No matter, come the fourth round of matches the TCCB had become so anxious they contrived an experiment to test various different makes and styles of ball. One morning at Lord's, various suits, including Tim Lamb, stood behind the nets while a sequence of Fraser, Cowans, myself and South Africa's Stephen Jefferies sent down a succession of deliveries with the various prototypes. The experiment was a farce. The net pitches were well worn and into their fourth day of use. You could have got lift and movement with an orange. Furthermore, the batting guinea pig was Mark Nicholas, a cultured stroke-player in favourable conditions, but never a man for a tricky wicket. He played and missed at virtually everything. Worst of all, the suits had no idea who was bowling with which make of ball.

Still, after a few minutes they'd apparently seen enough and went back to their ivory tower. Some weeks later, it was announced that on the strength of 'a thorough examination', a lower-seamed ball would be used for the 1990 season. We got hold of an example and it looked like . . . well, an orange. The decision transformed the game, rewrote the record books and terminated several bowlers' careers. I still have hallucinations about it. More of that later.

IN A TRANCE

Sunday 4 June, Middlesex v Hampshire, Lord's
Meanwhile I was having a lot of success with the ball and, predictably, none with the bat. Against Worcester I tricked Ian

Botham with a slower ball that I'd learned from watching him in his heyday. He was a bowler ahead of his time in the 70s with the sort of variety, including a clever little off-spinner, that is now almost a cliché. He was a sucker for his own medicine, however, and aiming something massive over the sightscreen to the one I held back, he was too early on the shot and poked it tamely to cover. 'Now *that*,' he said, passing a smirking Emburey on his way back to the pavilion, 'is how you bowl an off-break.'

How satisfying to deceive the game's greatest con artist, still the idol of all English cricketers and most Australians as well. What a triumphant feeling. He BOTHAM, landed like a haddock by me, Hughes, with a simple sleight of hand. It made the days of hardship, of feeling inferior, the worries and humiliations and injustices of this job, completely worthwhile.

But among the gods, we mortals soon crash back to earth. Facing Malcolm Marshall in the next Sunday match, I, the number 9, was more or less our last hope of victory in a pulsating finish. We needed eight runs from two overs, and one of the batsmen to come, Gatting, was incapacitated. In poor evening light Marshall came tearing in, and his first two balls fizzed past outside off stump while I was still getting into position. I gripped my bat tighter and moved earlier for the third, but the same thing happened. As the ball flashed by there was a small clicking sound before it thwacked into the keeper's gloves. The bowler came rushing down the pitch maniacally yelling '*Yeess!*' and all the fielders rushed round to congratulate him. 'Well bowled, Macco,' Spikes yelped. 'Only Norman to knock over now.'

The umpire was unmoved, however, and so was I, temporarily convinced I hadn't hit it. Eight wanted, still nine balls to go, I said to myself, almost calmly. That's OK. I looked around the field at the dismayed faces, and the bowler's disbelieving stare. Then I thought, 'Mmm, three of those balls are going to be bowled by Malcolm Marshall,' and, suddenly dazed and confused, I walked off.

It was stupid, and after a few steps, I emerged from the

trance and tried to turn back, but that looked even more stupid, so I carried on my way. 'Did you hit it?' the players asked in the dressing room when I arrived back. 'Yes . . . er, no . . . er, I'm not sure,' I stammered.

'I fink his arsehole fell out,' said Jamie Sykes, the twelfth man. He might have had a point.

I had been caught out trying to straddle the ethics of an amateur and the behaviour of a professional. I believed in reacting honestly, that is, walking, if you thought you were out, regardless of what was at stake. I had certainly been taught that at club level. But Australian attitudes were seeping rapidly into our society: there was no escape from *Neighbours*, Dame Edna and *Prisoner: Cell Block H*, and their cricket team were blitzing ours. Australian players didn't walk unless it suited them, hastening a growing trend for English cricketers too to choose their moments. Double standards ruled. Gatting had a fearful go at Nasser Hussain for not walking after a thick edge to the keeper, yet he himself had on occasion stood there having apparently nicked it to first slip. Gooch and Gower were equally inconsistent. 'The umpire's there to do a job,' they'd say, echoing the sentiments of generations of batsmen from Grace to Cowdrey. I guess you have to be calculating to get to the top. I wasn't.

CRACKERJACKS

At least my clown prince tag was gradually disappearing, though, as other more certifiable contenders came into view. Youngsters who occasionally threw their toys out of the pram, or made facile remarks, or got into night-time scrapes were far more interesting than my foibles. Though opposites in size and style, Sykes (big, smart) and Tufnell (thin, scruffy) were now a well-versed double act, always anxious to embellish their previous evening's activities during pre-match stretching. In one escapade they were driving around when a

WPC stopped them, then got out the breathalyser. Both players allegedly ran off, with the woman in pursuit. Sykes lumbered out of sight but Tufnell was apparently detained and later lost his licence. Gatting or Keith Brown had to give him a lift in every morning. At least it ensured he got there.

The Lord's groundsman, Mick Hunt, walked into the dressing room during a match one afternoon to check on our intentions. He found the usual array of bodies lounging about. Tufnell was asleep on a bench. 'You declaring soon, Skip?' Hunt asked. 'The trouble is, it takes about ten minutes to start the roller up these days.'

'Probably hasn't been serviced since about 1947,' Sykes suggested, slouched across an armchair.

'And to think that's a professional athlete,' the groundsman chuntered. 'If he was a racehorse he'd be dogmeat by now.'

'He's already got dogbreath,' said Fraser.

Two complex youngsters further distracted attention from my own eccentricities. Mark Ramprakash's pot was simmering all summer as he tried to prevent the humdrum atmosphere and rigid attitudes from infecting his raw talent, and it finally boiled over. Now nineteen, and in his first full season, he had become vexed by the relentless schedule, the high expectations and the antagonism from opposition fielders. His father's mixed background (he was a Guyanese of Indian stock) and the cocktail of influences in the dressing room only wound him up further.

When, after a run of low scores and five turgid hours in the field, he was mildly reproached by the acting captain, Downton, for failing to chase a ball with total commitment, he flipped. 'I don't *ever* want to hear my captain accuse me of that,' he railed as he flung the ball back. 'Not ever, ever, *ever*. I always give a hundred per cent.' He wouldn't be consoled, and minutes later in the dressing room he glowered at Downton, face to face, as he continued his diatribe at high volume, until other players intervened. It was a most unexpected outburst from an essentially polite, quietly spoken lad, and the club took no action. The players did. We nicknamed him Bloodaxe, or usually just plain Axe.

Ramprakash was an Anglo-Afro-Asian; Alex Barnett was on another planet. A promising slow bowler, he was hired as cover for Tufnell and epitomised the quirkiness of all left-arm spinners. An idiosyncratic, well-brought up lad, he had a personal agenda which occasionally materialised in stupid acts. On his first day at Lord's he turned up, without his cricket gear, in a leather jacket and jeans, burst past the pavilion doorman and wandered straight across the main square. It was a bit like marching on to the Centre Court at Wimbledon in football kit. He was spotted by some MCC minion and practically court-martialled. An intelligent chap prone to talking tripe, Barnett was soon christened Bungalow (nothing up top), Bungy for short.

We were reminded during the Cheltenham Festival of another eccentric individual who had once been in our midst. Nepo's antics had become more and more absurd the longer he'd stayed at Gloucester. By the end he was wandering about and sleeping in the same clothes for several days at a time, failing with the bat and flying into a rage when he lost his concentration at squash. Then he would down a pint of lager in one and thrash anyone with the audacity to take him on. Inevitably, the county had eventually let him go, but he was now back in the area, teaching in Cheltenham. The mind boggles.

But in the crackers league, the Sussex team took the biscuit. There was David Smith, Tufnell's first tormentor, a punchy character (although I always thought he was a nice, harmless bloke). There was Paul Parker, a manic fielder who ran to a different fielding position every over and read Virgil during the lunch interval; and a psycho fast bowler called Andy Babbington, who looked like an axe-murderer and mumbled, 'Come on, stick it up his nose' to himself as he walked back to his mark.

Babbington had inherited the legacy of another recent mad Sussex paceman, Adrian Jones, who tore in to bowl like a man possessed and frequently overstepped the line. After a string of no-balls at Hove one day, the Sussex committee – a rather stuck-up lot – became agitated, and eventually one elderly individual put down his gin and shouted 'Oh *come on*, Jones.' The bowler stopped dead in his follow through and shouted right across the field: 'Why don't you fucking get out here and see if you can do better?' He joined Somerset soon after that.

HAYNES' WHEEZES

Well, what's wrong with people showing they care? There's too much take-it-on-the-chin in our society. Why don't we show a bit of emotion, blow our tops a bit? Like Desmond Haynes. I have never met anyone who harangues himself quite so violently when he's out. 'AAAARRRRGGGGHHHH!' he'd thunder as soon as he got back to the sanctuary of the dressing room, forgetting that he was often in public earshot. At Headingley he was in such anguish at having dragged a ball from Sidebottom into the stumps that he stormed into the showers to cool off. Unfortunately, he pushed rather too vigorously against the glass door and it disintegrated, causing a small explosion.

Haynes' influence was massive. The rest of the top order all copied his exaggerated open stance, his preference for longer bats and the little punch of gloves to a partner when a boundary was struck. Soon after the Headingley incident, an irate Gatting accidentally shoved his hand through the dressing-room door at Lord's, badly cutting himself. Against the moving ball, Haynes was brilliant at farming the strike if a colleague was struggling (Mike Roseberry benefited from this); he gave frequent exhibitions of how to disseminate spinners, and loved discussing the game after play.

One day we chided him about the cynically slow over rate of the West Indies fast bowlers, which allowed them to get their breath back for the next rib-tickler. 'If we speeded our over rate up, we'd beat you in three days,' he railed. No argument there. Since 1979, when Haynes had made it into their side, the aggregate score in Tests was England 0, West Indies 17.

Haynes also suffered from very bad hay fever, something I'd noticed was common among Caribbean cricketers – which is why they all carry handkerchiefs. I realised that this weakness could be the answer to all England's problems. Forget selecting muscular batsmen who could hook or titches who could weave when the West Indies were in town. All we needed was a few players who could surreptitiously scatter grass seed around the wicket ends and watch the West Indians' eyes stream. We'd have to be sponsored by Sinex, of course. I suggested to Emburey that England might be keen on the idea. 'Don't talk shit,' he said, justifiably. He was grumpy because he'd lost his driving licence and was having to make do with a sponsored pushbike.

REBELS WITH A CAUSE

Tuesday 1 August, England v Australia, Old Trafford
Emburey wasn't the only one feeling sorry for himself. Ted Dexter, the chairman of selectors had suffered a few business problems since the 1987 crash and had scaled down his glamorous lifestyle. He'd sold his large pile on Ealing Common and moved into a modest townhouse overlooking my old cricket club. His experience was typical of the lower profile suddenly adopted by sponsors and other corporate types.

Dexter's fabulous array of vintage cars and sporty numbers had gone, to be replaced by a BMW 850 on which he could be regularly seen throttling the motorways on spying missions. He got the identity of a few players confused – he thought Syd Lawrence was Courtney Walsh and, having been to Taunton, reported that Peter Roebuck wouldn't make the grade but Jimmy Cook was worth looking at (he was South African). Overall, though, he was pretty rigorous.

One of the first decisions he made was to reappoint Gatting as England captain, but he was overruled through the interference of Ossie Wheatley who, as chairman of the board's cricket committee, had the power of veto. David Gower was elected instead, and turned out to be a disaster. He had a rather laissez-faire approach, which included a failure to attend a press conference because he had tickets for the theatre, and tended to let things drift on the field. Generally the team lacked spark, and they were trounced 4–0 by Allan Border's rampant Australians.

Gatting, who had been informed privately that he'd regained the England job before Wheatley exercised his veto, was hurt by the rejection and rumours began to emerge that he was involved in a rebel party to tour South Africa. He certainly seemed to be taking a lot of secret phone calls, and once or twice he was late for practice.

The rumours were confirmed on the last day of the fourth Test at Old Trafford. Gatting wasn't playing, but during it Gooch and Emburey – friends and previous co-rebels – sat in an anteroom of the pavilion and Emburey, who'd had an influence in assembling the squad, mumbled the occasional 'are you still going?' when prospective tourists wandered in. The party was announced that night. You couldn't really blame Test-match marginals like Paul Jarvis and Matthew Maynard for signing up, bearing in mind that England had tried twenty-nine players in the Ashes series. Their lives were shrouded in uncertainty, and £80,000 for two short winter tours was undeniably tempting. I would have gone if anyone had asked me, but no one did.

Gooch wasn't interested in the tour this time, and eventually Gatting was announced as captain. He had sackfuls of mail, and one morning I sifted through some of it on the dressing room table. Of the 230 envelopes I opened, 160 letters were supportive, 59 protesting, 10 rude or vindictive and the other contained only a picture of a large gorilla eating a banana. 'You're the dimmest England captain since the war,' read one, while another asked: 'When Marshall hit you on the head [in 1986] you must have suffered brain damage, or are you too thick-skinned?'

Some accused him of gross naïveté for admitting he knew nothing about apartheid. He was only being honest. There were so many hidden agendas in the media that few of us were really in possession of accurate, up-to-date facts about South Africa's status quo. As a fifteen-year-old simultaneously thumping a ball around in his back garden and eating a packet of crisps, Gatting could hardly have imagined that a few years later, not only would his batting technique and unremarkable evening activities be exposed, but his political acumen vilified. He was definitely a man more sinned against than sinning. Mostly, anyway.

NO SEASIDE RESPITE

August, The South Coast

With so much on your mind basics can sometimes be forgotten. While the South African business was still rumbling around, Middlesex were pitted against Hampshire in the semi-final of the NatWest Trophy. The Southampton ground was bursting to the gills, it was a glorious day and Gatting's battle talk was gathering momentum, though he didn't have to raise his voice – the visitors' dressing room at Hampshire's HQ is about the size of a garden shed and a good deal less well equipped.

'Come on, lads, we've played so well in this competition, let's not let it slip now,' he urged. 'It's a good wicket, so a solid start's important. And remember, no silly runs on the offside. Paul Terry's very quick.' A while later Gatting returned to the pavilion, run out attempting a tight single to Terry at cover.

As in the previous rounds, however, our bowling attack was too irrepressible to be dominated and we won an exciting match when, with Hampshire requiring 20 from 15 balls and

A Lot of Hard Yakka

Chris Smith 114 not out, Angus Fraser broke Smith's thumb with an unintentional beamer, and I managed, with my new run-up, to propel a leg-stump yorker at will. We had played brilliant all-round cricket in the sixty-over competition, and totally deserved to be in the final, and to win it. Ellcock had produced lightning, destructive spells; Fraser, Cowans and Emburey were miserly and I had chipped in with 10 wickets in the four rounds. All the batters had made runs.

But the county treadmill has this wondrous way of temporarily knocking you down to size. Four days in Weston-super-Mare interrupted our cup run and did us more harm than good. What a dreadful place to play first-class cricket. The venue was neither super nor first class. I quite liked the place on my first visit, seven years earlier, but by now I thought it was a downright shambles. When you're a novice professional cricketer trying to impress, every ground is a novelty and you don't mind the odd hardship. Wide-eyed enthusiasts see a good side to virtually anything. Once you're playing for your livelihood, trying to save face under pressure from lively young pretenders, you can't be doing with such inadequacies. A ropy wicket, no nets, an outfield like a ploughed field scattered with dried-up dog turds and shards of glass, no treatment room or decent showers and a changing room so small you have to kneel in other people's bags while you're rummaging in your own for a box. The umpires are shoved into an old caravan barely big enough to swing a mouse and their washing facility is a plastic bucket of lukewarm water.

People said it was important to take the game to the supporters, but this was the 1980s, not the era of the horse and cart. Surely even pensioners could drive the twenty or so miles to Taunton if they really wanted to watch cricket. I mean, you don't get Newcastle United staging a match at Whitley Bay, do you? In any case, from what I could make out, Weston in August is mainly full of rather overweight Brummies taking their kids to the beach for rides on sad-looking donkeys.

Cliff, Somerset's ailing dressing-room attendant, still

wearing the red smock the county gave him about 200 years ago, did his best to make up for the substandard facilities, frequently to-ing and fro-ing with a vast urn of tea borne on a small trailer. But the catering tent was so far away and he shuffled along so slowly that the tea was totally stewed by the time it arrived.

Our batsmen's techniques were in tatters after three days' exposure to the Weston wicket and the bowlers had to work hard against the local billy-blockers, Chris Tavaré and Richard Harden. On the Sunday we risked sprained ankles and broken jaws chasing leather on the treacherous outfield.

Let no one deceive you that forty-over games are a cake walk. No one. For a bowler, that eight-over spell, in those days off a short run, and the fielding afterwards is as debilitating as a day and a half's normal cricket. These matches are often balanced on a knife edge and every ball demands your utmost concentration and effort to make sure it's directed precisely where you intended and to avoid severe injury if the batsman happens to return it with interest.

You can't then skulk off to long-leg between overs for a breather, either. Boundary fielders have to be constantly alert to cutting off possible twos – any apparent slackness earns you an earful from the captain. Diving stops are of course de rigueur, as is running between positions to make sure you don't receive an over-rate fine. To lose one of these breathless tip-and-run skirmishes is to feel as exhausted and demoralised as the defeated crew in the Boat Race. The one consolation of the congested cricket season is you don't have to wait a whole year to avenge a defeat.

DEMOLISHED

2 September, Middlesex v Warwickshire, NatWest Final, Lord's
Middlesex's self-belief was more or less indestructible in 1989; it could certainly handle the odd dent. On the day of the

NatWest final, the team were ultra-confident and fresh, too, not having exerted themselves for several days, except guesting for Thetford Coachworks at a benefit day in Bury St Edmunds. We were meeting Warwickshire, then virtually neck-and-neck with *Crossroads* in the giving-Birmingham-a-bad-name ratings.

This was my fifth Lord's cup final, but the first for which the committee had had the wherewithal to organise a party for the team afterwards. As we had won our previous seven finals, there was huge expectation and a larger than usual collection of wives, girlfriends, parents, relatives, agents and other hangers-on clamouring for comps (we still only got four each). Newly engaged (I had proposed to Jan on a number 65 bus going to Kew Gardens) and having been recently award-ed a further two-year contract, I was unusually relaxed before the match. Perhaps too relaxed. On hearing that we were batting first, I predicted to some friends that I'd probably have to bowl the last over with ten to win.

My premonition was spot on. At 7.15 p.m. there were exactly nine runs separating the teams, and I was preparing to bowl the last over. It gave me lots of confidence that Gatting had entrusted me with the fate of the trophy, and I wasn't at all fazed that the outcome of these next six balls would determine whether each player could afford a new cooker or a new kitchen (the winning team would earn £22,000).

The light was quite gloomy when I set off to bowl the second ball, and the bespectacled Neil Smith was batting as if he needed a miner's lamp as well as thicker lenses. When he made contact with my trusty slower ball I thought for a split second that it had gone straight up in the air. 'Catch it!' I shouted confidently. After what seemed like an eternity, a man in the top tier of the Nursery End stand obliged. The ball had travelled fully 90yds for the only six of the match, and the Brummies in the crowd had gone berserk.

Three to win, four balls to go. Not much of a contest now. It's amazing how one piddling little ball can transform the entire mood of a packed stadium. I stared dumbly around, hardly able to believe what had happened. This certainly wasn't in my script. The Middlesex players were stunned into silence for almost the first time in living memory. Gatting was gobsmacked.

It's no good dwelling on these misfortunes, though. You've just got to get on with the game. I did. I bowled a wide. I felt stupid. God knows what they were saying in the commentary box. 'Dear, dear, fancy not being able to get one straight. Hughes' temperament has let him down at the vital moment. It must be nerves.' It wasn't, it was resignation, which is, if anything, less excusable. I felt culpable, and crap.

Two to win off four. Somehow, I bowled two dot balls. Suddenly there was hope. Just one more good yorker and we'd have a chance. I produced it, Smith jammed it straight back to me. I slipped and missed it. The batsmen ran the winning two while I sat dejectedly in mid-pitch, powerless to stop them or the onrushing ecstatic Warwickshire supporters.

A strange wave of relief engulfed me, despite one fat bloke jeering, 'You just lacked talent' and slapping me on the back. It was only when we were back in the dressing room, after all the presentations and players sportingly coming up and offering all sorts of other reasons why we lost, that deep depression began to take hold. I was like a child who has broken an expensive vase but only bursts into tears later when his parents get back from work.

Our first post-final dinner, held in a garish anteroom of the Regent's Park Hilton, was predictably muted. I stood up and made a martyrish speech declaring that it was all my fault and I didn't want any sympathy. I got it regardless. 'I shouldn't have let those four byes through,' Paul Downton said.

'No, no, I shouldn't have bowled that pissole yorker outside leg stump,' Emburey interrupted nobly. These post-mortems are the raison d'être of major sporting events. It matters not who won or lost, but how you place the blame.

And if I thought the issue would quietly expire over the next few days, I was horribly wrong. Wherever I went – pubs, dinners, benefit matches, parties – people brought it up, and still do now, aeons later, especially at Edgbaston. To add a finishing touch of irony, the demolition and rebuilding of the Nursery End stand where the six had landed began the day after the match. Neil Smith incorporated those last-over heroics into the England team's motivational video for the one-day internationals in 1996. And whenever it rains during their NatWest coverage, the BBC dredge it up, reminding me that I never did buy that new cooker.

The ball that went for six has become the single most important moment with which my whole cricket career is identified. 'You're that bloke who was panned out of the park by M.J.K. Smith's son,' punters chuckle. Still, I'd rather be partially identifiable than totally anonymous.

TEN-YEAR ITCH: 1990

bed partners • cannon fodder • down the order • Canterbury week • a decade of change • Haynes whips Akram • a cardboard climax • intimidatory batting • £50 a head

BED-MATES

Jan and I got married at the end of March. All our favourite members of the Middlesex team came and the reception was held in the pavilion of my old cricket club, which was refreshingly free of amateur snaps depicting the 1984 midsummer barbecue. My father had quite an influence. He 'gave my hair a little trim' before the nuptials and his great friend Leslie Crowther was the guest of honour. After the main speeches, which went on far too long (especially mine), Leslie reeled off a series of his classic jokes: 'What's the difference between a sheep and a Lada? It's marginally less embarrassing getting out of the back of a Lada.' And so on.

It was a glorious, sunny day to get hitched, offering no hint of the tribulations to come. They began that night, in fact. The dancing didn't finish until gone midnight, so rather than book into a hotel for three hours' kip before our 6.30 a.m. honeymoon flight from Gatwick, I led my wife and the hard core round to a friend's house for beer and steak pies. Not what you'd call romantic.

At about 3 a.m. I fancied a bit of shut-eye, but Jan was nowhere to be found. I discovered her upstairs, zonked out on top of a double bed beside our host's unconscious wife. There was no room for me, so I crashed out in the next bedroom, fully clothed. When the alarm woke me at five, a girl had fallen asleep next to me, but it wasn't Jan. I had spent my wedding night in bed with my sister.

We took a week's honeymoon in Sicily, which was enjoyable if only because at last I had found a valid reason to skip the annual pre-season gutbusting in the gym. But when we came back and were transferring all Jan's worldly goods from her flat to my house, I left the ignition keys briefly in our estate car packed full of books, china, clothes and valuable heirlooms. Having checked that we'd got everything, we came back downstairs to find the car had been nicked. After an exhaustive search I eventually found it three days later. There was nothing in the back except two empty paint tins. Already I'd taken one step forward and two back.

Mike Gatting had had his own disasters during the rebel tour to South Africa, but there was a good spirit in the Middlesex camp that April, brought about by a rejuvenated England. They'd won a Test in the Caribbean for the first time in a generation (Fraser was Middlesex's only representative), which was transmitted live by Sky TV. A revelation in itself. We'd all been glued to it, and Tony Greig's hysterical 'Goodnight, Charlie' seemed to have bidden good riddance to English cricket's ineptitude, even if Geoffrey Boycott's reaction to a dropped catch – ''E could've caught it in his moother's pinny' – had not.

A further local boost was the separation of the Siamese twins, Tufnell and Sykes. Despite a reasonable season in 1989, Sykes was deemed to be a disruptive influence by the committee, although none of them would ever admit it publicly. Certain members of the hierarchy pulled faces when he wandered about exclaiming, 'Look at 'im – 'is whooper fell out,' and you could see what they were thinking.

Overall it was a good move, although we missed Sykes's cruel humour and Bethnal Green anecdotes. His departure put the wind up Tufnell, channelling his focus, and he seemed to keep his obstreperous side under wraps for a while. He even cut his hair, and agreed to smoke outside when Emburey complained that the dressing room smelled like a lorry drivers' caff.

THE YEAR OF THE BAT

It was the pong of perspiration that dominated most changing areas in 1990, because bowlers toiled all day without getting anybody out. 'You're not going to like the balls we're using this season,' the umpire Alan Jones remarked one morning, pre-season, and he was right. They were even more orange-like than we'd feared. The leather was dull and unpolishable and the seam almost imperceptible. It was like bowling with a large red mothball. Their arrival coincided with new, TCCB-defined straw-coloured pitches and the hottest spring since 1929. It was, in short, the prologue to the Year of the Bat.

The only people who had a tougher assignment than the bowlers at The Oval were the Howes brothers in the scorebox. Surrey made 707, Lancashire replied with 863, and over a period of six days there were 2,760 runs. That's a lot of turning wheels and pulling cords. In the country as a whole there were two triple centuries and a 291 before May was a week old. Spikes, on a perilous one-year contract for the first time in ten years, grabbed a rare chance as Hampshire's number 3 to make a century and a fifty in the opening match before badly ricking his back. It denied him a great opportunity.

Middlesex managed to escape the carnage with a quiet three-day match in Cambridge, where there were no advertising hoardings or helmets and they ate jam tarts for tea. It still wasn't completely safe for some people. Having a drink one night in an out-of-the-way pub, Gatting was suddenly confronted by a psycho who called him a racist bastard and threw a pint over him. He was tempted to take the bloke outside but thought better of it and left quietly. Undaunted, the *Sun* still splashed the headline, 'GATTING IN RACIST PUB BRAWL' across its front page the next morning.

For a while we avoided the big cavalry charges because, even with Fraser troubled by a sore hip, we still had a good attack. I was slightly peeved that Cowans was described in the *Playfair Cricket Annual* as right-arm fast (his speed was so reduced by the years of toil that he was deceiving batsmen in the flight), whereas I still had an occasional bit of pace but was now listed as right-arm medium (I had always been fast medium before). It sounds trivial, but it has a significant effect on your self-esteem.

But that is nothing compared to the fear and loathing you experience when, after a long day in the field, the scorer arrives in the dressing room bearing a scrap of paper. The bowling figures. Harry Sharp dutifully hands them to the captain. 'Go on, read 'em out,' says one beleaguered trundler resigned to becoming a laughing stock. The captain proceeds to do so, accompanied by guffaws and gasps.

'I didn't go for a ton, did I?'

'A hundred and eighteen.'

'Shit, that's arch pongo. I've had a shocker. What about Tuffers?'

'Eighty-seven.'

'Huh. Didn't see him offering to bowl when the shit was flying.'

Just as every batsman seeks to score a hundred, every bowler wants to avoid conceding one. Some kept count all day and knew their tally; others preferred not to face the harsh reality. Gloucester's Syd Lawrence was fined by the other players for hiding the written evidence after a particularly trying day in the field, and Leicester's George Ferris visited the scorers before the end of the day, jokingly suggesting they could 'adjust' his analysis and reduce it to 1–98.

To add to the indignity, as the demoralised bowler sits, head in hands, absorbing the hard facts and waiting for his bath to fill up, one of the slip fielders will try to nip into it. 'Oi, what are you having a wash for?' Fraser once challenged Emburey. 'You've been standing like a cardboard cut-out all day.'

'Well, if you'd bent your back I might have had something to do,' Emburey replied, lowering himself into the water.

LOOKING DOWN THE BARREL

Wednesday 25 July, Canterbury Week

By early June we were leading the championship and the Sunday League. The team was supremely confident. To put it another way, there were a lot of big egos. Desmond Haynes admitted he didn't know how to get out and it looked like it as he lashed Essex for 220 not out, spending the entire match at Ilford on the field. His ebullience was infectious. 'Man,' he said, 'I don't think I'll *ever* retire. I just *lurve* playing cricket.'

He was so excited by the prospect of facing his great friend Malcolm Marshall on a shirt-front at Bournemouth that he shouted through the dressing-room wall, 'I'm gonna give you some *drives*, boy!' as he padded up.

'You better bring a stepladder,' Marshall warned. In his over-enthusiasm, Haynes got out for a duck at the other end.

Nothing diminished his exuberance, though, and it rubbed off on his young partner, Micky Roseberry, who kept pulling near half-volleys over mid-wicket, at last living up to his nickname – Zorro, the flashing blade. There was a lot of provocative slapping of gloves and loud calling. Mark Ramprakash was channelling his volatility into giving bowlers a good spanking, while Gatting and the dependable Keith Brown were cutting them to death. Brown had a fine season, and it was announced during a televised Sunday match that he'd been awarded his county cap. 'Why doesn't he wear it, then,' Geoff Boycott commented, 'instead of that ridiculous pork-pie 'at?'

If we won the toss in a home championship game, the bowlers usually did little else but bask in the sun at the Nursery End the first day, although that occasionally meant a mad dash back to the pavilion to get padded up if there was a sudden middle-order collapse. Once I didn't have time to put on my socks before going in to bat. Despite nudging the age of thirty-one, I didn't really set a particularly good example.

With the ball our unit was probing and ruthlessly effective, notably Tufnell, whose attitude and fielding had improved

100 per cent, though his dress sense – unstructured jackets, crumpled trousers, mock-croc shoes and tie at half-mast – was still appalling. It didn't stop him attracting women. Most of them seemed to want to mother him.

I was seriously affected by the state of the balls we were using. My bowling was gun-barrel straight – no one was having any trouble with it, particularly not wicketkeeper Downton, as I never got anything past the bat. At times when I was up against Gooch or Hick or Jimmy Cook, it was truly cannon versus fodder. I was so innocuous that Gatting didn't even bother to give me a bowl in one match. As I also made no runs in that contest, I had what Sykes would have delightedly referred to as 'a fresh-air game'.

It's depressing when as a senior you slide down the pecking order, or get ignored or dropped, a bit like being asked to move into a smaller office because some new, uppity salesman has suddenly become flavour of the month. For a time you wallow in paranoia, convinced that the boss is picking on you for some unfathomable reason. In county cricket we play so much that people don't notice their own gradual deterioration and advancing impotence. Bowlers way past their sell-by date still delude themselves that they haven't lost an ounce of penetration: just listen to Fred Trueman. 'I could bool as fast as Pringle and I retired twenty-five years ago,' he'll bluster on *Test Match Special*. No one ever has the guts to point out sportsmen's fading powers and declining speed, which is a shame, as it would save expanding men a lot of park-football injuries.

Gatting's decision to demote me was utterly sound. When I was offered a long bowl, against Kent at Canterbury, they clocked up 449–2. My run-up was perfect, but the old nip off the pitch had gone and the shorter balls that batsmen used to weave hurriedly away from were being clobbered over square leg for four.

Canterbury Week is not, it must be said, the place to rediscover ruthlessness. It has a soothing, old-fashioned ambience created by assorted ex-servicemen and thesps taking their annual trip down memory lane with their blue-rinsed partners. There's probably been the same conviviality, the same ladies' hat competition and the same pile of empty Chablis crates ever since the event was founded in 1842. To complete the festival flavour, a dozen stripey marquees ring the ground, patronised by the East Kent Yeomanry, the Old Stagers, the Purchasers, the Band of Brothers and the High Sheriff. There's a real ale tent, too.

I circumnavigated the ground on the last afternoon as Gatting and Ramprakash tore headlong into the Kent attack, and was foolishly tempted by the liquid hospitality in various tents. We were coasting to victory, so I had a pint, then another, and another, washed down with a couple of Pimm's. I felt quite light-headed. Suddenly, there was a crash of wickets, I had to rush back to the dressing room to pad up, and before I knew it I was taking guard in the middle faced with the task of hitting 12 to win off the last over. I missed every ball.

Thank goodness it didn't cost Middlesex the championship. In the last two months the team lost only once, on a diabolical wicket at Derby which resembled a lunar landscape. Despite the usual Test calls and a serious eye injury suffered by our Mr Reliable, Paul Downton – struck by a bail at Basingstoke – we remained top of the table from mid-June onwards.

FAST HANDS

Friday 17 August, NatWest Semi-Final, Old Trafford
Our title progress was disrupted by a tedious, weather-ruined NatWest semi-final. The rain was torrential for thirty-six hours, consigning us to Manchester for three aimless days. We passed one lunchtime visiting Angus Fraser's Uncle Brian's fish-and-chip shop under a viaduct by the Manchester Ship Canal. Behind the chrome fryer and food display was a pre-war sitting-room area where we were plied with mushy peas and

potato fritters until we felt decidedly bilious. Uncle Brian was something of a jolly larrikin, while Gus, who had a much more privileged life, could be a grumpy git. On that basis maybe Geoff Boycott's brother is a compulsive party animal.

Fraser was a marvellous bowler then, of course, but even he could do nothing to protect us from the slashing Lancastrian rapiers, and when the match finally resumed, they sliced up the target of 297 with ease. The anxious waiting around, the unrefined arrogance of their batsmen and the morale-sapping sight of hordes of Lancashire supporters swarming into the ground like ants when the grapevine relayed the news that their team were cruising to victory was extremely inhibiting. No wonder they're so hard to beat on their home turf.

My most vivid memory of the game was the duel between the two most accomplished one-day cricketers in the world, Desmond Haynes and Wasim Akram. It was on a par with Daniel versus Greenidge five years earlier. Haynes already had fourteen one-day international hundreds to his name and wasn't fazed by anyone, even a bowler who ran up in a furious hurry to unleash an explosion of bouncers and yorkers in apparently random order.

Akram's preliminaries to actually letting go of the ball are so frenzied it's a wonder he doesn't trip over. I have seen him hurtle up to the stumps behind the umpire, pop out to slam one into the keeper's gloves via the batsman's pads, and carry on up the pitch yelling hysterically for lbw, while the confused batsman stands looking this way and that, wondering what the hell happened. None of this mattered to Haynes. He hooked the bouncers, walked across his stumps and daringly swatted the length balls over mid-wicket. He somehow managed to whip perfect yorkers through square leg or glide them just out of the wicketkeeper's reach. He wielded the bat alternately like a cudgel and a hoe, and finished 149 not out. Akram sportingly applauded him as the players walked off. Even then his hands moved faster than a Chinese noodle-maker's.

A DECADE OF CHANGE

The Lancashire players' upgraded image symbolised cricket's transformation during the 1980s – the span of my own career thus far. Here they were now, driving into the ground in shiny hatchbacks and wearing double-breasted Cecil Gee suits, silk ties and salon hairstyles. Some had agents and mobile phones and had befriended local boutique-owners who arrived on rainy days with rails of pleated trousers and loud shirts for them to choose from. They took their swishy arrogance and gym-honed bodies on to the field in the manner of their mates over the road at Manchester United. They could all bat and bowl and field and hit massive sixes, and their play was compulsive viewing.

Yet ten years earlier Lancashire had been a rabble, with one star player (Clive Lloyd) who failed to lift them above the mediocre. They turned up in moderate saloon cars, wore dowdy blazers and nasty brown shirts (didn't we all), fielded ponderously and had a wicketkeeper who batted at number 11. 'A night on the Boddy' certainly didn't mean fitness training, and their overall appearance was clubby and unprofessional, but they had a good time and told excellent jokes.

Elsewhere in 1980 there had been forty ex-public-schoolboys playing county cricket and twenty-two past or present Oxbridge students. Half the county captains were university or public-school educated. Middlesex, who supplied the nucleus of the England team, had a dynamic mix of university boys, West Indian immigrants and streetwise Londoners. Self-expression was encouraged and players turned up in all sorts of garb. The ambience in the dressing room was bubbly and stimulating and would frequently be enhanced by members of the opposition popping in for a chat. We often had a beer with them after play and no one suggested that it was unhealthy to mix socially with your adversaries. Personally, I thought it was all part of the fun of the fair.

The transference of the Middlesex captaincy from Brearley (City of London School, Cambridge University) to Gatting

(John Kelly Boys' High School) in 1983 coincided with a change in outlook throughout the game. Dressing rooms became more disciplinarian, a regimental approach to preparation and behaviour was adopted and class distinction was gradually blurred by the inexorable advance of 'professionalism'. Contact with the opposition diminished (an Australian coach at Kent virtually forbade it), and in 1990, Geoff Miller, the only remaining player who unfailingly visited the opposing team's dressing room after play to thank them for the game, had retired. He was also the last man to field at slip with a whoopee cushion up his jumper.

The nouveau county cricket had spawned a performance stereotype who was slightly cocooned from the real world by his relentless schedule, bought ordinary High Street clothes and married a bottle-blonde air stewardess/secretary/PA. Few modern players had the inclination to stray beyond the immediate vicinity of their hotel on tour. Travel was an ordeal rather than an adventure.

Perhaps because of the relatively low salaries (this was my eleventh season and I was still earning only £14,000) and comparatively undynamic atmosphere, there were half as many public-school-educated county cricketers in 1990 as there had been a decade before, and most were regarded with casual interest and labelled 'jazz hats'. Ex-Oxbridge students were also down from twenty-two to nine. One was Michael Atherton, who, in his early days at Lancashire, had found the letters F.E.C. stencilled on his locker. This was assumed to signify Future England Captain. The gnarled pros responsible later admitted it stood for Fucking Educated Cunt.

As a result of a rather less enlightened approach to the game verging on that of pro football, conformism ruled and the typical 1990s cricketer was a decent, regular middlebrow man who read the *Daily Mail* and Wilbur Smith novels and (except in Lancashire) dressed at C&A. This might help explain why in general England's recent performances have been pretty uninspiring. Many of the more prominent players daub the slogan 'Form is temporary. Class is permanent' on the lids of their bulging coffins. It isn't class they lack, but charisma.

HARVEST

Saturday 22 September, Sussex v Middlesex, Hove
I went to the NatWest final as a spectator. Having bowled vital overs in the climax to the previous two years' competitions, I felt slightly sadistic as I envisaged all the anxiety on the pitch while I sipped a Pimm's at the Allen Stand bar. The match was effectively all over by 11.15 a.m. by which time Philip DeFreitas (then of Lancashire) had knocked over Northants' top five at a personal cost of 19. It failed to clinch DeFreitas his place on the winter tour – I could never understand why a startling performance in a one-day final should be used as a serious guide, anyway.

One who had made it into the England party was a certain Philip Clive Roderick Tufnell. Quite an advance, considering that he had almost been sacked twelve months previously. His knack of luring batsmen down the pitch with the ball on an invisible string was his greatest asset, but his temperament was still questionable. Gatting blew a gasket every time Tufnell got bolshy about field settings or strategies: like Edmonds, he occasionally directed a whole over down the leg side if he didn't get his own way.

It was odd, too, that whereas he was perfectly confident trying to stem the batsmen's cavalry charge on a flat wicket, teasing and tantalising, with the bat he became a quivering wreck when facing anyone who had more than a four-pace run-up. On one occasion, sent in as nightwatchman to weather the last three balls of the day from the Sussex speed merchant Tony Pigott, Tufnell clad himself in armour, then backed away in unconcealed terror from the first ball and slashed it wildly over the slips for four. He attempted to do the same to the second and lost his off stump. Gatting therefore had to come in for one delivery. He was not amused.

The season still had four days to run after the tour party announcement, and Middlesex were one victory away from becoming champions. Standing in our way were Sussex, but they obligingly lay down, as any reputable bottom-of-the-table team tends to do. On the third day, we had more trouble with the traffic on the A27 than with the Sussex batting. Someone in the Middlesex office had decreed that we would stay in an Elizabethan, beamed pub in the olde-worlde village of Alfriston rather than at our usual Trust House Forte number on the Hove beachfront. All very well until you get stuck behind a combine-harvester in a no-overtaking zone and arrive at the ground twenty minutes late.

On that decisive third day, we went through the loosening-up routine on automatic pilot. Stretching and a few gentle hits into the boards were all that anyone could be bothered with by this time of year. Nets were only for freaks. Then it was back to the dark, cluttered dressing room to check the weather forecast on Ceefax. Essex were harrying us at the top of the table, but their match at The Oval was going to be disrupted by rain. All we had to do was bowl out Sussex for less than 240 to win by an innings and claim our crown.

The wicket was flat and the doubts lingered for a while, but two balls suddenly kept low and Sussex declined to 19–2. We smirked at the sight of David Smith, a dangerous player, thumping a hoarding with his bat on the way off. It was 70–4 at lunch, when, over steak and chips, we discussed the Essex position (still raining) and the credentials of Emma the perky blonde waitress, who later married Ian Salisbury.

I had rather too much to eat and bowled an insipid spell afterwards. Gatting's 'double teapot' pose was very much in evidence. 'Come on, keep it tidy, lads,' he kept admonishing, without actually looking in my direction. I still hadn't learned that I was always put on immediately post-lunch as the only bowler who gamely charged in with a full stomach and didn't complain about feeling nauseous.

Ten-Year Itch: 1990

Anxiety levels were high as players wondered whether we'd stumble at the last hurdle, and the field was quiet apart from Gatting's goading and the seagulls whining overhead. Fraser diffused the tension with a couple of quick wickets, and then Tufnell, on as a substitute, took a blinding catch on the boundary in front of the pavilion. The Cat, curled up on the couch in the players' viewing room for most of the match, had woken up.

Taking the final two wickets in successive balls so, at last, had I. We were champions – and I was on a hat-trick with my first ball of the next season.

Clinching the championship is a strange sensation. It's the culmination of five months' team-work, of map-reading and exhausting drives, of sharing rooms in tasteless motorway-side hotels, of cramming shut bags full of dirty gear, of practice on damp, patchy nets, of knee niggles and scraped elbows and rowdy arguments over silly card games, of ecstasy and agony and sometimes apathy, all compressed into a few smiles and handshakes and the presentation of a giant cardboard cheque for £40,000 (£3,500 per man) in front of a few pensioners sitting in stripey deckchairs and shrouded in blankets. There's more atmosphere in a doctor's waiting room.

We were invited into the Sussex committee room for a drink, a noble gesture considering that they had finished with the wooden spoon. But then, in spite of the changes in the game, cricket is still replete with traditional English cordiality. The quaint habit of applauding a member of the opposition when he's just caned you for a hundred isn't the type of behaviour you'll find in other sports. I'm not aware of the Everton players ever having patted Ian Rush on the back when he'd just completed a hat-trick against them.

There was a dilapidated old wicker chair in the committee room. 'Sign of the times here, I suppose,' I ventured to one tweedy old buffer.

'No, no, it's a valuable relic. It's Ranjitsinhji's,' he replied, rather peeved. Why do we insist on nostalgically hanging on to useless old rubbish? It's a sign of our current inferiority complex, I suppose – clinging hopefully to illustrious images of the past because we can't face the present. We are all escapists at heart.

And generally reluctant to participate in extravagant celebration. Usually the euphoria of winning the championship peters out in a long, sober drive to get home before dark and is punctured by the arrival of a seasonal P45 on your doormat. With this title, Middlesex's fourth in ten years, things were different. The match was over a day early and we were still booked in at the pub, so the office staff, some Second XI players and even Jim the physio joined the team on the razzle. There were toasts and informal speeches and Tufnell bought a round. I underlined that latter fact in my diary and added several exclamation marks.

The whole season had the same unreal ring to it. Ball paid total homage to bat from start to finish. Ten players had passed 2,000 runs, Graham Gooch averaged 101.70, there were 428 hundreds and 32 doubles and someone wrote that it was easier to get past a Lord's gateman than an outside edge. Teams were regularly chasing 400 on the last day and getting them, and cricket-loving John Major, then chancellor of the exchequer, must have given serious thought to devaluing the run. Yet amid all this, old fuddy-duddies still waffled on about the dangers of too many short-pitched deliveries.

What about some legislation against intimidatory *batting*?

PASSING THE BUCKET

Autumn

The benefit year is English cricket's greatest anachronism. The very idea that a player should be rewarded for his years of 'service' is rooted in class chauvinism. County administrators even have the gall to announce that they have 'granted' Smithers a benefit (it's never written into contracts so that the 'gift' is not liable to tax) and then entirely wash their hands of it. Maybe I'm cynical about this, but I'm convinced that counties subconsciously use the benefit year to handcuff players. The officers have a guilty conscience about their conspicuous lack of profit and therefore the low salaries, but are also aware that impoverished players will stay awhile if this carrot is dangled in front of them. Generally, they're right.

'Simon Hughes has been awarded a benefit by Middlesex in 1991,' ran a news item in the July 1990 issue of the *Cricketer* magazine. It was probably the most favourable thing written about me all year. A lot of people must have read it, because they were coming up to me and saying, 'I didn't know you were retiring,' which I wasn't, of course. It's a *benefit*, not a state pension. I noticed that none of these sympathisers did the decent thing and offered to be on my organising committee.

This is the first headache. Trying to assemble a group of energetic movers and shakers who are not only willing to give up their time to dream up events, but also to pressurise their friends and acquaintances into buying tickets for them. Laundering money for me: that's what it boils down to. Not surprisingly, candidates are hard to find.

Some beneficiaries resort to hiring professional fund-raisers, which, if it is done subtly, is probably the best option. I mean we uncommercially minded cricketers are hardly experts in the shark-infested waters of corporate hospitality and client entertainment. The only thing we can offer is the attendance of 'celebrities' at functions, but this rarely lives up to its billing. Beleaguered organisers are usually obliged to replace the advertised Mike Gatting or Desmond Haynes or Ian Botham with Ed Rossiter who once played for Buckinghamshire Schoolboys.

Basically, a benefit is an exercise in contriving and running a small business for a year. People who set up small commercial outfits usually have some accounting knowledge, available funds, a small workforce and some office space. Most cricketers think spreadsheets are old-fashioned pitch covers, are frequently overdrawn and have to make space for a small desk in the spare room among the mounds of surplus kit. The workforce is their wife. Don't ever bother to try and phone a beneficiary. He'll always either be engaged or out in search of donors. Just as you can recognise a cricketer by the fielding scars on his elbows, you can immediately identify a beneficiary because one ear is flatter to his head. For about fifteen months he metamorphoses from a tanned athlete into a pallid telephone salesman. He has to design a brochure, sell advertising, book venues months ahead, persuade stars of stage, screen and sport to attend dinners, lug around boxes of bats and prints to be signed, woo potential sponsors and mailshoot punters.

The process usually starts about midsummer the year before, when he begins shadowing the current beneficiary to see how the events work, meet some of the trusty drumbeaters, ask anyone in a suit for his or her business card and generally put the word around. He inherits a database of benevolent individuals and their companies, though when he rings the number given he often finds the person concerned hasn't worked there since 1982.

Usually benefit brochures are full of sycophantic tributes to the player from the stars of the game. I found the idea of producing something like this deeply embarrassing. What was there nice or interesting to say about me? 'The day Hughesy beat me twice outside the off stump,' by Viv Richards. 'Yozzer's great diving stop at backward cover,' from David Gower, that sort of thing. Hardly a rattling good read. So I put together an anthology of cricket writing in the 1980s instead, with a little section about me at the end, the contributors – my father and two college friends. The *pièce de resistance* was a complimentary message from one I.T. Botham – badly typed, but totally unsolicited.

As the first non-Test-playing beneficiary at Middlesex for a decade, I was reluctant to lean on the usual diligent fundraisers, who had in any case bled everyone they knew, however vaguely, to death. So I tried investing in new talent. In other words, my old university mates. The trouble was, few of them had risen far enough up the corporate ladder to have any real clout, and to compound the problem, there was a serious recession out there. Anyone whose previous conspicuous wealth had a Lloyds bias was now drinking Perrier instead of Perignon.

Not surprisingly, my benefit committee meetings achieved little except the exchange of gossip over a few cans of Guinness. None of the participants really had much of a clue, and to be honest, neither did I. Trial and error was the prevalent philosophy and we wasted an age debating the design of the benefit tie. After a string of hopeless prototypes, I ended up styling it on something my wife Jan had bought in Italy in green, blue and purple stripes. I resisted the temptation to have 'Yozzer 1991' embroidered on the bottom.

A reasonable calendar of events did emerge, however (about forty in all), thanks in no small measure to the availability – and popularity – of a little room in the top right-hand turret of the Lord's pavilion which few people beyond the inner sanctum know about. During the summer this is the exclusive domain of MCC committeemen slavering over a four-course lunch. In the winter, though, it could be hired for black-tie evening functions at a giveaway price. They even let you bring in your own booze. Good old Nancy stayed behind with her loyal staff to prepare traditional Irish stodge which was eagerly devoured by red-faced city types, who, once slightly the worse for wear, gamely bid for signed bats and rugby balls and generously supported the raffle – especially if my sister was selling the tickets in one of her low-cut dresses.

And my father's acting contacts, allied to my sporting ones, spawned a distinguished list of personalities – Barry Norman, Brian Johnston, Stephen Fry, Cliff Morgan, Leslie Crowther and Dave Allen, for instance – who all generously gave up their time to speak, searching dutifully at some point for some kind words to say about me ('He's a good chap and a real trier'), and the tightly packed room had a powerful intimacy. Most importantly, if you sold all sixty tickets at £50 a head, which usually wasn't difficult, given the prestige of the venue, you finished the night a good £3,000 better off.

Bigger events were much harder to sell. There were four other southern beneficiaries – David East (Essex), Mark Benson (Kent), Mark Nicholas (Hampshire) and Tony Pigott (Sussex) – all vying for support in the Square Mile, often through the same contacts. Consequently, many of these harassed pinstripes had had their fill of large sporting dinners at the Grosvenor or various banqueting suites, and I got a lot of probably-nots for my big March launch. I should have been thick-skinned enough to shrug off rejections, but initially I found it all rather depressing, and doubtless I wasn't much fun at home. Jan was under pressure herself in an understaffed solicitors' office, and we became crotchety with each other, which just exacerbated the situation.

CASUALTY: 1991

a ghastly ride • sticking the knife in • Tufnell
over the top • Irish session • strange tender •
the chairman's office • cards and money • new
faces old haunts

TWENTY SECONDS

The Group 4 Security firm might have become a metaphor for laxity, but three of their namesake, our little original Training Group 4, were still managing to keep their heads above water. While I was immersed in my benefit at Middlesex, Spikes and the Rat were embarking on an arduous self-improvement programme in the Hampshire indoor nets. After a decade of fluctuating fortunes in the county game, they had finally realised, as I had done two years earlier, the value of a disciplined approach and were determined to leave nothing to chance.

In Spikes' case, the metamorphosis was vital, since he'd been inactive for most of 1990 with a back injury, started a small business importing wine from South Africa and ended up drinking a lot of it himself. His subsequent bodily expansion had earned him the new nickname Jocky (as in Wilson), and he knew he had to get back into shape for the new season. I, on the other hand, was about to become a physical and emotional wreck.

One of my early benefit functions was an unorthodox winter dinner in the Carlton Hotel, St Moritz, Switzerland. Now, don't get the wrong idea here, I wasn't suddenly rubbing shoulders with Prince Multimark von Schadenfreude or Wing Commander Poncey-Carr. Some imaginative friends had rigged up a long weekend playing cricket on St Moritz's frozen lake taking in a few rides down the Cresta Run, and had managed to attract local sponsorship. On the dubious premise that I could have an auction of cricketing memorabilia on the Saturday night, I was press-ganged into going. Wooed by the resort's glamorous image and David Gower's recommendation, Mark Nicholas and Chris Cowdrey came too.

A Lot of Hard Yakka

A 25-over match on ice at 6,500ft and -15°C is not quite as ridiculous as it sounds. With the artificial-matting wicket, an outfield of compacted snow framed by little orange boundary flags and players in ski gloves and Ray-Bans, you can actually have a reasonable game. That is until the ice under the pitch thaws, then refreezes in ridges making the surface a corrugated minefield. But the cricket wasn't the real reason for being there, in case you hadn't guessed. A short distance from the gaggle of fur shops and glitzy cafés selling strudels and schnitzels, the main road rises up over a small hill. On the other side you turn down an icy path which leads to what looks like the bridge of a ship looming out of the snow: the clubhouse of the Cresta Club.

Loudspeakers relay the upper-class tones of Lt-Col Digby Willoughby, the master of Cresta Run ceremonies. 'Fitzherbert and Whitman to the box . . . Come, come, Higgins, you must be properly attired on the ice – hurry up, man! . . . Perkins next rider.' And a bell dings, followed by eerie scraping sounds as another toboggan sets off down the treacherous, mile-long ice chute bearing a masochist clad in nothing more than plus-fours and a motorcycle helmet. When this human missile arrives at the bottom of the run, miraculously still intact, Willoughby barks: 'And Ponsonby-Smythe has alighted at the charming village of Cellerina.'

Beautiful people in expensive gabardines, fur mufflers and cool shades cram the sun-drenched pavilion balcony or perch on a rostrum at the notorious Shuttlecock corner, a 90-degree turn responsible for many spectacular falls. The rickety old sledges, some bearing RAF logos, attain speeds of 60mph as they hurtle down the mountain, their rider's nose 10ins from the ice. It's terrifying enough watching from a safe distance; to volunteer for the experience is sheer lunacy. I wasn't doing it under any circumstances.

'I'm not doing it under any circumstances,' I said adamantly several times, having resisted the lure of skiing all my career for fear of injury. Apart from anything else, a trip on the Cresta costs £150. You do get a potential five rides for that, but to my mind that was a penalty rather than a bonus.

But of course, peer pressure is the invidious core of boysy society, a go-on-one-for-the-road temptation it's hard to resist. Your companions make you feel inadequate if you withstand their persuasions, as if you answer to an inferior god (i.e. common sense). I was bewitched by their spell and dumbly fell into line. This meant rolling up at 7.15 a.m. to get kitted out in elbow pads and prehistoric-looking shoes equipped with metal prongs and then listening to the improbably tanned Lt-Col Willoughby's 'death talk'. 'You might come out into the straw at Shuttlecock,' he said, hardly instilling the novices with optimism, 'and when you get up I want you to wave your arms to show me you're unharmed. Then take your toboggan down to the road and you will be collected.'

The fateful moment arrived an hour later. With no tuition apart from a brief explanation of where to hold on to your projectile, you're set on to the ice by a balaclava-ed Swiss assistant wearing large spiked boots. 'Don't forget to drag your feet,' he said as Willoughby announced, 'Hughes next rider' and dinged the bell.

I forgot, and was immediately out of control. A fairground rollercoaster was nothing compared to this. I zigzagged from side to side in the precipitous channel, rapidly picking up speed, shot round the first bend at about 45mph and positioned myself too high up the side to negotiate Shuttlecock, a tight left-hander. I flew over the edge and rolled over and over, my helmeted head rattling against hard ice. I had completely missed the safety straw and came to rest 25yds from the run. 'Good God, Hughes, that was a ghastly ride,' Willoughby declared over the tannoy. 'Take your toboggan down to the road.'

I noticed a stabbing pain in my right shoulder as I waved my arms, and I couldn't lift the sledge. I stood there, feeling stupid and helpless, and experiencing a flashback to the aftermath of being hit for six in the last over of the NatWest final. *'Hughes, take your toboggan down to the road. You're holding everyone up!*' A Swiss man lunged over to help. There was a large lump protruding from my shoulder blade. I staggered up the hill with Willoughby still haranguing me, and hung about shivering for a good half-hour until someone could drive me to a clinic. I'd had twenty seconds on the Cresta Run for my £150 investment, and you don't get a refund. It took the specialist about the same length of time to determine that I had broken my collarbone.

'It should heal in four weeks,' the doctor said, putting me in a figure-of-eight sling. That was a relief. I could get over the inconvenience well before the start of the season without Middlesex ever knowing. I wouldn't be flavour of the month if they found out what had happened, having not exactly complied with the request to 'ensure you stay fit in the winter months'. If I had to suffer nothing more serious than my wife's irritation – 'You total divot,' she said when she saw me – then there was little to worry about.

OUT OF THE PICTURE

Wednesday 10 April

Some hope. Also in our party was a *Daily Express* journalist, invited along to write a colour piece on the cricket. He had been at the Cresta that morning and had heard what happened, even if he hadn't seen it. 'Don't mention how I did this, if you don't mind,' I said naïvely. Not only did he promptly ring up the Middlesex secretary to get a comment, but he also probed Mike Gatting for a reaction, having broken the news to him. 'It's not my concern what players get up to in the winter,' Gatting said loyally.

The incident had a crippling influence on my life. The injury impaired my driving and two days later I lost control of a Range Rover in an icy St Moritz car park, badly damaging a Porsche and two BMWs. If you're going to have a prang, don't choose the most conspicuously wealthy town in

Switzerland for it. In fact, it's probably better not to drive anywhere if you've just broken your collarbone.

Worse, it didn't mend in time for Middlesex's first few matches, and this was to prove far more significant than I realised at the time. I was still allowed to go on the pre-season trip to the Algarve, a week of light training, golf and nightclubbing that left us less fit when we returned than we had been when we set off. I wasn't able to bowl, run or play golf, but it's miraculous how a few beers and thumping Europop can alleviate physical pain.

And for Jan it was one foul-up too many. I should have read the signs before, but I didn't until it was too late and she had met someone else.

It's funny how you look at the situation afterwards and wonder how you could have been so blind. The symptoms had been staring me in the face for weeks. The irascibility, the lack of affection, the unanswered phone when you rang home from abroad. Whether you have conveniently ignored what has been happening, or simply deluded yourself is hard to say, but stark, naked reality certainly pings open your eyes like ice blocks down the spine.

Jan was pretty and bright and complicated and I thought I'd never find anyone else I fancied this much, so I tried desperately to save the marriage. I couldn't bear the thought of being single again and *out there*. But for her we had passed the point of no return.

We had it out on 9 April and the agonising went on most of the night and into the following morning, so I was absent from the Middlesex photocall, the most important date in the pre-season calendar, when a posse of press men take individual mugshots and pictures of the team posing, in this case, with the championship trophy. Missing that is like being ill at home on the day of the school photo – you virtually cease to exist if you're not in it.

When I got into the dressing room late that morning Gatting exclaimed, 'Where the hell have you been?' in front of everyone. Before he could launch into a tirade, I cut in, more vehemently than I ever had in my life, 'Look, *don't* start,' I warned. 'Something serious has happened. Just *leave* it.' To his eternal credit, he did.

Men are not as good as women at expressing their emotions, and professional sportsmen are in an invidious position when ravaged by personal crises. It's just not done to say to the captain, 'Er, sorry, my wife's just left me, and I don't think I'll be able to bowl a good out-swinger today.' You have to give the impression of being tough and chipper even if you're fraught and confused and wondering whether the cad who stole your missus is better in bed. Your team is a collection of acquaintances rather than real friends, so there is no one to confide in. If you do blurt out the truth, as likely as not someone will offer a consoling line like: 'Well, you're not exactly an oil painting, are you?'

I sought solace in the Rev. Andrew Wingfield-Digby, a cricket nut and reputable player who happened to be at Lord's that day. He was doing the rounds of the counties offering his services as a kind of spiritual counsellor. I was a convinced atheist but found his rationality and sympathy invaluable at the time. I could explain the situation to him without fear of a severe ribbing and develop some kind of sensible response to the split-up. Wingfield-Digby did valuable work with the England team over the next couple of years, until he was unceremoniously swept out by Ray Illingworth's new broom in the summer of 1994. Introspective players like Chris Lewis, Graeme Hick and Robin Smith definitely benefited from his presence.

Jan and I made several attempts at a reconciliation, but all to no avail, and finally we amicably went our separate ways. There were no arguments about money and little dispute over possessions – there were plenty of wedding-present decanters and ornamental bowls to go round – and luckily no kids were involved. Well, none except me and her, anyway. I had finally qualified for the Middlesex divorcees society – almost a prerequisite for playing for the county. Brearley, Emburey, Barlow (twice), Tufnell, the late Wilf Slack and Cowans were all fully paid-up members. Come to think of it, Edrich and Compton had about ten wives between them.

Cricketers are more often beset by marriage problems than most other sportsmen, and in retrospect it's easy to see why. It has nothing to do with making teas or getting green stains out of whites. Lest anyone needs reminding, cricket takes an interminable time to play, and in the summer the husbands are always away, forcing the wives to be self-sufficient. In the winter they are always at home (except when on an England tour – and then they are abroad for much longer periods than other sports tourists) and tend to get under their partners' feet. Players' moods fluctuate with their fortunes on the cricketing rollercoaster which lurches alarmingly up and down the condensed peaks and troughs. Success is relayed blow by blow; failure leaves them sitting in morose silence. They continue the cynical dressing-room piss-taking at the domestic dinner table, showing particular insensitivity when addressing any of the wife's neuroses. When girls fret about the cut of a skirt or the colour of a top they've just bought, they probably don't want to be dismissed with, 'Well, it'd look all right on Elle MacPherson.'

You wonder how the longest-serving other halves, the Mrs Gattings and Mrs Bothams, have survived. It's probably through a combination of inner strength, bloody-mindedness and the fact that their husbands are not away part of the time, but virtually all of it.

THE HAT-TRICK DELIVERY

Thursday 16 May, Cambridge
Inevitably I wasn't all there for the first month of the season, and it was probably just as well my damaged collarbone prohibited me from playing. When I did finally get an outing, at Fenner's, it was eight months since I had last bowled in earnest – the two wickets in two balls to clinch the 1990 championship at Hove.

A Lot of Hard Yakka

Cowans and Ellcock took the new ball and the build-up to my big moment was further disrupted by a sudden shower. After the stoppage, Emburey, the acting captain, said, 'OK, Yozzer, you start from the Pavilion End.' John Crawley was batting. This was my chance to go into the record books with the longest-spanning hat-trick in history.

An attacking field was stationed – three slips, two gullies and a short leg. I marked out my run-up carefully, loosened up ferociously and tried a couple of practice deliveries to mid-off. Then I told everyone, including a couple of local photographers, to be ready, and gave Crawley a meaningful stare. I tore to the wicket wind-assisted, leaped vigorously into the delivery stride . . . and bowled a wide. I didn't take a wicket in the match, never mind the over.

CAT ON HOT BRICKS

Monday 24 June, Sheffield

Benefits are all-consuming, which can be quite valuable if the rest of your life is in turmoil. You need every minute you can get to run a one-year business with an eventual turnover of around £300,000, and actually having to play cricket or contemplate single life is a negligible side issue. I was in the Middlesex XI to play the West Indies tourists, and spent almost the entire match on my feet: when I wasn't bowling or fielding, I was rushing between dressing rooms getting bats signed by the two teams and then hawking them round hospitality boxes before lunch. I returned at tea to collect the money. In the match my bowling got a bit of a pasting. For once I had a decent excuse.

I became so preoccupied that I drove around to matches on autopilot, and on one occasion found myself lost in Sheffield town centre with no idea of where I was going. I used memory dial-up on my mobile phone to try to ring the Middlesex office but got through instead to my occasional drinking partner

Henry Kelly on the set of *Going for Gold*. He wasn't a lot of help directing me to the ground at Abbeydale Park, but at least I booked him to speak at a dinner.

No wonder I couldn't find Abbeydale. It's so far out of Sheffield it's almost in the Peak District, and used to be in Derbyshire until the county boundaries were changed after the war. The surrounding tree-lined avenues and salubrious neighbourhoods are certainly a world apart from Sheffield's grime and deprivation. The ground itself sloped so much you had to park your car in gear for fear it might burst down an embankment and shoot across the pitch behind the bowler's arm.

Yorkshire players still talked in hushed tones about the time Wayne Daniel, playing at Sheffield for the West Indies, got so much vicious lift he put three local batsmen in hospital, so I was interested to see what the pitch would be like. A green flier puts the veteran seam bowler under pressure because he is expected to take wickets, but it does make a pleasant change from lifeless featherbeds. In the intervening years, however, someone had sapped the Abbeydale pitch of its succulent juices, rendering it another dead animal.

This meant the spinners did a lot of bowling, which ought to have pleased Phil Tufnell, who was vying to get back into the England squad after some erratic performances in Australia. But he seemed to have got out of bed on the wrong side before the third day and became very stroppy when he couldn't have the field he wanted to set. A series of outbursts culminated in a mega-tantrum when a mishit drive cleared deep mid-off without going for six. Tufnell was livid and blamed Gatting for failing to position the man on the fence and the fielder himself for failing to soar 20ft off the ground to make the catch. He swore, kicked the turf and refused to go on until he got his own way, as children often do in supermarkets, knowing that their parents will give in rather than create a spectacle.

Gatting had seen it all before. His patience snapped and after an altercation which must have been audible to everyone within a two-mile radius, he sent Tufnell off the field and threatened to punish him. Public humiliation had become the only way to control him. Tufnell came over all sheepish after the game, holding up his hand in conciliation, though he had further angered Gatting by taking a risky single in the last over of the game, obliging me to play out time to salvage a nail-biting draw.

As I said, Tufnell was nicknamed the Cat chiefly because he spent a lot of time asleep, but the sobriquet developed extra piquancy as he began to reveal a dark centre of self-obsession and worry. He had become more concerned about how his action looked when he bowled than about whether he was doing a good job for the team, and he sought constant reassurance. 'It is coming out all right, innit?' he'd mutter to me at mid-off, having been smacked through the covers, adding at the end of his spell, 'I didn't get cut too much, did I?'

At the crease he had a reputation for being scared of any bowler with a mean expression, irrespective of how fast he was. 'I'm not obviously backing away, am I?' he'd twitter in between overs, conscious that fast bowlers and jittery batsmen have the same relationship as Rottweilers and nervous post-men. He was a perfectly capable tail-ender, but he preferred going in number 11 because when he was out he didn't have to walk off the field on his own. He got a bit twitchy whenever the TCCB drug-testers turned up and divided up the scorecard into little pieces, picking out two names at random. He didn't want to get in trouble for taking cough mixture or catarrh remedies. 'What am I going to have to do? What will it show up?' he exclaimed nervously once when his name was called. 'Probably that your blood's yellow,' someone said.

Many less enlightened counties wouldn't have tolerated Tufnell, and he put the England selectors in a dilemma, too. They knew he was the canniest left-arm spinner in the country, with excellent control and a devilish ball-on-a-string delivery which lured countless batsmen out of their ground with fatal results. He could also be a boon in the dressing room with his eccentric mannerisms and acerbic wit. He came out with occasional brilliant one-liners and was often good company. The downside was this excessive navel-gazing and a question-mark over his resilience under fire, which had already been exposed in Australia.

Gooch was perturbed by him and so, later, was Atherton, particularly when he went AWOL in the Caribbean, but Gatting handled him superbly. He respected Tufnell's ability and inestimable value, and allowed him plenty of leeway, but he did put his foot down if he strayed too far out of line. Gatting threatened suspension during the tantrum in the Yorkshire game and afterwards stuck to his guns. Tufnell was 'expelled' for a week.

IRISH INTERLUDE

26 June, Dublin

Seven days' compulsory relief from the county treadmill might be a godsend if it spared you a boring time in Derby or Leicester, but Tufnell's punishment coincided with a trip to Dublin, where Middlesex were playing Ireland in the NatWest. As far as 'domestic' cricketing venues go, this is the crème de la crème. The hospitality is, to use a Truemanism, 'oonbi-leevable', the city is a jewel and the national cricket team a pushover. Dublin beckons you with its warmth and humility and animation and radiant girls with hypnotic blue eyes. You have no qualms (and no choice) about making the visit a seventy-two-hour party.

The Irish have this amazing habit of welcoming you as if they haven't seen an English visitor since the Reverend Ian Paisley first vented his spleen on the airwaves. They seem to be genuinely surprised that you'd bother to dip into their insignificant little world. 'Bejaysus, yis nat fram London are yis?' they exclaim. 'Oi was dere meself in nointeen fiftee-tree. Oi'll bet it's still a mervelis place.' Their cricketers fawn over you like long-lost brothers and eagerly lead the way to their favourite dens of iniquity. If this is a crafty plan to weaken the visitors' resolve with a dozen pints of Guinness, it rarely works. The home players are the ones who end up horizontal.

John Emburey almost became a victim, however. The sixty-over match was spread over two days because of a sharp storm during the Irish reply, which soon reduced the flaky Clontarf pitch to the consistency of soggy Weetabix. The drinking in the clubhouse therefore started early, and finished late – Emburey and I were still stumbling about the hotel foyer at gone 4 a.m. It was only when I got to bed that I remembered I still had ten overs to bowl in the match, whereas he, the ultimate pro, had already completed his stint of twelve (at a miserly cost of 13). He spent the following morning indisposed on the physio's couch – only about the second time he'd been off the field in his entire eighteen-year career – while I laboured gingerly through my spell.

Two Iranian Shekels

Wednesday 3 July, Middlesex v Essex, Lord's
The curse was still with me when we flew back to immediately begin a three-day match at Lord's. A hot, stifling morning broke a sequence of showers and the sun drew the moisture up from the ground, making the atmosphere and pitch clammy. We should have bowled Essex out for 150, but alcoholic sweat was still seeping out of our pores and by midday they'd already rattled up 90. A large proportion of these runs were scored off my first spell, which was liberally sprinkled with long hops and full tosses. When an understandably irritated Gatting sighed, 'Have a blow, Yozzer,' after my sixth over had cost 13, Graham Gooch, 46 not out, said: 'Oh, are you coming off? I was rather enjoying that.'

We lost the game by a mile and I then contracted a knee injury, so I was out of the team. All the same, this was probably not the reason why my benefit collections on subsequent

Sundays at Lord's contained such an odd assortment of tender. I took the unprecedented step of persuading flirtatious girlfriends in short skirts to go round with the buckets instead of the loyal old supporters who normally did it, and they regularly brought in £1,000 plus. The English currency – mostly coins but sometimes the odd fiver – was always augmented by francs, dollars, fruit-machine tokens and any other shrapnel people happened to have in their pockets.

It was the usual practice for the MCC to broadcast the proceeds over the tannoy once they had been counted, and one Sunday I got them to announce: 'Simon Hughes thanks everyone who donated to today's benefit collection, which raised 1,230 pounds, 30 pence, 70 Canadian cents, 50 pesetas, 1 Kenyan shilling and 2 Iranian shekels.' It got a better response than anything I'd ever achieved on the field, and all the collectors chuckled with self-satisfaction. We weren't quite so amused when the next morning we read that Bryan Robson's benefit match at Old Trafford had raised £340,000.

LORD'S GIVETH AND LORD'S TAKETH AWAY

Friday 12 July, Middlesex Office
My injury freed me to hang about at Test matches cornering any legends who happened to be popping in to sign my prints or replica scorecards for auction. These included Garfield Sobers, loitering at the Grace Gates while the steward searched for his umbrella; Sunil Gavaskar, a BBC teatime guest, R.E.S. Wyatt, England's oldest surviving captain, and still perspicacious; and Compton and Miller, who were hobbling out of a hospitality tent. 'DeFreitas a Test bowler? Pah!' Compton was saying.

I also had more time to compose articles and filed a strong column about the inadequacies of county coaches after Mickey Stewart had been unfairly denounced for paying a fleeting visit to Derby to patch up Devon Malcolm's bowling action.

A Lot of Hard Yakka

'Most counties employ a full-time coach who travels everywhere with the first team,' I wrote. 'But apart from a distant glance at the nets, supervision of fielding practice and organising the teatime sandwiches, many are little more than administrators. Hordes of young players complain that their coach never says anything to them.'

This got me in hot water on two counts. First, I had neglected to have the piece vetted by the Middlesex secretary, Joe Hardstaff (though this was more accidental than deliberate), and second, it was seen as something of a poisonous barb at our own coach, Don Bennett. Although I thought him rather one dimensional, and he certainly wasn't everyone's cup of tea, he'd done his utmost for Middlesex since his debut in 1950 (he became coach in the 1970s) and understandably, he took it badly and remained terse for the rest of the summer. The committee also took a dim view, particularly as I had been warned before about failing to get my copy scrutinised. After two short hearings with the hierarchy, I was fined £500.

My disintegrated knee was operated on a week before my nominated benefit match, a Sunday League game against Lancashire, denying me any chance of playing. Gatting allowed me to toss up and auction the job of twelfth man, bought by a high-flying executive who was appropriately made to grovel around for spare gloves and sweaters in players' coffins. (Some hadn't been cleaned out for several years, so it could be a bit like putting your hand in a lucky dip, except that old stained jockstraps, worn-down studs and smelly insoles hardly constituted favourable prizes.) My reward for the day was 40 per cent of the gate receipts, which amounted to £8,435. Not quite in Bryan Robson's league, but then I didn't risk breaking a leg every time I went for the ball.

Indeed, a pair of creaking knees wasn't an insufferable consequence of 4,000 overs into the wind over eleven years, and I was confident of a decent comeback, until one morning I was called into the secretary's office. 'The chairman of cricket would like to see you,' he said.

Bob Gale, a Middlesex player of the previous generation,

sat at a desk in the next room. A corpulent figure with a benign face hiding behind large rectangular glasses, he looked unusually grave. 'Simon,' he began earnestly, 'I'm sorry to have to tell you that the club might not be offering you a contract next season.' I was dumbstruck. 'The committee remarked you haven't been taking wickets like you used to, and you have been picking up a few more injuries lately.'

'But one had nothing to do with cricket,' I protested anxiously, alluding to my accident on the Cresta Run.

'It's just a warning,' the chairman went on. 'I don't like having to say it; you've been a marvellous servant to Middlesex.' It brought to mind Bradman's oft-quoted remark: 'Batsmen are the darlings of the committees; bowlers are cricket's labourers.'

'What can I do?' I asked helplessly.

'You can go and take wickets in the second team and prove you've still got some firepower,' he answered. I looked down despondently at my bandaged knee and returned an expression of dismay and non-comprehension. 'Do your best,' he added. 'The decision hasn't been made yet.' The use of the word 'yet' left a bitter aftertaste. Had they really made up their minds, and were just breaking it to me gently, or could they be swayed in my favour over the next few weeks?

HIT THE ROAD, JACK

Monday 26 August

I knew Middlesex would announce the new contracts in early September, so there wasn't much time. I had a fortnight to get fit and make an impact. I worked harder on my fitness than I ever had before and opened the bowling for the Second XI ten days later at Southgate in front of their one regular supporter, Kay, a tireless octogenarian, and a few anonymous passers-by. I took five wickets in the first innings, and made a few runs in the second, watched by Gatting, who turned up on the last day. Would it make a difference? I asked hopefully. He pulled a resigned face and said it probably wouldn't.

Early the following week I was summoned to see Gale again. I was bricking it. With as much sympathy as he could muster, he informed me that the committee would not be offering me another contract. 'They thank you for all you've done for Middlesex,' he said by way of consolation.

The reality hit me immediately and I was crying as soon as I'd left the room. I'd been sacked, got the bullet, been cast on to that terrible heap of withered arms and legs. All those years of toil seemed to have vaporised and I felt spent and worthless, like an old washing machine thrown on the tip. Cricket defined me, gave me a position and an identity. Accountants might collect Van Morrison albums, bankers go parachuting at weekends, computer-programmers participate in the Campaign for Real Ale. They have some leisure pursuit to get fixated about and take their minds off their job. Cricket was my job *and* my hobby. Without it I didn't know who I was, or what I was going to do.

No one prepares for this moment, or expects it. The longer your career goes on, the more you delude yourself that you still have a value and that experience carries more weight than youth. You take your own competence for granted and sniff privately at young pretenders, reclining in silent relief if one of them gets his comeuppance on the field. It's mean and uncharitable, but it's vital to abide by the laws of the jungle. If you don't erect the barricade, your home will be invaded.

Just because you're older it doesn't necessarily mean you're wiser. I pondered the wisdom of having attempted the Cresta Run a few weeks before the start of the season. As my abbreviated ride had effectively cost me £3,000 in medical fees and car repairs, my marriage and now my job, it wouldn't probably rank as one of the greatest decisions ever made.

To professional sportsmen, the pinnacle of success is not winning or being a hero, but gaining the overall respect of your colleagues as their Man of the Match or Player of the Season. The sack is their nadir, the ultimate rejection. It casts away virtually a lifetime of devotion bordering on addiction, of habitual behaviour, and of reliance on freebie gear. I hadn't bought a T-shirt or a pair of trainers for twelve years.

Venturing into the dressing room, you feel like an outsider, a person who doesn't belong, a state of mind reinforced by the realisation that someone has already taken over your locker. Players pull long, sympathetic expressions, as if you've just had a leg amputated. And, come to think of it, that would be just about the only thing worse.

Salvation

I was granted no sentimental leaving parties or misty-eyed final appearances or tokens of gratitude from the Middlesex committee. Nothing. Not a sausage. But 1991 was not a total *annus horribilis*: having heard me occasionally on radio, the BBC enlisted me to do some TV commentary on an end-of-season match between Essex and Victoria, the Sheffield Shield champions.

It satisfied another of my ambitions: to share the microphone with the incomparable Richie Benaud. He was a pleasure to work with and has a remarkable ability to make the most prescient comment on the game while his attention is apparently elsewhere. I was also surprised to discover that his sideways glance at the camera is not an in-vision affectation. He talks to everyone as if he's looking over their shoulder.

In October, with my Middlesex benefit engine still chugging along – a rather incongruous state of affairs, considering that I was no longer a registered player – I was contacted by Geoff Cook, the head honcho of English cricket's new eighteenth county, Durham. They would need some older lags to tide them over for a couple of years, he said, and I fitted the bill. He fitted mine, too – offering me £20,000, more than I'd ever earned before.

Money wasn't the principal reason for signing though. The

excitement of being in at the start of a new venture was one; my allegiance to Durham from my student days was another. The chance to play in the same team as Ian Botham, the most famous English cricketing figure since W.G. Grace, was the clinching factor. Was he really such an icon of victory and daredevilry and late nights as he was cracked up to be? Without a shadow of doubt.

REHAB: 1992

the eighteenth county • Botham and the dolcelatte • 5000 volt Jones • local heroes • Larkins' piece of piss • guard of honour • wooden spoon • striptease?

BOTHAM

My close association with English cricket's greatest showman began inauspiciously. I lured him to speak at my last benefit dinner, a celebrity-loaded event in Durham, and put him up overnight at a smart hotel. I stayed at a considerably less salubrious establishment up the road – more like a dosshouse than a hotel – with two attractive female friends I'd roped in to help. They were both single, and I was too, so the prospect of teaming up with one of them in the afterglow of a prestigious evening looked good.

My hopes were dashed as soon as I arrived in our shabby foyer. All dolled up waiting for the taxi, the girls had suddenly been ambushed by two local thugs who'd burst into reception, uttered various oaths and then spat at them. The girls were livid, mainly because crying had smudged their mascara. I tried to console them and verbally reproached myself for having not been there to defend them.

My sympathy fell on stony ground. Maybe they knew that in reality I'd have run a mile. 'Men are either scum or wimps,' one of them said, and the other backed her up. It didn't stop them flirting with the punters all evening, sitting on their laps and later exchanging phone numbers. Selective memories, women. Still, at least the evening nudged my benefit past the magic £100,000 mark, effectively doubling my earnings from twelve summers of county cricket. *Doubling*. And people wonder why we have benefits.

I didn't see Botham again for six months. He was abroad all winter and missed Durham's pre-season training, which mostly took place in a dingy indoor centre on wasteland by a main road, the sort of place you'd usually find a B&Q. He was present at the photocall on Good Friday at my old university ground, and afterwards he and I and Durham's overseas player, the Australian Dean Jones, retired to the students' favourite haunt, the Dun Cow, for a few pints of Castle Eden.

'Can I get a Durham badge for my helmet?' Jones asked as soon as we sat down. 'I can't play for a team and not be properly decked out. I hate all these geezers who wear their England gear on the field in a county game.' I was impressed by that. Botham promised to use his timeshare on the River Tay to take Jones fishing and the pair of them were soon slapping the table and laughing at each other's stories.

I found it odd that two men who had been locked in mortal combat and sledging each other during the World Cup only a month before could carry on now as if they'd always been bosom pals. But then, most exhibitionists practise this kind of duplicity. Rival politicians do it, so do barristers and chat-show hosts. The teeth-baring is really a mark of respect.

Botham's legendary winning powers were soon in evidence. Durham's inaugural home match was a Sunday League game against the one-day supremos, Lancashire. The Racecourse Ground, quintessentially English, overlooked by a cathedral, a castle and a prison – representatives of our three most regressive institutions – was full by one o'clock and the Battle of Portaloo had already begun. With only six toilets provided for 6,000 people, you needed to know you might want a waz at least half an hour before you actually did.

Having faced the first ball of the match, Botham didn't make many and his bowling was collared. But he took a flying catch to dismiss Neil Fairbrother and when Lancashire's last pair needed 10 to win off the final over (bowled by me), he pounced at short mid-wicket and threw down the stumps with the batsman inches short. The roar was tumultuous. 'All part of having a good scriptwriter,' he boasted, struggling off surrounded by joyous supporters. The pubs in Durham were still heaving at 4 a.m.

Two days later Botham rescued Durham's ailing innings

against Glamorgan, galvanised by the presence of his great friend Viv Richards in the field. 'Come on Watti, donledemoff-dehook,' Richards kept saying to the bowler Steve Watkin. Botham made 86, then came on to bowl his mesmerising medium-pacers and, having dismissed Maynard with a regulation half-volley, produced a piece of pure inspiration.

Richards had been propping forward apprehensively, desperate not to get out to his mate. Trying to turn an innocuous ball to leg, he got a leading edge which a 17st Botham grasped full length an inch above the turf. His dive caused a small tremor in the ground and an eruption in the crowd, but drew no reaction from Richards, who strolled off, blinking like a cat that is barely awake.

The season carried on in this vein. Botham's performances on the field fluctuated, but his overall impact was, like his body, vast (his calves are the diameter of chimney pots). He took useful wickets, played influential innings and cajoled colleagues, sometimes announcing in the dressing room that if he saw anyone not trying, 'they'll feel my boot against the seat of their pants'. His mere presence was enough to inhibit some opponents. Even when he got out to an atrocious shot, his self-belief remained intact and he blamed the pitch, the umpire or, on one occasion, a man flashing a mirror beside the sightscreen. A steward was dispatched to flush out the culprit, but none was found.

An impregnable ego is fundamental to any great sportsman. They cannot be seen to doubt their own superiority. Pride, some call it. Anyone who tampers with it risks being crushed underfoot, regardless of the situation. That in itself betrays a whiff of insecurity. What, Botham insecure? Judge for yourself.

We were having an Italian meal one night in Canterbury, and the head waiter had rolled out the red carpet, giving us the best table, drinks on the house, etc., as always happened when Botham walked into a restaurant. After dessert he fancied some cheese.

'Can you bring me some dolecetti?' he asked. The waiter looked blank.

'Don't you mean dolcelatte?' I intercepted.

'That's what I said, dolecetti,' he repeated.

'No, it's dolce*latte*,' I insisted, rather labouring the point.

There was a slight pause while he absorbed the information. Then he snapped: 'Well, how many bloody Test wickets did you get?'

This desire to always have the last word is embedded in his uncompromising personality. When I turned up on the third night of one of his charity walks, he was halfway through dinner with his entourage. 'Great to see you, Yozzer,' he said, 'but you're two days late. That's a pound in the kitty.'

'What for, to buy you a razor?' I retorted. His beloved moustache was for once submerged in a field of stubble.

'I shouldn't mention hair growth if I were you,' he countered. 'That's another pound for being balder than last time.'

For all his confrontational demeanour, he was extremely generous, and loved company. He threw lavish parties at his splendid pile in north Yorkshire, only partly to ensure that leading members of the opposition would crawl tentatively out of bed the next morning and succumb tamely to his bowling. During an away trip he laid on a magnificent golf day for the Durham team at a country club near Chepstow where he was a member. He invited me to stay at the family home one night and we sat round the dinner table with Kath and the kids, consuming roast chicken and New Zealand Sauvignon Blanc. They seemed happy and content and at ease with each other. Liam, then 15, and Ian behaved more like brothers than father and son.

I'd fallen asleep in my Nottingham hotel room the night before one match when the phone went. It was 2 a.m.

'Yoz, fancy sharing a bottle of burgundy?' Botham said.

'But Beefy, it's the middle of the night,' I whined.

'Look, I'm in the next-door room,' he went on. 'If you're not in here in five minutes I'll come and drag you out.'

I went of course. We sat talking for an hour about cricket politics and the ineptness of the TCCB while a Guns'n'Roses concert blared out on TV.

'Shall I order another bottle?' he said eventually, having drunk most of the first.

'No,' I said, and escaped to bed.

Wherever Botham was, he coveted attention, an audience. He craved the company of cricketing colleagues off the field as much as the applause and compliments on it. Did he have any *real* friends, I wondered? His wife, certainly. She stood up to him and his chequered past probably gave her a psychological authority. But it is hard for anyone else to really relate to him. There were any number of sidekicks willing to help out with this or that – the solicitor, the light-aircraft pilot, the local publican who supplied barrels of beer and racing tips. There was mutual trust and loyalty, but Botham's immense aura, which left everything else floundering in its wake, made his inner feelings inaccessible.

He was also a victim of his own popularity. He was a virtual prisoner in the pavilion, knowing he would be besieged by a starstruck public if he left it, and constantly burdened by requests for favours and fan mail. He got about fifteen letters a day from all sorts of loonies. One, from Cochin, India, read: 'Dear Mr Botham, We very much enjoyed the way you danced after taking a wicket in the World Cup. This is to ask you if you would be interested in importing cashew nuts from factories here in Kerala . . . You might be able to set up a shop.'

Bored in the dressing room, he snoozed, shuffled papers, or phoned Allan Lamb or Robin Smith with some snippet he'd gleaned on a filly running in the 3.30 at Redcar. When he'd exhausted all other possibilities, he passed the time thinking up silly nicknames: Durham's tall, lolloping captain, David Graveney, who fell over at the slightest hint of a long chase to the boundary, became Victor, the prostrate giraffe; I was Pluto (on another planet), then THE, which stood for The Hairy Egg.

Obviously, he had his own agenda. He turned up more or less when he liked and rarely practised, another of his little insecurities, in a way. Failure is so much more demeaning if you start out totally prepared. Instead, he spent the half-hour before a match using bats and balls to indulge in a putting game round the outfield with Wayne Larkins. The bowlers were mightily relieved that neither had much inclination to bat in the nets as it saved us constantly having to trudge half a mile to fetch the ball back.

Botham's sheer presence turned a match, any match, into an event. That was the key essence of it for me. Four-day cricket had become routine, a bit of a grind; one-day matches were formularised. The game was stocked with good, work-manlike pros; flair players were either left out or obliged to rein in their natural exuberance. There was very little imaginative or daring captaincy. County cricket had stagnated, and was at times soporific. Understandably, the 'crowd' were often about as animated as a bunch of waxworks.

But no one nodded off to sleep when *he* was batting or bowling (least of all the fielders), and at slip *he* was always liable to do something out of the ordinary, even if it was to blame a glinting, flapping tarpaulin 100yds away for causing him to shell a catch. Grounds were filling up again in expectation, and all Durham's one-day matches were sold out weeks in advance. It gave our existence as professional cricketers a tangible point. We were performers seeking a reaction, there to give pleasure (or pain), and to be enjoyed (or groaned at). Botham's name on the scoresheet ensured we weren't just a statistic in a newspaper. You can't knock that.

LOCAL WORSHIP

The euphoric Durham supporters had their own heroes. They loved Graveney for his honesty, his steadiness and reliability, his resilience to defeat and magnetic attraction to bouncers. They crooned at Paul Parker's brilliant fielding and courageous batting, blissfully unaware of his hyperactivity – he regularly strummed 'And Where Do You Go To, My Lovely?' on his guitar at five in the morning, read *Ulysses* on the hoof during the lunch interval and manically surfed the radio stations in the car on the way home. He made Chris Evans seem laid back.

Dean Jones was an invigorating asset, introducing novel fielding routines, playing brilliant innings, gibing at opponents from slip and motivating colleagues with enthusiastic encouragement. 'That's a top effort, you're doing fantastically,' he said as we met in mid-pitch after an over from Curtly Ambrose. He meant it, too, in spite of the fact that I'd just played and missed at all six deliveries. He was the most electrifying person I'd ever played with, and was appreciated by everyone except the opposition.

People marvelled, too, at the way Phil Bainbridge would mesmerise batsmen with his dribbly assortment of slow swingers and loopy slower balls, and was able to play nuggety innings on four hours' sleep and a bloodstream that was 40 per cent proof. 'Cos kick a bo agin a wo and 'ed it till it bosses,' he said in exaggerated Potteries-speak (meaning 'Let's kick a ball around and head it till it bursts'). Bainbridge was indestructible. Then there were the popular local diehards: Simon Brown, who sustained us with his dependable bowling, and Andy Fothergill, who kept us going with his spontaneous humour. 'He's that desperate after a few beers he'd shag a barber's floor,' he observed about one colleague.

Most of all they worshipped Ned. As time moves on, some things change, others remain constant. Musical and artistic tastes have shifted radically in the last twenty years, but Wayne Larkins's batting style has not altered one iota, and neither has his nickname, borrowed from the *Archers* character, Ned Larkins. Watch any rerun of Northants matches in the 1970s and you'll spot a solid moustachioed character with fuzzy hair who shuffles across his stumps and whips a startled bowler lazily over mid-wicket.

If you'd been at Darlington, Stockton, Gateshead Fell or any of the other Durham grounds in the 1990s, you would have seen exactly the same thing. The locks had gone greyer, the face was a little more wrinkled, the fingers had been bashed to bits, but the moustache was identical, the shuffle survived, the shots were still clean, crisp and effortless. The beauty of Larkins's batting was its unrefined purity, in stark contrast to his lungs and liver, which had had to endure umpteen fags a day and a predominantly liquid diet since youth.

The regal cover drive, the emphatic pull, the languid legside pick-up were all worth the admission money alone. He was more naturally gifted than any other batsman in the land, and no attack escaped his power. He took a century off every county he played against. One particular over in July 1992 summed up Larkins to a T. The Durham openers had to survive five overs in the evening against the Leicester fast bowler David Millns, rampaging down the hill at Grace Road.

Millns took an early wicket, and, with five minutes to go, tore at Larkins. The first two deliveries fizzed close to his jaw and thwacked into the keeper's gloves, still rising. I, the nightwatchman, stood quaking in my boots at the other end. The third was another flesh-seeking lifter. Larkins swayed back and thrashed it past cover.

The fourth spat from a length and nearly took his hand off; the fifth grazed his right shoulder. Certain he had Larkins for the taking, Millns sought a fuller length with the last, expecting a rattle of furniture. Larkins launched it through the covers and into the boundary boards with such force it rebounded back to the bowler. Walking up the wicket at the end of the over in shock, I expected some adrenaline-induced comment or morsel of advice. All he grunted was, 'Piece of piss,' and walked back.

Always an enigma, capable of taming the world's fastest bowlers yet strangely vulnerable to the innocuous dobber, Larkins's relaxed posture in the dressing room – puffing away in a corner, laughing infectiously – concealed a fierce competitiveness which only properly surfaced against the most demanding bowling or after his eighth pint. He was an immense admirer of Gordon Greenidge and had all his skill and panache but only a smidgen of his hunger. The difference between Greenidge's 7,558 Test runs and Larkins's 493 was simply attitude.

So, armed with his essentials – a chunky bat, a bottle of shampoo and twenty Benson & Hedges – he intoxicated middle England with his swashbuckling batting on the field and awesome stamina off it. He was a simple man of simple pleasures. Offer him a bouncy wicket, a hearty lunch and a few beers, and he was happy. I envied his natural talent, but I had also learned that personal gratification is so much more intense if it is harder to attain.

A NO-WIN SITUATION

July, Durham v Middlesex

Durham played Middlesex twice during the season. They were huge matches for me, and I was subconsciously fired up against my old colleagues. Every player wants to remind former team-mates of his value and to banish bad impressions. In the second round of the NatWest Trophy at Uxbridge I came on to bowl when Gatting had just taken guard, and I was determined not to let myself down. I gave him nothing and my accuracy surprised him. I took three wickets before a short stoppage for rain. On our way back out, Emburey, who hadn't yet faced a ball, said, 'I'd love to hang around long enough so I can carve you just once over extra cover!' He edged his first ball to the keeper and I finished with 4–41.

'Oh, Simon, why did you leave Middlesex?' a female supporter asked as I walked through the members' enclosure. 'We rather liked you.'

'Because I was asked to,' I replied matter-of-factly.

Two weeks after knocking Middlesex out of the NatWest (the satisfaction blemished by conscience), Durham were at Lord's for a championship match. It was weird being there as an opposing player, although the visitors' facilities were familiar as Middlesex had twice been obliged to move out of their home dressing room during my time there, having lost the pavilion 'toss' in cup finals. The stewards and other employees offered me a most gracious welcome back, and, walking out to bat on the Saturday, I was given a standing ovation by the crowd, and the players, led by Gatting and Emburey, formed a little guard of honour at the wicket. It made the hairs on the back of my neck (there weren't many on my head) stand on end. I suppose it was like experiencing your own obituary. It didn't, however, prevent Tufnell from mischievously suggesting to one of the pacemen, 'Come on, stick it up his nose,' when I hung around for a while.

Middlesex trounced our makeshift side in two and a half days and Durham's form gradually slipped. The atmosphere in the dressing room was always lively, but it lacked a hard overall edge, especially when Jones had to return home early. There were none of the cruel but galvanising barbs that winning teams thrive on. Although the county was desperate to avoid finishing bottom of the table, the ruthlessness and cocky self-belief just wasn't there.

The support was, though. Even on the last day of the season, when Durham were already confirmed as wooden-spoonists and about to be crucified by Lancashire, there was still a good smattering of well-wishers braving the autumnal air, and many climbed over the boards at the end of the match, shook us by the hand and thanked us for all our efforts. I had never seen this before, and it emphasised the exceptional warmth of the Durham people, who put their sportsmen on pedestals and always, always offer encouragement. We were recognised and fêted wherever we went in the area.

Captivated by my new identity and bewitched by all the admiring attention, I reclined at the bar of a cricket theme pub in London, unconcerned by the lateness of a friend. In this conducive environment, someone's bound to come up and ask me about the season, I thought. A youngish bloke did wander over and look at me in a comprehending sort of way. Then he said: 'Excuse me, you're not the strippagram are you, by any chance?'

LAST RITES: 1993

four-day extension • Sunday brunch • self-
service Gower • the twilight of the Gods • a
fine pair • it's all over now • dirty tricks

COLD REALITY

I knew 1993 would be my last season. Botham knew it would be his, too. Four-day cricket had arrived in full and Durham were rightly anxious to give their young players maximum opportunity. Anyway, Durham's too cold for old crocks. Also I'd been invited to become cricket correspondent of the *Independent on Sunday*. I'd gradually wind down my Durham commitments and do what I could for the paper, then retire from playing in September and take on the job full time. I was pleased with the arrangement; it gave me something to look forward to and would keep me in the game.

I kept a diary of the summer.

Wednesday 7 April, North York Moors
Twelve counties have jetted off to sunnier climes for pre-season training, but Durham's is in a dusty old gym. Back to square one for me, then. Only difference from thirteen years ago is we're at Ampleforth College in north Yorkshire, a school run by Benedictine monks. They're occasionally seen practising in the nets with pads buckled on underneath their black cassocks.

No bleep test, thank God; more skill work than lung exercise. Also every player is consulted by a psychologist and given a practical demonstration of first aid by a man from the Red Cross. We might not be any good, but at least now everyone can deal mentally with finishing bottom and is qualified to give the kiss of life if one of our batsmen is poleaxed.

Wednesday 28 April, Durham v Minor Counties, Hartlepool
Our first serious match, with the Benson & Hedges Cup now a straight knock-out. Two Botham sixes relieved the pressure of a tense chase. He's been a bit irritating lately – extremely

contemptuous of practice matches (deliberately letting balls through his legs), but fiercely competitive if it's for real. Also on the positive side, he's wangled us a good supply of those wrap-around Oakley sunglasses. Afterwards Peter Willey, making his debut as an umpire, used the players' showers.

'When have we got you again then, Will?' Botham asked.

'Oh, June, Gateshead Fell, against Middlesex. But you'll have lost interest by then, Beefy.'

We all laughed.

Sunday 9 May, Lancashire v Durham, Old Trafford

Graeme Fowler was straight back to his old Manchester haunt as Durham's new opening bat. He reckons joining a new county is like changing your girlfriend. 'You don't realise how bad the last one was until you get to know another.'

The preliminaries to our first fifty-over Sunday League match began quirkily at 11 a.m., when sixteen-year-old Liam Botham drilled a straight drive on to his father's shin on the practice ground.

'That's the last time I'm coming into the nets,' Beefy winced, conveniently forgetting that it was also the first time for about five years.

Our new polyester coloured clothing gave us nipple rash and as 'lunch' between innings was not until 3.10 p.m., I was famished midway through, and on the boundary had to ask a spectator to buy me a packet of crisps. When Mike Watkinson came in to bat, umpire Nigel Plews asked him what he wanted. Noticing the official's bright blue coat, Watkinson said, 'Six gallons and a can of oil, please.'

Saturday 15 May, Durham v Hampshire, Stockton

Our enjoyable viewing of the FA Cup final (Arsenal v Sheffield Wednesday) was rudely interrupted by umpires Meyer and Holder announcing that rain had abated and play would start at 4.15. Spikes is semi-content. Kept out of the Hampshire team by the arrival of David Gower, at least as twelfth man he could continue to watch the football, and it was freezing outside. They'd had snow on the hills nearby. I tried to bowl in three shirts, a tracksuit top and two sweaters on a pitch like rolled snot.

Gower made a fluent fifty. The fact that he's still keen for an England recall was emphasised by excellent shot selection, exquisite timing and the decision not to walk after gloving a catch to leg slip. Despite playing against Gower maybe twenty times, I don't feel I've ever really got to know him. People say he's shy, but to me he seems a deliberately closed person, almost totally self-sufficient. Affable, but he never lets his guard down.

Actually, star batsmen are generally hard to befriend. Gower, Gatting, Boycott, Hick and Atherton are men without close mates, probably because of the solitary nature of their job. A batsman's precarious existence and general isolation in the middle makes the leading protagonists self-absorbed and introverted. Only Gooch, of the real elite, seems to be able to switch the channelled focus on and off. Bowlers are more gregarious because they rely on other people – fielders and umpires – for their success.

Robin Smith is more open, but he still has a dark, superstitious side. He came out against us with a four-leafed clover taped to the back of his bat, proceeded to waltz up the wicket at me and unleashed a vicious straight drive which grazed my shoulder before I'd moved and then cannoned into the boundary. Bowling at someone with this power, I was the one who needed the four-leafed clover.

27–30 May, Durham v Kent, Darlington
I wasn't playing today (we're trying to give our young bowlers as much four-day experience as possible), so I drove Botham to the local infirmary for an X-ray on the knee damaged by Liam. He got a rousing ovation from the octogenarians in Outpatients when he entered, and several clambered eagerly to their feet to get autographs. I bet they're not like that at home.

A Lot of Hard Yakka

There didn't seem to be much wrong with *him*, either, when he launched a violent assault on the Kent bowlers in pursuit of their daunting Sunday score of 300. The umpires ran out of balls while he and Larkins were blazing 91 off the first twelve overs, but then it pelted with rain. Opening the bowling with the compulsory fielding restrictions (only two out in the first fifteen overs) is no fun in these games, and I was bowling at the death as well. Two consecutive dot balls are a major cause for celebration.

Friday 4 June, England v Australia, Old Trafford
Shane Warne bowled Mike Gatting with the ball of the decade. It also happened to be Warne's first delivery in an Ashes contest. It fizzed down a foot outside leg on a perfect length, bounced generously and turned virtually at right angles to flick the top of off stump. No wonder Gatting looked so bewildered – he couldn't have played it in his dreams. Neither could anyone else. It was all the more remarkable as Warne is even chubbier than Gatting, and resembled an overweight beach bum (mainly because he was one).

I watched the match from Grace Road, Leicester, where the ground is gradually improving but the lunches are still inedible: tinned boiled potatoes, stringy beans, meat like old boots and bottles of yukky orange fizz loaded with sediment. They'll never produce any good fatties on that diet.

10–14 June, Durham v Middlesex, Gateshead Fell
There had been a major countrywide deluge for three days, so we slumped around listlessly with Sony Walkmans and Sega Megadrives. There's no room to play cards – all the available table space was taken up with mountains of kit. The stuff we carry now! White gear, coloured gear, training gear, protective gear, headgear, cosmetics, lotions and potions, never mind bats, white and blue pads and four pairs of gloves. Our coffins are straining at the hinges. No wonder the kit van has already broken down twice this summer.

There is general agreement that four-day cricket is harder

and requires extra commitment, and that scheduling a fifty-over Sunday League match after the third day is therefore fatuous . No one – no one – likes the twelve o'clock start, not even the spectators.

THE TWILIGHT OF THE GODS

Thursday 17 June, Glamorgan v Durham, Colwyn Bay
The two most famous cricketers of our age, Ian Botham and Viv Richards, were playing out their last rites at a place which, ten days ago, stood under 3ft of water. It's a mediocre north Wales resort of campsites, council houses and blue rinses in teashops, more in keeping with a season of the Grumbleweeds than a clash of Titans.

But then, their encounters these days are a little geriatric compared to what they were. Botham lopes up to the wicket where he used to spring, bowling gentle, teasing seamers, although he's still capable of a vigorous bouncer when riled. Richards, now forty-one, is relatively circumspect, sizing up the bowlers quietly, like a grandfather surveying mischievous children.

Richards struck the rookie Durham paceman John Wood for three fours in an over, the last an imperious pull which said, 'Hey, sonny, don't bowl there to me.' Botham came on with some slow wobblers. Richards was getting into position too early and retreated into his shell.

'Hey, man, I've seen this before, I'm just gonna be takin' singles,' he said, and dabbed a wide one tentatively to third man.

'Yeah, and if you get out my end I'll dance round you all the way to the pavilion,' Botham chimed.

Richards didn't fall for the bait, lifting Graveney into the road instead, near some houses with roof tiles missing. 'That's Viv's handiwork last year,' the groundsman said. And then he was out, playing on to the off-spinner, Phil Berry, an anonymous dismissal to match the anonymous venue. Botham ended up taking four cheap wickets, and strode off saying, 'I should put in for a pay rise.' But he finished on the losing side.

Just look at their achievements. Richards has 114 hundreds, a triple century in a day for Somerset, 8,500 Test runs – more than any West Indian in history. He was never on the losing side as captain of his country. Botham has 383 Test wickets, 14 Test centuries. *Fourteen*. More than anything Graveney, May or Dexter managed. One year he hit eighty sixes in a season. They broke a thousand records, captured a million hearts. Yet at Colwyn Bay there was barely a soul left at the end to see these two greats together on a first-class field for the last time.

Monday 19 July, Durham v Australia, Durham University 'It took me five minutes to get out of bed on Friday,' Botham said. 'I thought, I don't need this any more. I've had ten operations – back, shoulder, wrist, knee, other knee, cheek . . .' He glanced outside at the rain. 'Look at that approaching thunderstorm. I tell you, there's that much metal in my body, if I get struck by lightning you'll all die.'

We were sitting in the Durham University Cricket Club pavilion, a place where, thirteen years before, I was regularly awarded the 'Career in Ruins' tie for some stupid misdemeanour. Here, now, on the last day of Durham's match against the Australians, Botham was pulling the plug on his own epic odyssey. Outside, waiting for the 'retirement' press conference was a throng of pressmen, camera crews, photographers and Sky's presenter Sue Barker in black leggings and a shocking pink plastic jacket to match her shocking pink nail varnish.

The interviews were conducted in a marquee over sandwiches and copious amounts of red plonk. In the afternoon the rain abated and Durham took the field, mainly in honour of the 3,000 people who'd turned up to see their hero for the last time. After fifteen overs, Botham was brought on to bowl and, still convinced that anything was possible, sent down a series of loopy long hops, determined to strangle one last Australian.

I sat in the pavilion with the tourists. Steve Waugh, the next man in, was on tenterhooks and others looked on expecting the worst.

'Cor blimey!' Allan Border exclaimed.

'What's he tried now?' Merv Hughes asked, lying down.

'One that Boony couldn't reach,' Shane Warne said.

'He'll snaffle him in a minute, you bet,' Hughes predicted. There was discernible reverence in all their voices.

It wasn't to be though, and after eleven fruitless overs, Botham took his sweater to a standing ovation. Even the old grumps who usually moaned about his lost commitment got to their feet. Then he kept wicket in batting gloves and no pads before leading the teams off. All the Australian players rose and applauded him, and many of us had lumps in our throats. 'That's part of my childhood gone,' the wicketkeeper Chris Scott said sadly.

The timing was right. He can still occasionally hypnotise batsmen or unleash a stroke of withering power, but his eyes are less keen, the Château Lafitte-induced gut is stretching the acrylic shirts, and once he lost his England place the motivation was gone. He kept pleading for rain so he could go off and play golf.

So we said goodbye to I.T. Botham, great all-rounder, anti-hero, fund-raiser, people person – the man who didn't so much preach a method as an attitude. Do you want it or don't you? If you do, go out and get it. If you don't, on yer bike son. The game will go on, but he will be hugely missed by everyone. He knows he'll miss us, too: as he was leaving, brandishing a half-drunk bottle of burgundy, he said: 'Right. Now I'm going to have a whopping big party for my retirement. And you're all coming, *aren't you*?'

I Think It's All Over

12–14 August, Northamptonshire v Durham, Northampton
Several bowlers were injured, so I ended up playing a four-day game. Actually, breakdowns are everywhere. England have used ten seamers in the Ashes series (and have already lost it 4–0) and the list of decent quickies who've been temporarily or permanently crippled in the last decade makes depressing reading: Foster, Fraser, Cowans, Botham, Lawrence, Dilley, Small, Jarvis (P.), Ilott, Millns, Igglesden, McCague, Thomas (G.) and Bicknell. The workload of ploughing up and down on hard, covered pitches and straining every sinew on Sundays bowling yorkers and throwing yourself around the outfield is just too much.

Curtly Ambrose has had his injuries, too, but there was nothing wrong with his pace in this match. He clattered through our second innings sending stumps flying, and I, having made nought first knock, came in at 87–9. I walked past Ambrose at the end of his run. He winked. I took guard and surveyed the field, which wasn't strictly necessary – they were all crouching virtually within touching distance. The first ball was on a length and reared up towards my head – the original spitting cobra. I punched it gently to gully to record my first ever 'pair'. No runs at all in my first season, and none in what was due to be my last match. I won't say that there was naff all in between, but it seems like a good point to end.

Monday 20 September, Darlington
I did play on several Sundays after that, which rather ruins the story. With the extra demands of four-day cricket, finishing bottom (again) was inevitable with our mix of inexperience, old lags and diffident captaincy, and the last few games were fairly forgettable. Botham's farewell party wasn't. It took place in the Imperial, a small Darlington brasserie full to the brim with his favourite booze (some claret or other) and he made a moving speech standing next to the cappuccino machine.

There was no dolcelatte on the menu. Then it all got rather
riotous and we improvised some intricate rugby moves using
an oval-shaped packet of coffee beans. I touched down for a
try, but the bag burst, scattering the contents all over the place.

This drew a range of responses, from laughter and applause
to severe irritation: a microcosm of my career, I suppose. But
then, isn't that the essence of being a paid sportsman – to get
a reaction? Ultimately, professional cricket is entertainment, a
spectacle with performers. Being in the Durham team with
cricket's greatest showman has made me into one again.

15 October

Then came the bad news. A new sports editor had arrived at
the *Independent on Sunday*, and he had ignored all the promises
made to me and appointed Derek Pringle (thirty Test appearances) as cricket correspondent. Even though I have been
writing a weekly column in the *Independent* for seven years,
they won't give me so much as a scrap of compensation. Off
the stage and into the pits.

THE MORNING AFTER

into the void • love on the fax • the Ambrose bell tolls • Lara pulls England to bits • Getty's gaff • 'Goodnight' • Shangri-La

NEW MAN

February 1994

Professional cricketers only really mature after they retire. Like being in the army, the job's all-consuming and everything's laid on. But when they enter the void outside they stop dreaming about tomorrow's century or bemoaning yesterday's dropped catch or slouching on the sofa watching old reruns rather than doing the washing up. They cease to be Jekylls in winter and Hydes in summer. Away from the playing arena and dressing-room oscillation, their moods fluctuate less (they might be grumpy all the time, but at least that's consistent) and their relationships improve. Once they've surfaced from their total immersion in sport, they can get on with real life.

Which, in my case, meant finding a wife, a job and a lifestyle. Nothing much, really. Influenced by two years with Botham, I went at it like a bull at a gate. I joined dating agencies, had parties, booked tickets to the Caribbean, took people from the *Daily Telegraph* out to lunch. Within a month I was sorted. They might have already had more columns than the Parthenon, but the *Telegraph* nonetheless agreed to take some comment pieces from England's tour of the West Indies, and I joined their team of freelance cricket writers.

On the relationship front, I met Tanya, a fashion PR, on 29 January. We went out three times, and on 16 February I proposed to her by fax from Kenya, where I was attending a tournament. It wasn't desperation, I just felt it was right. So did she. Half an hour later she accepted by fax. We decided on 10 June for the wedding. A major influence in the growing reputation of London Fashion Week, she supervised my gradual conversion from Army Surplus to Armani. Luckily, they sell jeans.

MINISTER OF DEFENCE

Tuesday 29 March 1994, West Indies v England, Port-of-Spain
In view of my pursuit of pure cricketing expression and unrefined exuberance, perhaps it was appropriate I should spend my first month as a serious cricket writer in the Caribbean. West Indian players aren't concerned with conformism and they don't know how to hold back. They live and die by the sword, and pride is their governor. Sometimes they'll scale peaks; at other times they'll plumb the depths. Either way, you know it'll be entertaining.

The fourth day of the third Test in Trinidad was pivotal to the series. West Indies were two up with three to play, but faltering at 143–5 in their second innings, only 67 ahead. Ambrose, who didn't normally say anything hugely relevant in the dressing room, complained that all the early batting had been a touch irresponsible, and implored the rest to sell their wickets dearly. They did, except Ambrose himself, who heaved inexplicably at Caddick and lost his middle pole. England needed 194 to win.

Richie Richardson was livid with Ambrose as the England batsmen prepared to survive the hour before stumps. 'You complain at us and then you bat like a rasshole?' he said, or words to that effect. 'You better make it up with the ball.' What followed was the most incredible, irresistible, destructive spell of fast bowling ever witnessed in the colour-TV era. Ambrose's first ball was fast, fullish, on an ideal line and cut back slightly to have Atherton palpably lbw. The sort of first ball openers dread. Atherton walked back disconsolately and went straight into the shower.

When he emerged, England were 27–6. Ambrose's eighth ball had beaten Smith's solid defensive prod for sheer pace; another ripped out Stewart's off stump. The remainder succumbed meekly, dazzled like rabbits in headlights. Each wicket was celebrated with that wild flailing of arms, like a boxer on speed and almost as frightening. By the close, England were 40–8 and Ambrose had taken 6–10.

The Morning After

You could pick holes in the batsmen's technique – say Atherton should have been forward or that Russell took his eye off the ball – but the bare fact is that no one could have withstood that onslaught: not Boycott, not Bradman, not Botham. Not even Batman. The pace was ferocious, the bounce fearsome, the accuracy faultless. David Holford, the West Indies manager, said: 'I saw Curtly's 7–1 in Perth; that was exciting. But this was more exciting.' The taxi-driver taking us back to the hotel was more succinct. 'Ambrose – he the West Indian minister of defence,' he said.

CERTAIN GENIUS

Monday 18 April 1994, West Indies v England, Antigua
The day before the fifth Test in Antigua, I drove through Swetes village, where Ambrose lives. It's not the sort of place you'd associate with the numero uno of fast bowling. A neglected tree-lined lane winds through a small settlement of tired weatherboard houses, most with little verandahs. A beaten-up old Datsun lies abandoned on the verge. The only sign of life is the inhabitants' colourful washing swaying on the lines. It would be the perfect setting for the old man playing the blues in the Budweiser ads. During West Indies Tests, Ambrose's mother, Hillie, is glued to the commentary, and if her son takes a wicket she runs outside into this road and rings a large bell. She'd have had serious arm-ache after Trinidad.

But that was nothing compared to the muscle seizure Brian Lara suffered after three days of the fifth Test. He batted for 12¾ hours, faced 535 balls, struck 45 boundaries, ran 195 in singles, twos and threes. His scorechart, each stroke recorded with a thin black line, looked like a huge plate of spaghetti. He was obliged to raise his bat more than fifteen times to acknowledge the applause for passing some landmark or other. The most important of these – OK the only one that anyone was really bothered about – was achieved at precisely 11.45 on 18 April, when Lara pulled Chris Lewis for four to surpass Gary Sobers' 365 not out, the highest individual score in Test cricket. To completely finish him off, afterwards he signed a thousand autographs.

Driving to the ground on that third day, we, the press, knew he was going to do it, and we said so. It just felt like it had to happen. There was such certainty in his progress to 320 not out overnight, the wicket was so flat and the bowling so innocuous. The West Indies had already won the series and were only four wickets down, so theoretically he could bat as long as he liked. The scenario was perfect.

Initially, on the third morning his strokeplay was sketchy, with an uppish waft and some playing and missing. The blistering off drives and featherlight glides just out of the wicketkeeper's reach were absent. Fraser beat him outside the off stump and said, with grudging respect, 'I suppose I can't really call you a lucky cunt when you're 340 not out.'

Then, having edged his way nervously to 361, he drove Fraser sumptuously through the covers to draw level with Sobers. In the next over, Lewis bounced, Lara swivelled and the record was his. Just to underline that the whole achievement was pre-destined, as he pulled the decisive boundary he brushed the stumps with his pad, dislodging a bail slightly. But it remained perched precariously out of its groove as the pitch was invaded. Most of the policemen who ran on were more interested in shaking Lara's hand than in controlling the crowd.

The most striking thing about his innings, apart from its length, was its purity. He played every shot in the book, all with a classic natural backlift, a free swing of the blade and a beautiful elasticity. He hit virtually everything along the ground and never once relied on his pad in defence. An old schoolfriend of Lara's, who'd first played with him as an eight-year-old in a backyard, explained why. 'Sometimes we used a scrunched-up evaporated milk can as the ball,' he said. 'If you miss it, it cut your leg.'

The Morning After

Quite apart from the on-field dramas, I have never experienced such a wonderful cricketing spectacle. The raw emotion on the spectators' faces, the rousing applause, the stallholders gaily selling rotis, Chikkey's throbbing disco during intervals and breaks, Gravy the cross-dresser performing on a rostrum, the iron band roaming the ground, banging anything from pans to hub caps in syncopated rhythm. The uninhibited carnival atmosphere is spellbinding, and the din carried on late into the evening behind the main stand. If there's no room in heaven when I die, I'll accept a West Indian cricket ground.

Socially Adjusted

Summer 1994

I still occasionally lapsed into the negligence of my previous life, turning up to Heathrow for our June honeymoon without my passport, for instance. They wouldn't let me on the flight to Paris, so Tanya and I had to consummate our marriage back home on the sitting-room sofa. I've never been much good at wedding nights.

Apart from a few days in France, I spent my first summer out of cricket at cricket. Watching rather than participating. What struck me most was that writing about the game wasn't as agonising as playing it. Journalists have intellectual pressures and skilled competition, and it is a problem cleverly squeezing six hours' play into 250 words. But there were no nerves; you didn't have anyone bawling, 'Save the one, for God's sake,' or bollocking you for occasionally losing concentration. If you accidentally missed the ball, some kind person would usually tell you what had happened. You weren't obliged to turn up two hours before the start or spend ages in the nets unravelling some flaw, and you weren't sore and achy when you woke up the next morning. Sportswriting is challenging and enjoyable, but compared to playing, it's less fraught and more controlled. And therefore, it is slightly less gratifying.

Revisiting old familiar pastures, it seemed odd at first parking in back streets, showing passes at gates and heading for press boxes rather than pavilions, and players are a little wary of former colleagues who've jumped the fence. 'Shh, press,' they would hiss semi-conspiratorially when I came across them. Many even reverted to calling me Simon instead of Yozzer.

Feeling compromised, I politely rejected invitations to most dressing rooms, but I did go into the Middlesex one at the behest of the vice-captain, John Carr, himself in the middle of a Lara-like run spree. Discussion centred on his bizarre stance, and the ire of Jamie Sykes, now a taxi driver, who had complained vigorously to my newspaper about the way I had portrayed him in an article.

'Does that mean I could sue Boycs for describing me as fat and old?' Gatting asked.

'No, you can't argue with the truth,' Keith Brown said.

Did I miss playing? people asked. Not the persistent uncertainty, or the nagging pain, or the perpetual snoring of my hotel room-mate, no. But I did miss the buzz of performance and the quest for achievement. Which is where TV commentary comes in. Calling a game as it happens in the company of former greats *is* exciting and the closest substitute to actually being out there. Manning the microphone creates the same sort of pressure and surges of adrenaline as, say, fielding at deep square leg. It's mostly run-of-the-mill stuff, but occasionally and unexpectedly something more demanding comes along: an awkward catch, a dramatic incident. Will you be able to deal with it and breathe a sigh of satisfaction, or will you make a frightful faux pas? You can never be sure. It's alluring if you're that way inclined.

THE ENGLISH IDYLL

Sunday 4 September 1994, Wormsley

The only matches I took part in were for the Lord's Taverners or on John Paul Getty's ground in Buckinghamshire. It was really an escape. I couldn't face playing for a serious club team and, as an ex-pro required to deliver every week, I was tired of the expectations. I still enjoyed the game and was keen to play, but as a performer rather than a producer. Added to that, club pitches always seem so slow and lifeless after first-class ones, and county bowlers soon come to resemble cantankerous old trundlers.

Playing for the Taverners was a chill-out. The matches were fun, raised funds and brought together people from different branches of the entertainment world. David Frost and Richard Stilgoe, Tim Rice and Julian Wilson. Will Carling captained one match. He looked decidedly nervous before batting, but then smote two large sixes. 'I'm teaching him to relax with yoga,' his then wife, Julia, said looking on, 'but I can't get him into the lotus position. His thighs are too big.'

But a game on Getty's estate at Wormsley, hewn out of an escarpment in the Chilterns, is the ultimate cricketing experience in my book. The ambience is quintessentially English: oaks and beeches and sycamores lining the slopes, cows meandering between fields, a breeze wafting up the valley and billowing the white marquees and girls' long floaty dresses. With the thatched pavilion and scorebox, the manicured outfield, the smart guests sipping champagne, the setting is chocolate-box perfect. When you're receiving annual income of £94 million (£10,800 an hour) just from your assets, you can have all the perfection you desire.

Bearing in mind what Getty has been through (chronic heroin and alcohol addition, the loss of a beautiful wife to an overdose, the kidnap of a son, his ear cut off and sent through the post), you can see why he enjoys the aesthetic pleasure and dreamy tempo of cricket. Mick Jagger, a useful schoolboy player, introduced him to it in the early 70s when they were drying out together in some Chelsea rehab clinic, and now he's a total convert, staging matches, making huge donations, surrounding himself with old legends: Compton, Miller, Bedser, Cowdrey.

Sitting on a wooden picnic table, Getty admires the 30,000 trees he's planted, an imported red kite wheeling overhead, and gazes affectionately at the game. The pitch is blemishless, the play is competitive but chivalrous, there's a good mix of past and present in the team and interesting guests for lunch – John Mortimer and Jeremy Paxman at our table, the Jaggers, Mick and his brother, Chris, at the next. Unfortunately, I'm still being put on to bowl directly after consuming a four-course meal.

Later you are allowed into the grounds of Getty's mansion (which features a private cinema where he sometimes sits alone watching films of old Test matches) and given a tour of his priceless collection of original manuscripts and documents, housed in a mock castle. There's the first-ever page of printed matter, Samuel Pepys's diaries, hundreds of embroidered bindings and ancient bibles, and a fourteenth-century copy of the Magna Carta.

At the close of play Getty claps ecstatically, irrespective of the result; there are handshakes and smiles and more champagne, and players in their old county sweaters saying, 'I say, you haven't lost it, old lad,' to each other. All that in exchange for a few overs into the breeze is a fair swap. I'd happily search out this divine environment in the next life, if only the umpires would give lbws.

CLOSE INSPECTION

Saturday 13 May 1995, The Duchess of Norfolk's XI v West Indies, Arundel

Money infiltrates everything eventually. During the winter of 1994–5, the reputation of our sacred game was further ravaged by financial manoeuvres. Huge wagers were being gambled in illegal betting shops in Asia, and bribery allegations surfaced involving the Pakistan team, reminding me that in the dying minutes of a tourist match, one of their players had jovially offered me £100 to give up my wicket so that Pakistan could edge closer to the £50,000 Tetley challenge for beating eight counties. 'You'll have to give me more than that,' I said. They won anyway.

And in TV boardrooms cricket, like most other sports, was being kicked around like the commodity it had become as the broadcasters scrapped over rights. Their snarly conflicts would have been good TV in themselves. Eventually the TCCB reaped £58 million from Sky and the BBC for four years' coverage of county and Test cricket. Fifty-eight million pounds! When Middlesex won both the championship and Gillette Cup in my first year, 1980, the club's income from television and broadcasting was £5,763.

The players will eventually benefit, though hopefully they'll never lose sight of the fact that they're being paid to do something they love. But being a pro is tougher now. Four-day cricket is an arduous struggle, international demands have doubled, physical preparation is more rigorous. Where once a clumsy mistake was excused by the game's amateur ethos, now it is brutally exposed by 'spin vision' – the super slo-mo camera that zooms in with amazing clarity on every grisly error and humiliatingly replays it over and over to the intrigued viewer. A batsman's hopeless stuttery footwork, the crooked defence, the butterfingered fielder, the pitiful long hop, the attempted out-swinger travelling down all wonky before being pummelled. 'I'm glad they didn't have it in my day,' Vic Marks said before bowling some off spin in a charity match. 'It would've just showed the ball coming out of my hand dead straight. I'd have been carted everywhere.'

The sight of Syd Lawrence tear-arsing in to bowl in this same exhibition match, and then, after four overs, hobbling around like a Vietnam vet, knees cracking like bowls of Rice Krispies, didn't dissuade me from having one last go on the big coconut shy. I accepted an invitation to play for the Duchess of Norfolk's XI against the West Indies at Arundel, the traditional tour opener. Although I had not played seriously for a year, the lure of a final chance to splay a Test player's stumps on the big stage was magnetic.

I came on to bowl first change when Carl Hooper was on 19. My first ball, on a fullish length just outside off stump, swung a little and might have induced an edge a decade earlier. With a wonderful flourish of arms, Hooper deposited it into the car park over extra cover. Luckily, not one of the camera crews was filming at the time, but the public announcer was watching. 'Morning, Simon,' he boomed over the tannoy. What he should have said was, 'Goodnight.'

EUREKA!

Sunday 30 June 1996, Hampshire v India, Southampton
Follow optimism's twisting thread long enough and it will lead somewhere. After years of fluctuations and trudging hopefully to auditions and hearing nothing, my father was suddenly chosen to play General Franco in the film *Evita*. He spent a fortnight in Budapest recording various scenes featuring just him and Madonna.

Meanwhile, Kevan James had returned to Hampshire after a moderate 1995 season and a winter working in a windowless office for Southern Electric. Energised and enthused by the appointment of a new coach (Malcolm Marshall) and a new captain (John Stephenson), and by a motivational talk from Ian Botham, he felt buoyant and ready to continue his search for Shangri-La.

At the end of June, in his seventeenth season, he found it. He dismissed four Indian Test batsmen – Rathore, Tendulkar, Dravid and Manjrekar – in four consecutive deliveries. It was the first time for twenty-four years that this feat had been achieved in English first-class cricket. He wasn't at all perturbed that the only TV cameraman on the ground had left ten minutes before his spell began. He wasn't finished, either. The next day, batting up the order, he scored 103, becoming the first cricketer ever, anywhere, to take 4 in 4 *and* score a century in the same match. No one else had managed it, not Procter, Imran, Botham, Hadlee, Miller, not Benaud, not any of the old masters. No one. Only Kevan David James, born 18 March 1961, Lambeth. He'd finally become someone and shed his rotten old nickname, Spikes. Now his colleagues were calling him God.

'It's fantastic, unreal. I've waited all my life for this,' he said afterwards. 'I've thought about giving up millions of times, always worried about whether I'd be playing the next game. I didn't know where I'd be from one week to the next. Now I can say it was worth it.'

The worry, the pain, the torment, the heartless comments and unexpected disappointments, the love–hate relationship and the hard yakka, is *all* worth it. Worth it for the buzz, the achievement, the satisfaction, the camaraderie, the outdoor life, the public support, the ounce of fame, and the abiding fascination of the game itself. Worth it for Allan Lamb coming up and saying: 'Jeez, you were unplayable the first time I faced you – all those out-swingers, in-swingers and slower balls. Quite a fackin' handful.'

I looked up that game in *Wisden* the other day. He got 159.

If you enjoyed this book here is a selection of other bestselling non-fiction titles from Headline

Headline books are available at your local bookshop or newsagent. Alternatively, books can be ordered direct from the publisher. Just tick the titles you want and fill in the form below. Prices and availability subject to change without notice.

Buy four books from the selection above and get free postage and packaging and delivery within 48 hours. Just send a cheque or postal order made payable to Bookpoint Ltd to the value of the total cover price of the four books. Alternatively, if you wish to buy fewer than four books the following postage and packaging applies:

UK and BFPO £4.30 for one book; £6.30 for two books; £8.30 for three books.

Overseas and Eire: £4.80 for one book; £7.10 for 2 or 3 books (surface mail)

Please enclose a cheque or postal order made payable to *Bookpoint Limited*, and send to: Headline Publishing Ltd, 39 Milton Park, Abingdon, OXON OX14 4TD, UK.
Email Address: orders@bookpoint.co.uk

If you would prefer to pay by credit card, our call team would be delighted to take your order by telephone. Our direct line 01235 400 414 (lines open 9.00 am–6.00 pm Monday to Saturday 24 hour message answering service). Alternatively you can send a fax on 01235 400 454.

Name ....

Address ....

....

....

If you would prefer to pay by credit card, please complete:
Please debit my Visa/Access/Diner's Card/American Express (delete as applicable) card number:

Signature .... Expiry Date ....